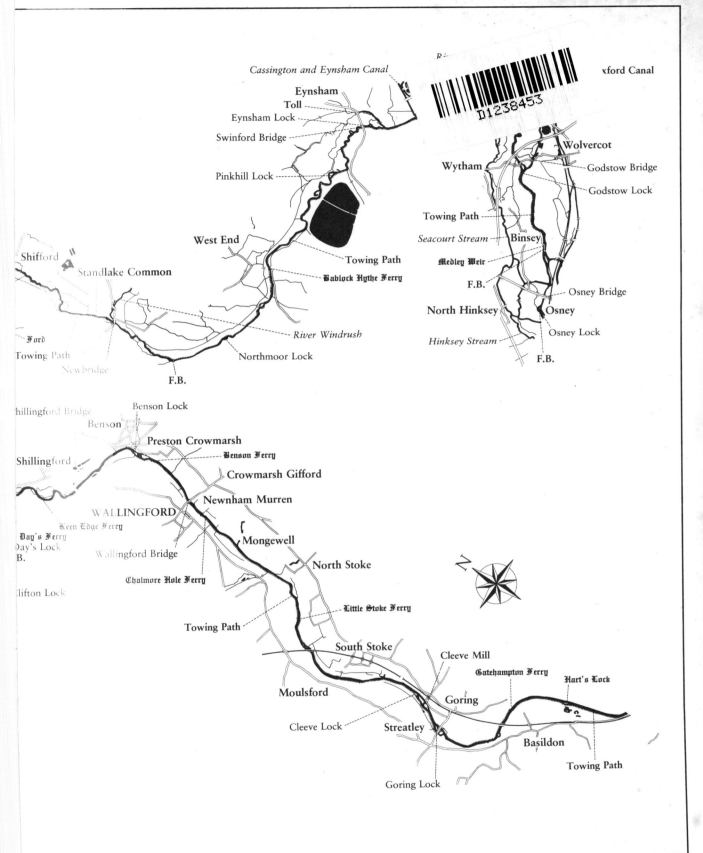

Cassington and Eynsham Canal

xford Canal

Eynsham
Toll
Eynsham Lock
Swinford Bridge
Pinkhill Lock

Wolvercot
Godstow Bridge
Godstow Lock
Wytham

Towing Path
Seacourt Stream
Binsey

West End
Towing Path
Bablock Hythe Ferry

Medley Weir
F.B.
Osney Bridge

Shifford
Standlake **Common**

River Windrush
Northmoor Lock

North Hinksey
Osney
Osney Lock

Hinksey Stream
F.B.

Ford
Towing Path
Newbridge
F.B.

hillingford Bridge
Benson Lock
Benson
Preston Crowmarsh
Benson Ferry
Crowmarsh Gifford
Newnham Murren

Shillingford

WALLINGFORD
Keen Edge Ferry
Mongewell

Day's Ferry
Day's Lock
B.
Wallingford Bridge
North Stoke

lifton Lock
Chalmore Hole Ferry

Little Stoke Ferry

Towing Path

South Stoke
Cleeve Mill
Gatehampton Ferry
Hart's Lock

Moulsford
Goring

Cleeve Lock
Streatley
Basildon
Towing Path

Goring Lock

D1238453

To Daddy.

with love from Jill xx

The Thames

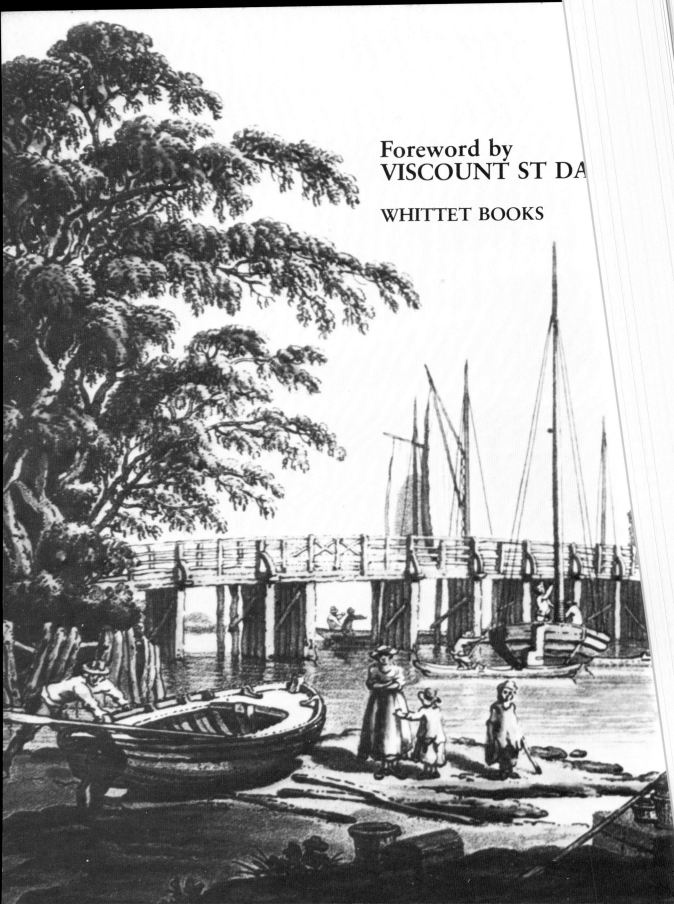

Foreword by
VISCOUNT ST DA

WHITTET BOOKS

The *Thames*

from source to tideway

Peter H. Chaplin

First published 1982
© 1982 by Peter H. Chaplin

Foreword © 1982 by Viscount St Davids

Whittet Books Ltd,
The Oil Mills, Weybridge, Surrey

Design by John Saunders

British Library Cataloguing in Publication Data
Chaplin, Peter
    The Thames from source to tideway.
    1. Thames Valley – Description and travel
    I. Title
    914.2'04   DA670.T2
    ISBN 0-905483-27-8

Typeset by Inforum Ltd, Portsmouth
Printed in Hong Kong
by South China Printing Co.

CONTENTS

FOREWORD

I have been delighted to be asked to write an Introduction to this book, written by my old friend Peter Harrison Chaplin. This is a book by a man who has spent his working life in preserving and improving the structure of rivers, particularly this one; at the same time he is able to appreciate not only the small technicalities but also the beauty of the river and its busy life of all kinds.

I have loved the Thames all my life. I was born near it, and as a child I was often taken on it up to Kew and Hampton Court. I was at a private school near Ascot, and when my parents took me out we went to Bray or Maidenhead and got an electric canoe. At Eton I was a wet-bob and used to row up to Queen's Eyot, and sailed with the Sailing Club below Romney Lock. Since then I have had a number of craft, often on the Thames, including a small barge-yacht of my own design which I lived on for six years. We have just sold our little electric canal cruiser *Emys*, and this summer will see us again on the Thames with our new electric river and canal cruiser *Silver Sail*. I have been lucky to have met and known many of the outstanding people of the river and its tributaries whose names now appear in this book. Harry Stevens, who owned the River Wey and left it to the National Trust, was an old friend; I knew T. B. Rixon, the greatest punting champion of all time, and was luckily able to inherit and preserve some of his equipment; Sir Alan Herbert, who knew and loved the

Thames and wrote so much about it, was a waterways and parliamentary friend of mine. He wrote an Introduction to my Inland Cruising book, though he insisted that it be put in as an Intrusion. I have always thought it to be the best part of the book.

But no Introduction, or Intrusion, could outshine this book by my old friend. It contains a mass of detail, quite a lot of it new to me, which will enrich what I hope may be many navigations of this much loved river. I only wish he had found space for the many facts that he said he has had to leave out. But what he has managed to include is splendid, and to have all this material, which would otherwise have been lost or hopelessly scattered, presented to us by a real expert is the sort of treat which does not happen very often.

The Thames has been both a highway and a line of defence for the traditional 'time out of mind'. Trade and prosperity have flowed on it. London itself owes its existence to the fact that it is the furthest place upstream that a sea-going ship can reach and the lowest point downstream which is bridged. The river was a main artery carrying everything from kings to turnips.

The navigators were far from having it all their own way, with the obstructions built by fishermen and millers and the difficulties of working a non-continuous towpath. There was almost always either too much water or too little, with the millers needing most of it to turn their wheels. The disputes could be rough; today we only have arguments between small boats and speeding power-craft.

I know nobody who could have set all this out better, and Peter Chaplin is a happy man, for his business and his pleasure run side by side, and his sons follow him both in their preferences and in their skill with the pen.

I will keep a copy of this book to hand cruise the Thames. There is alway pleasure, wherever one may be, in know history and development of a place, an not imagine a better book for this except possibly a fatter one!

March 16th, 1982   *Viscount St L*

To W. E. (Bill) Chaplin and my wife, Elizabeth,
more popularly known as Betty

ACKNOWLEDGMENTS

First of all, heartfelt thanks to my old friend Reg Bolland, not only for his help and encouragement but for the memory of happy canoeing explorations on waters outside the navigational limits. Hugh McKnight deserves a special thank you for his excellent photographic work, with particular credit for producing good prints from old and shabby negatives, and also making engrossing pictures of various artefacts. I am deeply indebted to many friends for their help in numerous ways: David Pickin, Len Webster, Ian Crouch, John Bates, Brian Hillsdon, Mark Edwards, Michael Turk, George Kenton, Keith French and fellow committee members of the Thames Traditional Boat Society, besides others, who over the years have helped to make this book possible; with respectful mention of some old timers who have passed on, such as Louis 'Jube' Waldock, John Constable (Snr), George Odell and dear old 'Mister Brown' of Thornycroft's. Finally a word of appreciation

for two of my contemporaries since Vick Woods, who was an outstandi man, and Bernard Hunt, best descr maestro of piling.

All illustrations not otherwise cr from the author's own private colle author and publishers gratefully ack permission to reproduce the illustra appear on the following pages: John E Bates and Son (Boatbuilders) Ltd, 125 126, 127, 145; Reg Bolland, 128 (bot Norman Ellis, 111; Eton College Boat Keith French of French Brothers, 85 Malcolm Head, 171, 174; Brian Hi 87, 106, 107 (top), 116 (top), 117, Tony Hobbs of Hobbs and Sons Lt (top), 156; Hugh McKnight, 15, 60, (top), 142, 155 (bottom), 159, 161, 1 Mitchell, 89, 91, 93, 94, 109 (top), David Pickin of Windsor Boats (bottom), 108, 157; Peter Powell, 1

1

THE THAMES FROM BIRTH TO EARLY MIDDLE AGE

The Thames, in common with other rivers such as the Tame, Team, Teme, Thame and Tamar, in England, and other river names of obvious similarity in other countries, derives its name from the Sanskrit word *tamas*, meaning 'darkness'. The Thames, like the other rivers mentioned, tends to be dark or cloudy as opposed to the clear running streams of the chalk hills. The name Isis, which Oxford circles in particular use for the Thames above its junction with the Thame, is at best a poetic myth and at worst an intellectual affectation. The following extract from Boydell's *History of the River Thames*, published in 1793, proves that pedants are not new to us:

Perhaps it may be with saftey affirmed that it (the River Thames) never occurs in any charter or authentic history, under the name of Isis, which indeed, is not so much

Thames Head, 1960. Gregory Manning together with Paul and Tom Chaplin canoeing on the infant river not long before walls with drainage holes had been built athwart the stream.

as heard of but among scholars; the common people, from its head to Oxford calling it by no other name than that of Thames ... All our historians who mention the incursions of Ethelwold into Wiltshire A.D. 905, or of Canute A.D. 1016, tell us that they passed over the Thames at Cricklade. It may, indeed, be added, as no mean authority that, the spot, from whence the first spring of the river issues, is now, and according to the tradition of the country, ever has been called the Thames Head.

The formation of the Thames

It seems almost discourteous to enquire or even state the age of such a wonderful old fellow as the River Thames; however, if statistics are of interest, it is good to know that he was flowing, in all probability, prior to the great upheavals and earth spasms that took place around 30 million years ago. Then the crust of our earth was being pushed around like a piece of dough, rising to create mountains in some areas, ridges in others, with the resulting valleys providing gulleys to take the rain from the high ground.

The colossal movements that forced the Alps into their majestic form also affected south eastern Britain, like the outer ripples of a tidal wave. These ripples had a profound effect on the clay-covered chalklands of the Thames Valley, pushing them up to form ridges and giving the surface a wrinkled terrain as though it were a large succulent fruit dried by scorching sunshine. Previously the chalklands had been part of the Jurassic sea some 140 million years ago; in this sea, over a period of something like 25 million years, the chalk was formed from the shells of marine creatures, who were progenitors of the flints that were to be of such importance to ancient man for making tools for his own use, and for trading. These great forces emanating from the bowels of the earth must have played a tremendous part in the formative years of the Thames Valley, with the great Ice Age bringing it through to adulthood. The Ice Age commenced in the region of 2 million years ago and geologi-

cal history indicates that there were fo glacial periods, each of which was foll an interglacial spell when climatic cc became much better and temp increased, with consequent – albeit tem recession of the ice.

In its youth, over 2 million years Thames, rising in what we now kno Cotswolds, would have had swampy are channels of flowing water, gravel ba pools of water in an irregular pattern on running possibly some 20 miles nort present channel; it had no estuary of its it was then (a million years ago) a tribut Rhine, when England was physically p Continent. As the ice pushed its wa much shaping of the Thames Valley to in the form of modification rather than of a fresh landscape. One dramatic ch an exception: the helping hand given by cutting the Goring Gap, so enabling the to flow southwards towards Reading, met and joined forces with the River flow on to Marlow before swinging Beaconsfield and then more or less follc line of the Vale of St Albans; it then c Essex in a purposeful manner, for wate its own level and seeking the easiest cou no time to relax and linger in the for lagoons or swamps, would be busy c course and building up the banks wi times of flood or high water.

This process, over a period of time th to visualize, enabled the river to work i away from the Vale of St Albans, gra form its present course. This moveme wards was no doubt expedited by tilti land combined with a little pressure fro cap north of the Chilterns. The land ti precipitated by the action of North surges which gradually eroded la occupied by the Dogger Bank and the Dover; the sandy shoals of the Nortl forever moving and South East Englar sinking as is witnessed by the great neec plete the Thames Barrier and increase t of London's river banks.

Although this book is about the

'beyond the flux of the tide', or in modern terms 'the upper river', we shall extend its scope where necessary in order to maintain a clear perspective. Today, the non-tidal Thames is clearly defined as the river above Teddington (the name being derived from the Anglo-Saxon 'Tuddas Farm', or 'enclosure'. The old myth that Teddington means 'tide ending town' is no better than a corny music hall joke). Over the centuries the line of demarcation has varied. Way back in Roman times the tide came no further upstream than their London Bridge, which again indicates how much the South East of England has tilted over the centuries. The tide could be felt progressively further upstream; later reports give evidence of spring tides just about making their presence known at Kingston. However, the tidal state of affairs was considerably altered with the building of the first all-stone London Bridge in 1191; the piers and the elliptical projections of masonry around them, known as 'starlings' or

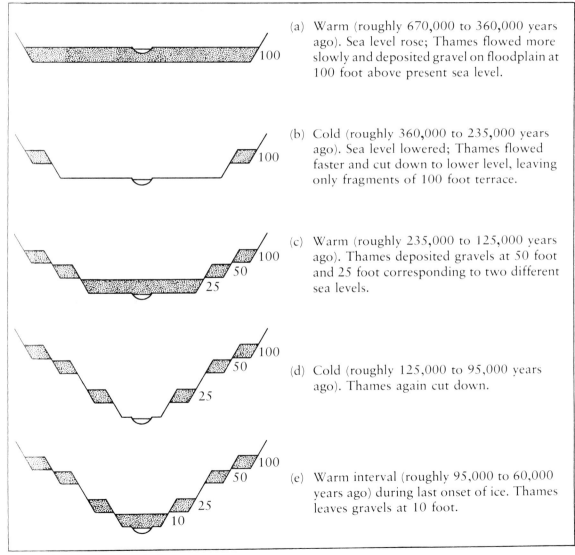

(a) Warm (roughly 670,000 to 360,000 years ago). Sea level rose; Thames flowed more slowly and deposited gravel on floodplain at 100 foot above present sea level.

(b) Cold (roughly 360,000 to 235,000 years ago). Sea level lowered; Thames flowed faster and cut down to lower level, leaving only fragments of 100 foot terrace.

(c) Warm (roughly 235,000 to 125,000 years ago). Thames deposited gravels at 50 foot and 25 foot corresponding to two different sea levels.

(d) Cold (roughly 125,000 to 95,000 years ago). Thames again cut down.

(e) Warm interval (roughly 95,000 to 60,000 years ago) during last onset of ice. Thames leaves gravels at 10 foot.

Effects of glaciation on river bed.

'splitwaters', which guide the flow so as to pre-vent the piers being struck by too strong a cur-rent, tended to act as a dam and restricted the flow of the tide.

When you realize that the Roman buildings at Tilbury were at least 12 feet lower than the present level of high tide, the term 'tilting' of South East England begins to have real signifi-cance. The river is, of course, still changing although its movements are restricted to some extent by the activities of water engineers; the subject of river maintenance and control will, however, be dealt with in Chapter 14.

When a glaciation took place, the ice cap would absorb a prodigious quantity of water, so causing a reduction in sea levels which resulted in the river cutting through the floodplain until the next thaw. The river cut down to great depths – an early channel exists about 100 feet below our present estuary, whilst our present floodplain is several hundred feet lower than in the Ice Age. At the next thaw there would be a fantastic rise in sea level, causing the Thames to back up. The result would be a diminution of flow and subsequent reduction in scouring action, with the formation of a vast floodplain which gathered a healthy deposit of alluvium over the enormous expanses of sand and gravel laid down by glacial action.

The last severe glaciation may well have drawn to a close some 18,000 to 20,000 years ago, the sort of time that is almost meaningless until one realizes that dwarf birches and willows were growing in the earlier interglacial periods. The first willow of pre-historic times to be named in horticultural works is that delightful specimen *Salix repens* that is so popular amongst gardeners today. Two other lovely willows, namely *Salix herbacea* and *Salix reticulata*, both of which are native of this country, are thought to have existed in the Pleistocene (in plain Eng-lish, 'most recent') period, which was about one million years ago.

Early man

Primitive stone implements found in Thames gravels suggest that man has roamed the valley

Salix repens, a delightful dwarf willow of the t in the Thames Valley during the interglacial

and lived by the Thames from anc possibly as long ago as 300 thou before Christ. He was the Acheulian craftmanship in shaping flint tools, axe found at Bell Weir, a sickle a polished stone axes at Old Win nymede and Walton, surpassed thos decessor, the Chellean man, whos been found in the valley of a Tham the Wey. As the Ice Age began its Mesolithic man started his penetr Thames Valley; these Mesolithic, Stone Age, peoples were a trifle mo in their way of living, with a wic implements for hunting, fishing a they became adept at making tool and shaping timber and by exper been found that one man using a fl fell a 12-inch diameter tree in thir

One can imagine these people, tribes of about four score persons, crude rafts or hollowing out tree tr rudimentary canoes. These early have been hewn in a pretty crud main hollowing out being effecte Later dug-outs, like the one foun ton, which was about 18 feet lon carried three people, were 'fully fashioned' with the skilful use of an adze (a sharp axe-like cutting tool, but with the blade set at right angles to the shaft). On this particular canoe the adze marks in the wood were just discernible.

The earliest navigators would, in all probability, have used rafts made of logs lashed together with vines or hide thongs; in the slow flowing river they would have been easy to tow, or pole along; with a large flat deck area they could carry reasonable loads, and there is little doubt that ancient man found 'rafting' an ideal way of transporting his family and belongings when moving to a new settlement.

The dug-out canoe was heavy in relation to its size and would not have been popular on reaches

Peter Chaplin and Fred Saunders with the dug-out canoe that Fred dredged up near Beasley's Ait, Sunbury, in October 1966. The canoe is now in Reading Museum.

where shallows abounded, for it would have been difficult to carry. This factor led to the development of hide-covered and, later, timber-sheathed boats. The first hide-covered craft were coracles which were just large enough to take one man on a fishing expedition, for which purpose they are still used in parts of Wales to this day. Many people, possibly due to tourism, associate the ancestry of the coracle with Wales; in fact this ancient form of water transport was developed in India and Tibet, before Stone Age man was using coracles on the Thames. The coracle was made by building a framework of withies (whippy young branches of willow) and covering them with hide which would be laced into place with thongs of the same material. Modern coracles are much the same except the covering is now of tarred canvas. Coracles could only be put to efficient use in fast-moving rivers, assuming that no attempt was made to propel them against the current, for, whilst fairly easy to steer, they are very difficult to move with a paddle, like a canoe. On an upstream journey, they are usually slung across the shoulders and carried.

From the coracle would have been developed the skin-covered boat with frame and a keel to facilitate progress against the current. Steering would have been crude, no doubt with an oar; and power supplied by oarsmen, or perhaps a sail, so as to make use of a following wind in the same way as the ancient curraghs of Ireland. A craft so described might possibly carry a score of people, be used for transporting timber, distributing requirements for local populations such as tools, pottery and reeds for thatching. Julius Caesar seems to have known about such boats being used in Britain; in Spain he copied the idea for transporting his troops across the River Segre.

On a river such as the Thames it is doubtful if skin-clad boats would ever have been used to any extent; but later there would have been no shortage of heavier craft, for the Thames Valley provided a bountiful supply of excellent timber for boat building. With the advent of the Neolithic (or Late Stone Age) culture, new and improved techniques in flint working were

introduced by immigrants from the Mediterranean lands: no doubt these techniques were
reflected in their boat design and building. No
relics have come to light, but these early boats
would have been flat-bottomed, punt-like craft,
possibly rather like a raft with sides and ends: a
functional design for the Thames. These folk
from the Mediterranean area were good sailors
who presumably first settled in the West Country, whence they spread towards the Cotswolds
and so into the Thames Valley; which is, in
current terms, a logical approach, bearing in
mind that a river is always measured from its
source, with locks, weirs, bridges and other
salient features referred to in the same sequence.
Likewise left- and right-hand banks are so
named in a downstream progression: in other
words, upon going upstream the left-hand bank
is to starboard or right hand.

But from river navigation back to our forebears: somewhere around 2000 B.C. the Bronze
Age replaced the Neolithic period, after which
was an era of trading and prosperity. Various
archaeological excavations have revealed a
wealth of information and artefacts, the latest
great find being the Bronze Age site uncovered
during the building of the south bank abutments
for the M25 bridge, which is alongside Runnymede Bridge. This Bronze Age site probably
dated from the 8th or 9th century B.C. and
formed part of a large riverside settlement over-
laying a Stone Age (Neolithic) site situated some
6 feet below present river level. As well as Bronze
Age pottery and metalwork, some Stone Age
polished axes and pottery were found, and
waterlogged woodwork – including timber piles
– from both periods. These piles indicate a wharf
existed on the site. With the development of
boats, the Thames became an important highway for distribution and even for the
export–import trade. The position of the piles
shows that the Thames was then, as now, flowing on a well defined course, which is corrobo-
rated by the finding of remains of human habita-
tion at various sites along the river bank such as
at Bray and Cookham. More exciting still has
been the unearthing of dug-out canoes at both
Bourne End and Cookham.

The Celts

Some five centuries before the birth
saw the introduction of the Iron A
Thames, as Celtic people from Gaul c
Channel and spread over the country
one of their early settlements have bee
the Wittenham area as well as eviden
ing the Thames at Wallingford and Sh
Dorchester, due to its position where
joins the Thames, became of greater in
The Celts were not exactly peaceful i
– perhaps 'invaders' is a better descrip
name for London, reputed to be '
meant 'lake fort or town', which w
been a sizeable settlement on one of t
or bluffs of the lower Thames. With
of the Iron Age, the improvement in
subsequent progress in techniques w
been reflected in the building of boat
tenings, which were longer lasting, co
used, in place of thongs made from ar
or vegetable matter. By the same toke
would be more plentiful, albeit crude
of hewn timber; whilst the crossing
for both man and beast would mo
fording, for wherever the river was wi
invariably be shallow.

Somewhere around the first quarte
century B.C. the Belgae landed in Ken
ingly wasted no time in finding their
Thames Valley, where they rev
agricultural practices by introd
wheeled plough. However in the up
they met stiff opposition from the Do
held that important Thames tributar
(which joins the Thames at Abing
Roman times. The famous White H
of the downs at Uffington was the sy
Dobunni tribe.

The Romans

Whilst Julius Caesar's invasion of B
place in 55 B.C., the real conquest o
the Romans was under Claudius in A
Thames Valley was presumably an e
especially in the upper reaches where

mentioned Dobunni seemed to collaborate from the beginning. So it is with no great surprise that we find the Dobunni becoming Romano-British subjects with a high degree of civilization. Roman pile-driving techniques enabled them to build better wharves, whilst experienced Roman shipwrights produced stronger barges with improved carrying capacity. Merchandise carried would have been much the same as in the days of the Ancient Britons, but pottery would have been of greater variety; to thatching materials would have been added cargoes of roofing tiles; tools for the craftsman and equipment for the farmer would have been in great demand. The movement of grain must have been considerable, since some Roman farms in the Thames Valley grew up to 500 acres of this very important commodity; another substantial crop of the Thames Valley was flax. The Romans were fond of their gardens and imported most of their rose bushes from Greece; no doubt many consignments went to the upper reaches by barge, to be planted on sites now supplied by that Oxford grower of repute, John Mattocks. It is also very likely that fodder for horses of the Roman cavalry was, where possible, taken by water.

Whilst the Thames had long been a highway for commerce, it was the Romans with their organizing ability, skilled engineers and able craftsmen who set the pattern for many years to come. The campshedding (bank protection) and wharf that was uncovered at Trig Lane, London, a few years ago gave detailed evidence of the excellence of their design and construction: heavy timbers of squared English oak were used, incorporating sophisticated joints that would put many a riparian (riverbank) contractor of the present era to shame. Not only their king piles but also their sheathing boards were true, plumb and well driven to give real penetration of the river bed. Pile drivers of the Roman era were akin to the hand-operated units of the present century. The machine consists of a mast, at the top of which is mounted a grooved wheel for a rope; the wheel is sheathed to prevent the rope jumping off, whilst down the face of the mast are 'guides' along which a heavy flat-bottomed

weight runs. When the pile driver is set in position the weight is hauled to the top of the mast and then allowed to 'free fall' so that it strikes the top of the pile to be driven, true and square and with considerable impact. Larger piles and harder river beds gave rise to the need for heavier 'monkeys' (drop hammers). In turn this required greater manpower, and, so that a number of men could pull and let go in unison, a series of separate ropes, like bell-pulls, were spliced to the main rope. This gave rise to large pile drivers being nicknamed 'ringing engines'. One such piler was in use before the last war in the Remenham reach.

One can only assume that the same excellence of design, thoroughness of construction and robustness of materials went into the building of London Bridge in the days of the Roman occupation. The abutments probably consisted of massive squared oak beams laid in an interlocking pattern to form a large cube, to take and spread the weight.

Roman boat building was of an equally high standard; ships were immensely strong, the strakes of their hulls were of sturdy proportions and joined by mortises and tenons rather than being nailed to ribs, which method required the caulking of seams. Some 20 years ago evidence came to light of a Roman period flat-bottomed river barge adjacent to the Thames. This craft had apparently been abandoned in about the 2nd century A.D., but, unlike the Roman ships with their pegged mortise and tenon construction, her oak strakes were held in place with iron nails whilst her seams were caulked with slithers of hazel twigs. Her overall length was in the region of 55 feet whilst her beam was about 22 feet. She had a mast step (socket) and was probably steered with a long oar; besides supporting a sail under favourable conditions, the mast would have provided a towing point when she was being hauled by gangs of men. Roman barges must have had much in common with the later West Country barges.

Staines was an important Roman river crossing; from evidence that has come to light in the recent re-development of the town, it would appear that Staines, or 'Pontes', as it was known, was a greater trading centre than earlier information had revealed. When the Romans built their bridge at Pontes, it was surely no accident that it lay almost halfway between their Roman City of Londinium and the important garrison town of Silchester. It is highly probable that Pontes was an important transfer point for supplies and equipment destined for Silchester, to which the main road from Pontes ran: merchandise would have been of a very wide variety from armour to amphorae of wine and olive oil.

The timber piles for the bridge at Staines would have been driven with a rig as already described; furthermore the barge in which the piling frame was mounted could have been of true Roman style shell construction, which did not depend upon ribs for strength. Although the Romans were excellent stonemasons, the building of a wide arch for navigation posed problems. This difficulty would have been overcome by driving squared oak piles for bridge supports, then spanning the intervening navigation channel with long baulks of timber, upon which the roadway would be laid. The bridge crossed the Thames in the vicinity of the present landing stage, which is immediately downstream of the old (Victorian) town hall; it was approached by Tamesis Street, which was the Roman road from London to Silchester.

The Romans invariably provided an inn and posting-house where one of their roads crossed an important river, and Staines's famous 'Bush' inn may have had its roots in Roman history. The 'Bush' derives its name from the 'bush of evergreen' – the ivy leaves associated with Bacchus the God of Wine.

When the former Thames Conservancy dredged the Staines reach in 1955 the river bed yielded secrets of varying antiquity; in the reputed position of the bridge over which the Roman legions marched were found domestic items of the Roman era. Perhaps the day will come when the remains of a wharf are found, for Roman barges, as already described, would have been about their business on the river, delivering and collecting merchandise from this important station, others passing through on their way to,

or near, the present centres of Bray, Bo Hambleden, Reading, Goring, Dorcl Oxford. The Thames throughout its l well endowed with Roman settlemen potteries, villages and a goodly smatte ubiquitous villa, which surely indicate Romans, like us, enjoyed the delight by, or near, the river.

The Saxons

After a period of 300 years, in about with the great invasion of the Picts a the control and influence of the Rom to wane; trade diminished; constr wharves, dredging and other works abeyance, whilst settlements lost muc former importance. Saxons made raic land and penetrated the Thames as f chester. In about A.D. 411 the remaini troops were withdrawn from Brit which the Saxon raids became more in as they settled down in Britain v families, fighting and barbarism ensu ever the Saxons pushed ahead and as th they established hamlets all along the town names ending in 'ing', such as Re remnants of the Saxons, who came North Sea coast of Germany. Being u rivers and estuaries of their homel seemingly took the navigation of the 1 their stride.

In A.D. 597 St Augustine landed on Thanet, having been sent to England Gregory; details are non-existent but in which he sailed would probably ha Roman design with qualities of sound tion and good sea-worthiness. St A first mission was to convert Ethelber Kent to Christianity and then to found Canterbury. Within a century Britain land' as it was to be called, became C Feuds and struggles of the tribal chiefs and a civilizing influence commenced founding of three great monasteries a Thames – Westminster, Chertsey an don; Abbot Erkenwald founded Cherts in A.D. 666, a West Saxon Thane by th

Cissa founded Abingdon Abbey in A.D. 675 where, in 1084, William the Conqueror brought his son to be educated by the monks. In A.D. 635 St Birinus made a special visit to Wessex and at Dorchester he met Cyneglis, King of Wessex, whom he baptised in the Thames, so bringing Christianity to Wessex. The king endowed a bishopric for St Birinus and, upon establishing his see, he built Dorchester Cathedral; nothing remains of this Saxon edifice but in its place proudly stands one of the gems of the Thames — the beautiful Norman Abbey Church.

The Vikings

Peace in the valley of the Thames was as unpredictable as the rise and fall in the levels of the river and in a short period of time the Vikings stormed across the North Sea. They navigated the Thames, plundering, robbing and pillaging as they went. The rich undefended religious establishments were easy prey for these fierce pagan warriors; monks and nuns were killed and their treasures looted. By A.D. 870 the Vikings had penetrated as far upstream as Reading, where they fortified themselves and made forays up the Kennet valley.

The Viking boats were double-ended, that is with the sharpness of bow and stern almost identical; they were clincher (clinker) built (overlapping planks joined with thongs, later clenched with nails) of fairly light construction and with little freeboard amidships; due to their length in relation to beam they were termed 'longships'. Measurements varied considerably, but those going upriver could have been around 40 feet long with a beam of about 11 feet. Oars would have been about 10 foot long and presumably a short choppy stroke was best to get the boat moving. They were steered with a rudder hung on the 'steer' or starboard quarter. The Thames 'Peterboat' owes some of its ancestry to the longships as do whalers, Shetland and certain other coastal fishing craft.

King Alfred, who was a great ruler and regarded in high esteem for his hold upon the upper Thames, waged a long and unyielding war against the Danes, or Vikings as they are often termed, who were making life miserable for the inhabitants. Alfred pushed the Danes back downriver and then strengthened defences on all the fords on the upper river. In the year 899 he died, after which there were further raids including the burning of Oxford by a force of Danish invaders who went up the Thames. Just over a century after Alfred's death, the Danish King Cnut was ruling England, but he was a man of more temperate ways and England enjoyed peace once more. By about A.D. 1016 most of the place names in the Thames Valley were as we know them today.

The Normans

The Norman Conquest in 1066 saw William of Normandy sacking the Thames-side town of Southwark, then marching his army along the south side of the Thames to make a crossing at Wallingford, where he entered into Oxfordshire, then turning eastwards to subdue Hertfordshire. The Normans were practical: they built in stone instead of wood. They re-established no small number of religious orders and put drive and initiative into establishing civilization. Although Norman buildings were erected on Thames-side locations, few of them remain because many of the early buildings were of composite construction. Iffley church is a gem of Norman architecture, and the church at Sutton Courtenay dates from Norman times; this village was known as Sutton until the manor was acquired by Reginald Courtenay from the Crown in the 11th century. Sutton Courtenay is renowned for its magnificent stone-built Norman hall, constructed in the 12th century. It is a hall house and retains its original lancet windows and south door. Sutton was originally a Saxon village, of which evidence came to light when about thirty Saxon huts were excavated prior to the last war. Oxford, like many cathedrals, incorporates Norman work; Norman stones appear in some Reading churches, and at one time in a mill.

William the Conqueror was quick to appreciate the military importance of a hill by the south bank of the river a little upstream of Edward the Confessor's former palace at Old Windsor.

William lost no time in acquiring this hill and initially set up a palisaded castle with a moat around it – Windsor Castle was born! He started the round tower in the 12th century and set the pattern of an English castle for subsequent monarchs to follow. By about the 14th century Taynton stone was being used for the castle; as Taynton quarry is near the Windrush, the stone was most likely loaded into small flats which would have been poled downstream to Newbridge, where the Windrush flows into the Thames. At this point the stone would have been transferred to West Country barges port down to Windsor. 'Flat' is a name for a wide variety of craft that a commerce; a Thames flat is ess shallow-draught, flat-bottomed bo punt-like appearance, but very bea length of anything above 30 feet.

William the Conqueror ensured th the Thames Valley was preserved fo whilst all rights over the river became lished as a royal prerogative, as will b in the next chapter.

2

JURISDICTION OF THE THAMES TOGETHER WITH PROBLEMS OF NAVIGATION

The earliest records concerning the management of the Thames go back to 1065 and 1066 when Edward the Confessor made a decree concerning the 4 royal rivers, the Thames, the Trent, the Severn and Yorkshire Ouse. He ordered that mills and fisheries be destroyed and tribute to the king be not forgotten. Presumably he was endeavouring to have structures removed that caused delay and/or hazard to navigation. Weirs not only were constructed to aid navigation but also to aid the miller and the fisherman. The two latter caused impediments to passing traffic by respectively diverting water from the river and placing fixed obstacles in the stream.

Weirs and locks

Weirs of the period were very primitive and of three different types: firstly there was the navigation weir to help bargemasters proceed on their lawful way. It would be erected at the lower end of a set of shallows, so raising the depth of water

A primitive flash lock; on the right is the fixed framework with paddles and rymers in position, on the left the lock keeper is drawing the paddles prior to removing the top timbers so that a barge can pass through.

for a considerable distance upstream, the distance between such weirs being governed by the fall of the river bed. These weirs were mostly built of timber and brushwood, generally in two parallel rows or 'hedges', the intervening space being filled with chalk, stone, turves or similar local material. Sometimes the weir was built in the form of a timber footbridge, with a cill across the bed of the river, so that timbers could be held in position in order to form what was essentially a portable dam. Generally there was no means of regulating the flow of water; to enable barges and other craft to negotiate these weirs, a central span of 15 to 20 feet would be fitted with removable timbers, usually in the form of 'paddles' and 'rymers'. The construction of this opening section was such that a heavy beam of timber, referred to as a 'cill', was laid down on the river bed across the opening, where it was most thoroughly secured. Immediately above and parallel to the cill was another beam sited well above maximum water level; this upper beam was removable. Against and on the upstream side of these parallel beams were placed vertical rectangular boards, the 'paddles', each board being attached to the lower end of a long shaft. Between the paddles were inserted vertical timber

Paddles and rymers, Buscot Weir, 1979.

supports known as 'rymers', which w
in the cill. The pressure of the wate
paddles tight against the cill, whilst t
of the paddles and tops of the ryn
against the upper beam. In some
rymers were grooved to receive th
Over the upper beam additional tim
sometimes be laid to provide a reasor
way and improved access for handli
tackle.

Upon a craft wishing to pass up
paddles, rymers and cross tim
removed, so allowing the pent-up w
upper reach to rush through the op
the difference in levels had equalize
less!). The craft in question woul
hauled through the opening by ro
required much strain by gangs of r
more modern times, horses; sometim
would be situated on a convenien
hauling a boat through. Occasionally
to be 'poled' or 'shafted' through, whi
be described as a diabolical escapade
the method employed, it was a ve
task, for, in spite of the level of the u
having been lowered, the entire flow
would have to pass through the ope
weir. Coming downstream would b
ous but quite terrifying, as the craft
through the opening by the terrific ru
Not surprisingly, as time was money
operators, they often 'shot' the wei
way downstream rather than hang ar
ing for the levels to equalize. It was t
water through the narrow opening
that gave rise to the name 'flash' or
these primitive 'locks'. Whilst they m
ible for larger craft to navigate the riv
was very slow, for in the proces
through a lock a whole reach would
emptied.

Until 1350 the jurisdiction of th
longed to the Crown, whose prerogat
build weirs and flash locks as describ
the medium of special, but tempora
sions. That of course, did not sto
riparian landowner from building a
from which he extracted tolls on pa

The other two types of weir were for milling and fishing. The former would be constructed in much the same manner as a navigation weir, but positioned not only to build up a good head of water, but also to direct it into a leat for the turning of a mill wheel, for which large volumes of water were required. Sometimes a miller, rather than lose his head of water, would keep barges waiting for days before letting them through his weir and sometimes would wring heavy tolls from bargees on passing through. During ensuing arguments, the head of water would sometimes build up even higher, to the discomfort of low-lying farms, which were liable to be flooded.

The fishery weirs were somewhat different; sometimes they were referred to by the self-evident term 'fishery hedges', which were a crude type of trap set across the stream. There were structures of a more permanent nature called 'kidels' which caused a shallow to build up on their downstream side for the catching of lampreys; then there were peculiar structures known as 'eel-bucks' set into a framework in such a way that they could be raised or lowered quite easily. These various contraptions, although very desirable for providing good fresh food, were a menace to navigation, inasmuch as they invariably presented a physical obstruction to barges, whilst their effect on flow and direction of water could be a source of danger. Although attempts were made to clear away these weirs it must be remembered that lampreys (small, reddish-green worm-like creatures about 6 inches long and with inconspicuous fins) were once considered a great delicacy, often forming an important dish at State banquets and City functions, and lamprey pie was a dish enjoyed on the royal table.

Lastly there was a hybrid type of 'half weir' which helped navigation in shallow reaches where there were aits (islands). A weir would sometimes be erected from the appropriate bank, running across at an angle to the head of the island, in an endeavour to deflect water into the barge, or main, channel; this had a twofold effect of providing a greater depth of water and scouring the silt and gravel from the bed.

Jurisdiction of the Thames

In the year 1197 changes came about, inasmuch as Richard I, who had previously held all rights on the Thames, sold them to the Corporation of the City of London in order to raise funds for his crusades in Palestine. Although Richard sold his rights, it remained a royal prerogative to control the river until 1350, in which year Edward III passed an Act of Parliament against obstruction of the navigable highway of the river. The execution of this and subsequent early Acts was then, as far as the upper Thames is concerned, entrusted to various commissions. The reason was that the Corporation of the City of London, whilst empowered to look after the navigation of the entire river, only carried out its duties strictly as far west as Staines, where it erected a stone (known variously as the 'City Stone', 'London Stone' and 'City of London Stone') in the year 1285 to mark the limits of upper and lower Thames. This stone stands in Staines Lammas where the County Ditch (a branch of the River Colne) joins the Thames.

Until 1857 (when the Thames Conservancy was formed) the City of London signified its right of jurisdiction with an annual ceremony. The Lord Mayor travelled upriver in his State barge, with a crew of 8 watermen in their magnificent livery, which consisted of scarlet tunic and knee breeches, white stockings, black shoes with silver buckles, silver buttons to the tunic and a peaked cap of velvet which was shaped like a jockey's. Upon arriving at Staines Lammas, there was a formal disembarkation ceremony before the formation of a procession to the City Stone, where drinks were served and a toast drunk of 'God preserve the City of London'. In the latter years of the ceremony horseplay became accepted, from which developed the custom of 'bumping' the Mayor and Aldermen on the Stone. This ancient custom of the Lord Mayor and Aldermen making their annual pilgrimage to the City Stone was re-enacted in 1977, to celebrate the jubilee of Her Majesty Queen Elizabeth II.

Although the Corporation of London was the first organization empowered with the task of

The annual ceremony at the City Stone, Staines. Note mayoral and livery company barges, right foreground. Unfor
artist, C. Marshall, delineated the stone completely out of proportion (1835).

looking after the entire Thames, it would seem
for all practical purposes that Staines was the
upstream limit of their activities, which were
taken over with the formation of the Thames
Conservancy in 1857. Above Staines, other than
the work of the Oxford-Burcot Commission,
little action appears to have been taken regarding various Acts of Parliament, petitions and
sundry proposals, so it is not surprising that the
government was anxious to implement at least
some of the clauses laid down in Magna Carta in
1215. In plain English these clauses sorted out
the priority of weirs, giving preference to navigation, stopped millers from increasing the height
of their weirs, which often caused flooding due
to back-up of water (the average fall of the
Thames is only 20 inches per mile so there was a
great temptation for millers to obtain more
power by having an increased head of water).
Fishing weirs at that time were probably getting
too numerous and required some form of control.

Early pound locks and the Oxford–Burcot Commission

By the beginning of the 17th century c
were rife regarding the navigability o
between Oxford and Burcot; so bad
shallows that barges travelling upstre
unload cargoes and send them to C
road, and vice versa. In 1605 James I
Act appointing eighteen commissione
powers 'for the clearing and perfectir
Thames between Oxford and Burco
Oxford-Burcot Commission was ina
although ineffectual in its early years,
the late 1620s built the first pound I
locks as we now know them) on the T
Iffley and Sandford respectively, foll
one at the top end of the 'Swift Dit
navigation channel that by-passed the
shallows on the approach to Abingdc
three pound locks remained the only or
type on the Thames until the building
ter's pound lock at Maidenhead in 17
    The Swift Ditch, now sluggish ar
overgrown, leaves the main river on the
a little upstream of Abingdon Lock; the
of the original Swift Ditch Lock now fo

of an overspill weir built in 1967 and the water cascading over it runs along the original channel until it re-unites with the Thames a few yards beyond the very beautiful old Culham Bridge, the construction of which was completed in 1422. From the main river the view of this fine, but disused bridge is masked by the present timber towpath bridge. The new Culham Bridge, sited just upstream of the old one, was opened to traffic in the late 1920s; in due course the old bridge was declared an ancient monument and is now cared for accordingly. Barges using the wharves at Abingdon had to approach them from Culham; the reason was that the wharves were in the downstream part of the town, below the point on the right bank where that sizeable Thames tributary the River Ock flows into the main stream, so giving greater depth of water and helping to keep the bed scoured. The pound locks built by the Oxford-Burcot Commission are the type with which we are familiar today, although the prefix 'pound' or 'cistern' has long since been dropped.

The first English lock of this type dates back to the 16th century when one was built in the Exeter Ship Canal. Pound locks are reputed to have originated in China, but the first known example on the River Lek in Holland dates from 1373. Basically a lock is a chamber capable of containing a barge or barges; it is usually sited in a 'cut' or artificial channel in close proximity to a weir. The lock is fitted with gates at each end, with sluices to allow the ingress and exit of water. Water levels either side of the lock correspond with those of the adjacent weir; within the lock, levels are controlled by opening and closing the respective sluices, so enabling the appropriate gates to be opened to allow a barge to enter and be raised or lowered, as the case may be, to proceed onto the next reach. Pound locks were a great improvement over flash-locks which were not only time consuming to negotiate but extremely wasteful of water. The building of pound locks was a protracted business; for example, Boulter's flash lock, which was with the exception of Romney (built in 1797) the furthest downstream lock until early in the 19th century, was not replaced with a pound lock until 1772.

The present navigation channel through Abingdon was re-opened in 1790, which led to the abandonment of the Swift Ditch route. The

Old Windsor Lock. This is the original lock built in 1822. Although not old by navigational standards, it shows clearly what is meant by a 'turf sided' lock (circa 1880).

term 're-opened' is used advisedly, for somewhere around A.D. 963 the monks of Abingdon Abbey had dredged and improved the river alongside the abbey and through the town, rather than send craft down the Swift Ditch; and various reports suggest that the present navigable channel had been used intermittently for some hundreds of years.

The Thames Navigation Commissioners

The Thames Navigation Commissioners were appointed under an Act of 1751, which gave scope for a possible total membership of 600. The commission was very unwieldy, which was not surprising in view of the fact that every landowner worth more than £100 per year in the 7 counties bordering the upper river was eligible for membership, together with the mayors of all Thames-side towns and representatives of Oxford University. A full meeting of the body would have been impossible, for at that time there would not have been a large enough building available. However, any 3 commissioners were entitled to inspect the various river works; this had the beneficial effect of stopping certain abuses, and informing the more enlightened commissioners what was going on and how urgent it was that the navigation be improved. Ideas formulated and put forward, largely through public opinion, and to an extent parliament, resulted in a more effective Thames Act in 1770. But the commission was further swollen in numbers by the addition of all Members of Parliament in the riparian counties, the Corporation of the City of London, the clergy from riparian parishes as well as other dignitaries, together with the proprietors of the Wey Navigation. In spite of these prodigious numbers it only required a quorum of 11 to carry out business. And so in the last quarter of the 18th century real progress was seen with regard to navigational works. The new commission had considerable powers. It could build and maintain towpaths and to this end could acquire land by compulsory purchase. It could buy up old flash locks and weirs, and of course construct new pound locks. It paved the way for the future, and

A TABLE shewing the TOLLS payable on the THAMES and ISIS Navigation, from...back, in each passage at the POUND-LOCKS, and at the OLD LOCKS and WEIRS; — And also CARRIAGE downward and upward by the Rivers Thames and Isis, and of Land-carriage to and...under mentioned and LONDON; — And also the TIME generally taken in Navigating a Barge, fro...downward by the afsistance of the Stream, and upward from London to fuch Places by Horfe-

	Tolls at the Poundlocks by the Ton each passage	Tolls at the Old locks and Weirs For 5 tons each passage	Prices of Watercarriage downward by the ton.	Upward by the ton.	Price of land carriage each way by the Ton.
	£. s. d.	£. s. d.	£. s. d.	£. s. d.	£. s. d.
STAINES - - -	2	—	- 5 0	- 7 0	1 0 0
WINDSOR - - -	3¼	—	- 6 0	- 8 0	1 6 8
MAIDENHEAD -	3½	—	- 7 6	- 9 6	1 10 0
MARLOW - - -	6½	3	- 9 0	- 11 6	2 0 0
HENLEY - - -	11	7¼	- 10 6	- 13 6	2 5 0
READING - - -	1 5	1 2½	- 12 0	- 16 0	2 10 0
WALLINGFORD -	1 11	2 10½	- 14 0	- 18 0	3 0 0
ABINGDON - -	2 2	4 2½	- 16 6	1 3 0	3 10 0
OXFORD - - -	2 6½	6 7	- 19 0	1 5 0	4 0 0
LECHLADE - -	3 3½	8 9½	1 10 0	2 0 0	5 0 0

This is an extract from Zachary Allnutt's *Acc...Navigation, Staines to Lechlade* circa 1790.

just as well, for the 19th century bro...great increases in river traffic – a large...boating for recreational purposes and t...of steam for commercial and passenger...

Zachary Allnutt, secretary to the co...ers, in his *Account of Navigation, S...Lechlade* (circa 1790) writes as follov...

The River Thames appears to be th...ancient navigable river in the Kingd...this navigation was formerly carried...very large barges of 200 tons, drawir...feet of water, passing down by force...stream through old flash locks or p...four or five feet, which made a rap...dangerous torrent, causing shoals a...structions; and being haled (towed)...upward passage against the stream, in...places by 12 or 14 horses, and in...by gangs of from 50 to 80 men. This...of navigation was found so inconv...and expensive, that in 1771 an Act o...liament was passed for improving...navigation between London and Cric...with a further Act vesting that pa...tween the City of London and Staines...city of London . . . the management...upper part to be in the hands of the N...ation Commissioners who held six ge...meetings a year, at London, Win...Marlow, Reading, Wallingford...Oxford. General meetings are empov...to borrow £75,000 for carrying on...

completing the works, and to pay interest for the same not exceeding 5%. The General Meetings are authorised to lay tolls not exceeding four pence a ton at each poundlock. – To set the price of carriage, and hire of horses for towing. – To regulate the height of water by setting water marks, to prevent flooding of adjacent lands, and to keep sufficient depth of water for navigation. – To remove all nuisances and obstructions, prevent impositions. To make bye laws and regulations, for the better carrying on the said navigation. In pursuance of these powers, the commissioners have borrowed £60,800 and have laid out same, and the surplus of the tolls in the improvement of the navigation from Staines to Lechlade by erecting poundlocks, making horse-towing paths and other necessary works … A sufficient head of water, is (in general) kept up by the poundlocks, for barges drawing not more than 3 ft 10 inches, the allowed depth to be navigated both downwards and upwards with safety, certainty and expedition. – And the downward passage particularly, (being the most important trade) is the best navigation possible, by the assistance of the stream, which at all times conveys the barges to the London markets with less delay or expense than any other navigation. All goods are regularly received at the several wharfs in London and along the Thames Banks and from thence conveyed to and from several places westward to Staines, Windsor … Maidenhead … Marlow … Henley … Reading … Wallingford … Abingdon and Oxford in barges not exceeding 120 ft. in length, 18 ft. breadth and 4 ft. depth.

At a general meeting of the commissioners held in Oxford Town Hall, on April 29th, 1855, a resolution was passed

That low water marks be fixed at Oxford water works, Folley Bridge, at Osney Mill, City Mill, Godstow weir and pound and at such other places the Commissioners may

think fit, and that the system of running flashes on the river be abolished, (the old habit of opening weirs, to let a 'flash' or flush of water down to help barges navigate the shallows in the reach below; they were haphazard and wasteful of water; in 1826 the commissioners had tried to improve the situation by arranging for two regular flashes to be let through the weirs each week, for which they scheduled a strict timetable; a flash took just about three days to travel from Lechlade to Sonning). … Yet above Oxford there exists hardly any other mode – the only plan for retaining water being by private weirs … it was recommended that Mr. Treacher, the general surveyor attended to the matter …

John Treacher was a carpenter who later went into business as a contractor and builder; by 1770 he was well established and constructed pound locks for the commissioners at various points, including Marlow and Hambleden, after which the Treacher concern specialized in all forms of river work. In 1787 John Treacher became surveyor to the Thames Commissioners, which position he held until his death in 1802, when he was succeeded by his son, also a John, who in 1835 was succeeded in turn by his son, George. John Treacher Jnr before taking over his late father's position had been appointed general engineer to the commission on September 30th, 1795.

The commission turned its attention to weirs, and many were improved by replacing the old 'paddle and rymer' type (as described in details of flash weirs) with improved fixed structures having large paddles running in grooves cut in the vertical supports. Attached to these paddles were a pair of chains taken up and round wooden axles positioned just below the upper cross beam of the weir. The axles were turned by inserting a spike into an appropriate hole and heaving away. When in the desired position the axle was restrained with a short chain and hook. This was a great improvement in obtaining, and maintaining, control of the flow.

Until the 18th century towpaths were almost non-existent; furthermore towing was generally carried out by gangs of men, delighting in the name of 'halers', who mostly waded along the foreshore. It was the commissioners who under their powers acquired land, built towpaths and established ferries at the points where the towpath had to change from one bank to another. The ferries are dealt with in the chapter on River Crossings, but the following extracts on towpaths give an insight into their construction:

Thames Commissioners report 1775. At Walton a new towing path hath been raised out of the bed of the river and now nearly completed ... the height is sufficient to enable the towing horses to go in safety in the highest navigable water. A good towpath is likewise made over Mr. Field's wharf and over a piece of ground belonging to Mr. Palmer of Walton for which he asked £100 ... A path formed and gravelled over the ait ground above Staines Bridge being 483 yards long and a large towing bridge is now making there and in a short time will be finished (it being

remembered that the Staines brid[g] period was further downstream, from what is now the public landin[g] Town Hall, to just below the Swan At Staines, for want of a horse tow[] (Middx side) men are hired to to[w] two miles, which is a hinderance [of] two hours. The towpath change[s] Surrey shore at the bridge.

A 1771 report states:

At Boveney it is ordered that a hor[s]ing path be made under the directio[n] General Surveyor as soon as conv[e] possible. Ordered that as soon as th[e] towing path be completed betwee[n] sor Bridge and Maidenhead Bridg[e] not exceeding three pence per ton b[] from all barges passing through W[] Bridge.

On July 29th, 1771, the commission[e]

to pay half the annual value of l[a] which towing paths are to be ma[d]

Bowles's map of the Thames (1788).

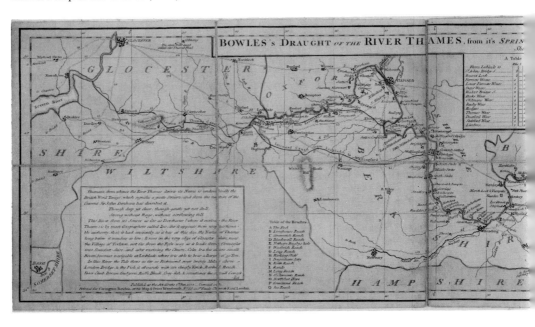

rent for the liberty of passing over such land as long as used and to keep repaired such paths, bridges and gates as necessary. In case where a footpath existed, no payment to be made for 9 feet, but rent for a further 9 ft. will be paid.

In August 1772: 'Towpath ordered to be constructed between Hedsor and Spade Oak and thence to Marlow Lock on the Bucks side of the river.'

In 1811 it was decreed that 'a towpath be made above and below Caversham Bridge as directed'. This section was a relative latecomer, for a little further upstream, at Purley, a horse towing path had been built in 1778, subject to the following: 'Towpath to pass at back of Purley Church so as to avoid Mr. Waldridge's orchard and yard.' This towpath was part of the route from Caversham, through Freebody's Mead, then through Freebody's Wharf and after the by-pass at Purley, on to Mapledurham. In 1787 the towpath above Pangbourne was continued towards Goring along the old foot towing path. In 1801 the towpath at Wallingford Bridge was altered – just ten years after estimates were prepared for making a towpath from Godstow to Osney. To render a topical ending to these towpath notes, it is worth recording that re-gravelling of the towpath in the Remenham reach in 1980–81 was probably the first time since 1783, when:

> The Surveyor having informed the Committee that he hath but one ballast boat, the other being employed at present as a ferry boat and therefore could not gravel the horse towing path between Henley and Remenham according to the order of the meeting of January 1783, ordered that he do immediately proceed to build another horse ferry boat and in the meantime do hire a boat and employ three gangs of men.

The river was divided into sections for maintenance and administrative purposes, the sections being:

No. 1   City of London – Staines (controlled by City of London)
No. 2.   Staines – Boulter's Lock
No. 3.   Boulter's – Mapledurham
No. 4.   Mapledurham – Shillingford
No. 5.   Shillingford – Oxford
No. 6.   Oxford – Cricklade
Nos. 2 – 6 controlled by Thames Navigation Commissioners

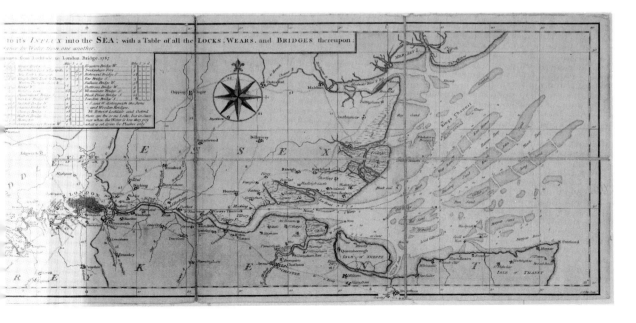

The charging and collection of tolls was a large undertaking, and fines for passing through a lock without paying a toll were substantial. For example, in March 1818 Kerry Harding was fined £10 for forcing a passage through Caversham Lock without paying a toll. On the other hand the commissioners were helpful to those who had accidents; in 1815 Wm Freebody had his tolls remitted after his barge *Britannia* had been sunk; the same applied to Tom Balding's *Friendship*, and many many others. In 1824 it was decided that the penalty for overloading barges (double tolls) was to be strictly enforced and that handbills were to be printed and displayed at locks.

In the 1750s the Corporation of London appointed a Navigation Committee to improve the river west of London. Much urgent work was needed, for shoals abounded, so causing great hindrance to traffic. There were no locks in the area under their immediate jurisdiction, and towing paths – for men, let alone horses – were either non-existent or badly eroded. In other words the river below Staines was in a sad and sorry state, and in an endeavour to expedite improvements the corporation looked into the possibility of various alternative schemes,

including canals with appropriate main river, which will be describ directly.

James Brindley's report

In May 1768, in the reign of George was passed for: 'Improving and com Navigation of the Rivers Thames an the City of London to the town of Cr the County of Wilts.' Salient points fr will come to light in a later chapter wh with barge traffic. Although barge t steadily increasing, little was done t the navigation, furthermore the st maintenance on existing works was highest standard. It is not surprising th find that on July 27th, 1770, the con the County Council of the City of instructed the great canal engineer, Jan ley, to survey the river from Boulter's Mortlake with a view to improving th tion. In his report to the committee states:

> Pursuant to your instructions, dat July, 1770, I have made a Survey River Thames, from Boulters Lo

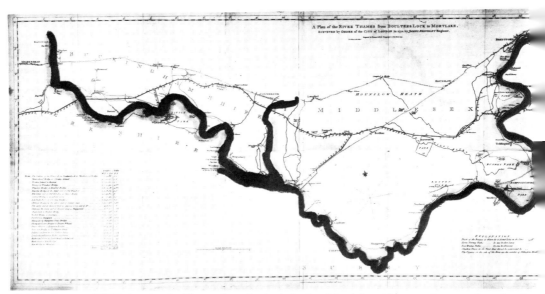

Brindley's map of 1770 showing the Thames from Boulter's Lock to Mortlake with route of proposed canal and co 'cuts'.

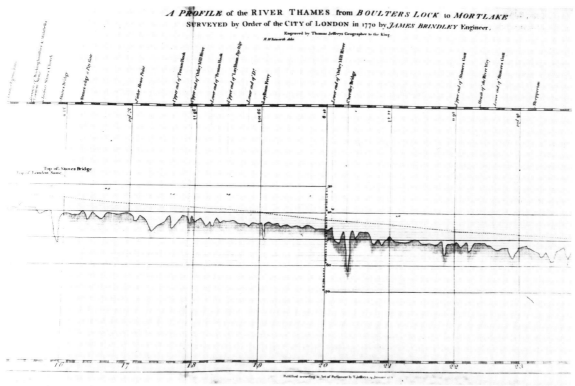

A reproduction of a small section of the profile of the River Thames prepared in 1770 by James Brindley.

Mortlake in Surrey, and have made a plan and profile of same, with a level and fall line, remarking the different falls from one town to another; and likewise have examined the most material Obstructions and Inconveniences that attend the present Navigation, which are considerable and many; for it hath been found by Experience, to be impassable for Barges in Time of Flood, which in most years continues several Months during the Winter, and is out of the Power of Art to Remedy. It likewise is impassable in Time of long Droughts, for want of sufficient Depth of Water; but this Difficulty may be removed, and the most effectual way to do it, would be by making Dams and (Cistern) Locks, the Dams to pound up one to another; the Number of which may be ascertained by the profile, which I suppose, will be about twelve, for if they be made to pound more

than five or six Feet, some of the adjacent Lands will be laid under water, or be subject to be soon flooded, as may be seen by the Surface of it, which are represented (by marks) in the Profile. But the Expence of improving so large a River in this Way, will be so great, that I suppose it will not be put into practice.

It is impossible for me to tell what the Expence would be, but dare make bold to say, it will be five or six times the Expence of making a Canal, and when done, will be far from being so safe and speedy a Conveyance; yet the River may be made better than it is, and that at no very extraordinary Expence. The Method that I would propose is, to contract the Channel in the shallow and broad Places, most of which are marked in the plan. By this means a sufficient Depth of Water, I suppose, may be obtained in all Places, or at least may be made much better than it is, but the Fall will remain the same, and the Current increase by the increased Depth of Water, consequently will require more Strength of Men and Horses to draw the Barges against the stream; yet by this Means it may be rendered much more certain than it is, and an easy Navigation downwards (except in Time of Flood) but the greater Labour and Expence of taking a Vessel upwards cannot be taken away by any Method that I know of, but by making a Canal, by Means of which, most Places upon the Banks of the River, may be supplied by collateral Cut for it is practicable to make Branches from the main Canal to fall into the River wheresoever it may be most useful to the County, viz. one may be made to communicate with the River above Windsor Bridge; the length will be about a mile, and the Fall or Lockage ten feet. Another cut may very easily be made from near West Bedfont, to the lower end of Staines; the Length will be about two Miles and seven furlongs, and the Fall twenty six feet. And whenever it is thought proper, another may be made to communicate with the River at or near Shepperton; this would be convenient to the Guildford Navigation, and the several Places down the Stream to Kingston. By these collateral Cuts, all the places upon the River (at least above Kingston) may be much better, cheaper and more certainly supplied with their commodities, than ever they were, or ever can be by the River Navigation alone, supposing the shallow places to be contracted (as mentioned before) so that vessels have a sufficient depth of water . . .

. . . Upon examining that part of the River between Mortlake and Richmond Gardens, I find much Time is lost, particularly in Neap Tides, owing to the Shoals and Sandbanks, arising on or towards the Towing Side, between those two places, which cannot be passed over for a great part of the Tide of Ebb, so vessels not being able to

reach this Place before High Wat
remain till the next tide, which th
not do, as the Towing Path begins
lake, could they have a sufficient I
Water to float them up: To rem
Inconvenience, I would propose a
be made across the River, somew
tween Mortlake and Kew Bridge,
Lock at each End; this would rec
Vessels from London that could sa
Tide to this Place, and by being com
Towing Path, would proceed up
Canal, or towards Kingston, witho
derance or delay.

. . . The Expence of this Dam, a
locks (from the best Accounts I ha
able to get of the Price of Materials)
about £17,500.

December 12, 1770   JAMES BRINI

A footnote to the above report reads a

Mr. Brindley stated on the 16th Jun
I am credibly informed that the exp
taking a Vessel of 100 or 120 Ton
Isleworth to Sunning, and back a
Isleworth, is 80l. and sometimes
which, by the Canal, at the tonna
posed, will be 16l. and may easily
formed in fifteen Hours, consec
there will be a clear Saving to the Pul
64l. out of 80l. upon every v
Besides this is not all the advanta
will acrue to the Publick from the
for in the present Navigation of the
they are three weeks in going up,
near long in coming down, often
great Loss and Disappointment
Proprietor in the Damage of his G

At a slightly later date Brindley carri
further survey with a view to exten
Isleworth–Maidenhead canal to Sonn
these proposals were discussed, pulle
re-discussed and finally put aside. But
Brindley's enthusiasm for his well c
plans spurred the Corporation of Lon
action and greatly stimulated the work.

in hand, of the Thames Navigation Commissioners. It is interesting to note that Charles Truss, the Corporation of London's clerk of navigation works, was an advocate of making canals rather than improving the natural river. The so-called ait at Staines, about a couple of miles below Staines Bridge and against the Surrey bank, is called Truss's Island; there is a monumental stone on the bank engraved with the City of London Arms and bears the legend 'Truss's Island 1774. Rt Hon. Fredk. Bull Lord Mayor'. This island, now really part of the mainland, is marked on maps as Savory's weir. No doubts this dates from the time when the backwater was sizeable and in which was sited a fishery weir.

19th century improvements

In 1797 a lock was built at Romney; the first below Boulter's! From then on things began to stir, albeit very slowly, so that by the beginning of the 19th century plans were in hand for improving the navigation of the river. Implementation of these plans commenced with the building of locks, the first to open being Teddington in 1811 followed by Sunbury in 1812, then Shepperton in 1813 (January) and Chertsey in September of that year. Penton Hook was opened in March 1815 and Molesey five months later. The late 18th century saw more activity upriver. The flash lock at Marsh near Henley dating from the 16th century was replaced with a pound lock in 1773; in the same year a pound lock was opened at Shiplake. These came under a programme of building eight new pound locks under an Act of 1771; the first of these eight was Sonning Lock. Whitchurch had its first pound lock in 1787 after 200 years of flash locks. Goring and Cleeve received their new locks in the same year, likewise replacing flash units. Hart's Lock (above Pangbourne), which was more of a hindrance than a help to navigation, ceased operating in 1800 and within a short time all trace of it was lost.

Most of the navigation works above Staines were carried out by the previously mentioned Thames Commissioners; those downstream mainly by the Corporation of the City of London.

When the commissioners met for their routine meeting in October 1833 they received their first warning about the imminent threat of railways; almost immediately they took steps to oppose them and it seems for the next few years they soldiered on, but with an income dwindling from the reduction in barge traffic. By 1850 the financial position had become very serious, and not surprisingly a flood of economic controls were instituted, but to no avail; the organization continued to decline. The Corporation of London was suffering much the same fate and was in a desperate situation with regard to its navigation responsibilities. In 1855 it needed £30,000 to carry out urgent and essential works. The government refused to help but eventually implemented their threat to set up a new authority; the corporation was first to be taken over, the commissioners not being absorbed until 9 years later. In 1857 the Thames Conservancy was formed to take over the river from Staines to

An early Thames Conservancy schedule of charges for pleasure craft.

Yantlet Creek in the Thames estuary and the City of London gave up all its rights. In 1866, as a result of a further Act of Parliament, the Thames Conservancy extended its jurisdiction to Cricklade. Then in 1908 the tidal portion of the river (from Teddington to the Nore) was passed to the then newly formed Port of London Authority.

The last lock and weir to be built on the Thames (not to be confused with enlarging, re-building or 'doubling up' of existing locks) was Shifford in 1898. On the river above Oxford, flash locks remained until long after the acceptance of pound locks; those at Eaton Hastings, Eynsham, Kings' and Medley existed into the present century; Eaton was the last flash lock to remain in use; it was removed in 1938. The term 'pound lock' remained in the river vocabulary for many years, although in fact by 1867 Conservancy officials had been told to drop the term and simply use the word 'lock'.

Water authorities

In 1971 a report was published by the Central Advisory Water Committee on the future management of water in England and Wales. This was followed by a white paper on the re-organization of water and sewage services; this culminated in the Water Act 1973, which received Royal Assent in July of that year. The Act is very comprehensive and more embracing than previous enactments dealing with water and river management; the most outstanding item of the Act was the abolition of river authorities, statutory water boards and joint sewerage boards and committees, and the transfer of their functions to new regional water authorities, who also took over the responsibilities of local authorities for water supply and sewerage.

All river authorities, together with the Conservators of the River Thames, the Lee Conservancy Catchment Board and certain other statutory water undertakings as well as all joint sewerage boards and committees were abolished on April 1st, 1974. The functions of those bodies were transferred on that date to the newly formed water authorities, who also assumed

new powers and duties with regard to and amenity in connection with wat

Ten regional water authorities we nine for England and one for Wales. established by an order made by the S State for the Environment and the N Agriculture. These ten authorities exer functions on and after April 1st, 1 navigation powers of the former Tha servancy, together with many oth including the all important task of lan are now carried out by the Tham Authority and, in particular, the Tha servancy Division of that Authority. diction of the new authority for purposes is the same as that enjoyed Thames Conservancy, i.e. from Cri Teddington. The Thames catchment a 3,845 square miles and the total lengt in that area amounts to 2,000 miles.

The greatest innovation with Thames locks was their mechanization lock to receive an experimental syste was electro-mechanical, was Mapled 1956. Cookham Lock was re-built i

The young Chaplin brothers inspecting the new electro-mechanical gear at Mapledurham Lock which made it the first power-operated lock on th

with mechanical operation, again, actuated by electric motors. However, electric power proved unsatisfactory, largely because electric motors did not enjoy having their rotations changed quickly, at times even instantly. Nevertheless this bold experiment paid off and sowed the seed, as usually happens in such cases, for an alternative and better system in the form of that all-powerful and reliable medium, hydraulics. The very first hydraulic system was fitted to Shiplake Lock in 1961 and from then on a programme was initiated for mechanizing all locks from Teddington to Godstow.

In 1976 came a breakthrough with lock tolls: the old-fashioned, time consuming way of paying the lock keeper was to buy a twelve-month lock pass, for which was issued an enamel plate bearing the name of the boat, or even to obtain at the first lock encountered, a journey pass; now the authority announced that: 'Boats, in respect of which valid registration certificates are in force, are entitled to pass through any of the locks on the River Thames within the jurisdiction of the authority (including Blake's Lock on the River Kennet) without payment of toll.'

A selection of Thames Conservancy registration plates. 1948 was the last issue of vitrious enamel plates. 1949 saw the introduction of the acrylic variety. The oval plate on the left was issued for hire boats. The upper figure (90) indicated the owner (in this case L. Waldock) and the lower figure (60) the number of boats held. 'Red Imp' plate was a lock pass for a powered craft.

3

Our great river is so dependent upon its tributaries, be they diminutive brooks or navigable watercourses, that no book on the Thames could be considered complete without giving a brief mention of the catchment area with an outline of the most important facts and features. The Thames catchment area was determined in 1931, after the Land Drainage Act of the previous year, and its superficial extent is some 3,845 square miles, drained by innumerable brooks, streams and rivers, which culminate in 38 main tributaries feeding the river between Thames Head and Teddington.

The **Cherwell**, beloved by generations of Oxford students, and possibly best known to tourists where it flows under Magdalen Bridge, past the magnificent tower of the same name, is a river of great charm. From its source near Charwelton it flows down to the Thames through vast acres of unspoilt Northamptonshire and Oxfordshire. The source, incidentally, is not so very far from two other watersheds, the River Nene and the Warwickshire Avon. Those who travel upon the Oxford Canal will be familiar with the Cherwell where it joins the canal, and other stretches of it where it runs in close company. To the north of Banbury the river is crossed by Trafford Bridge – a pleasant little structure with two dignified arches which in its day has supported vast traffic, for it carries the old Welsh Way, which once crossed the Warwickshire Avon at Offenham, and was used by

drovers taking their herds from Wa country fairs. Down below Banbu Brook, of steamboat fame, helps tc waters of the Cherwell.

The **River Windrush**, which flow Thames a little upstream of the 'Ros inn at Newbridge was once the lif Witney, for its waters were essential duction of those famous blankets. N the river provide power for the mills i sheep-rearing area, but the nitrous c the water had properties peculiar to t the blanket maker. The river rises w Cotswolds near Cutsdean and flo attractive tourist centres such as P the-Water, Burford and Minster Lo below Bourton the waters of the W augmented by those of the dimin Dickler, which is in all probabili important tributary.

The **River Lambourne** is a chalk s rises on the Berkshire Downs and ca cold waters to the Kennet at New eleven miles distant. Like many chal has 'swallow holes' where the river d certain seasons, not necessarily drought, to follow its own subterra In recent years the Lambourne Valle the news due to various ground-wa for which the valley is geologically logically suitable. Thames Water ha of boreholes to pump water into the

A charming Victorian scene showing a single skiff among water lilies (*Nymphaea alba*), which are now very scarce. Note eel bucks in right background.

from water-bearing strata during dry summer periods, so making water available for abstraction on the main river. Once pumping is stopped the ground water system is replenished by percolation resulting from rainfall. The maximum depth of these boreholes is 700 feet; the ground space they occupy is negligible, and vast reservoir schemes are obviated.

The Kennet itself is a very lovely river indeed, rising not far from the largest man-made mound in Europe, Silbury Hill, the haunt of archaeologists. The Kennet is famous for trout, but to boating folk it is associated with the Kennet and Avon Canal, of which it forms part in places, and runs in close proximity elsewhere. The Enborne, with its attendant Kingsclere Brook, which at one time was well endowed with mills, along with other streams, bring waters down from Hampshire to the Kennet which in turn helps to swell the Thames. Other Hampshire rivers are the Whitewater, Blackwater (after which two Thames Water launches are named), Fleet Brook and River Hart, all of which flow into the River Loddon, which joins the Thames at Wargrave

after welling up from the Hampshire countryside not too far from Basingstoke.

Hampshire also holds the source of the **River Wey**, which rises near Alton and rapidly collects water from a number of Hampshire and Surrey streams and rivulets. The lower part of the Wey was made navigable under Acts of Parliament passed in 1651 and 1681–3. The 15-mile long navigation, Weybridge to Guildford, was constructed by building a dozen locks and cutting about ten miles of artificial channel. The navigation was continued a further four miles upstream to Godalming in 1764. The Basingstoke Canal joined the river in 1796 and in 1816 a link was made with the South Coast by the construction of the Wey and Arun Canal.

The **River Colne** rises in Hertfordshire, in the Hatfield area, not far from the infant River Lea. A little below St Albans the Colne is joined by the River Ver which rises near Markyate and flows past the remains of the famous Roman town Verulamium. The rivers Bulbourne, Gade, Chess, Alderbourne and Pinn are but a few of the Colne's many tributaries, whilst the Colne itself splits into many branches before it joins the Thames. The most upstream outlet is the Colne Brook at Wraysbury, then the Wraysbury River at Bell Weir, the County Ditch alongside the City Stone, the main stream of the Colne by the cinema at Staines and the final offshoot, the River Ash, at Sunbury. This array of water-courses may have had some bearing on the Roman name for Staines, which was 'Pontes', meaning bridges.

From a horticultural point of view it is inter-esting to recall that watercress started to be grown as a commercial crop in the first quarter of last century and that some of the earliest beds were alongside the Misbourne and the Gade; both of these rivers find their way down to the Colne, although the Misbourne lives up to its name, for not infrequently, like the Lambourne, the bed of the river is dry. Being a chalk stream, the water is received by swallow holes, from time to time.

The Colne Valley Regional Park is the result of a far-sighted and excellent scheme put forward many years ago. It stretches from Staines in the south to Rickmansworth in the north and embraces all the rivers, lakes, gravel workings and reservoirs in the area plus of course the

Grand Union Canal with its attendan Arm. It forms a superb amenity area fo of boating, water skiing, fishing, wall watching and so on. Believe it or not, area of this Regional Park is 15 per ce than the Norfolk Broads!

Up at Dorchester, south east of O Thame joins the Thames after a seri derful meanders and passing a mill o last one, Overy Mill, has been restored and dates back to before D

The River Churn is the third tribu Thames going downstream (the othe the Swill Brook and the Derry Brook is made of the Churn in particular source is so easy to find at the well kr Springs, just off the main Cirencest tenham road, a short distance beyon of Coberly.

In concluding this chapter, ment made of the River Evenlode. At one used for commercial traffic, and to f passage of craft a canal was cut to last three miles of the river; this wa the Cassington Cut. Today this d can be observed below Eynsham L

4

RIVER CROSSINGS

Fords

In the dim and very distant past, when weirs and flash locks were few and far between, and little or no ballasting (dredging) was done to increase the depth of water, the Thames with its modest flow and abundance of gravelly shallows must have presented many suitable sites for fording. Some of the sites are obvious to this day by their names, such as Shifford, Duxford, Oxford, Shillingford, Wallingford. In 64 B.C. Caesar is reputed to have crossed the river at Coway Sale in the Walton reach, which was the one place that could be passed on foot. It was inevitable that

An early Thames ford, from a wood engraving by H.R. Robertson and W.J. Palmer.

with the construction of more efficient weirs, better locks, ballasting and general navigational improvements the shallow areas gradually receded so that the old-established fords became ferry crossings. According to legend a few of these fords have been re-used in times of drought, the crossing at South Stoke being one of them, when in a hot summer at the end of last century harvest wagons crossed the river, no doubt providing a welcome cooler for the horses.

Ferries

As ferries became established, punts and wherries were not always sufficient, for, as well as pedestrians, and what today we would term 'light parcel traffic', it was sometimes necessary to convey animals, and at major points light horse-drawn vehicles needed to be taken across. For this sort of traffic 'flats' were used, usually carrying one vehicle at a time; their swim ends (sloping up as on a punt) facilitated beaching, whilst the inside of the swims, when suitably planked, formed excellent loading and unload-

ing ramps. Such flats were mostly pol… the river, but some were worked ac… rope, which passed through guide po… ferryboat, and pulled the boat by win… on a windlass-operated drum on the ap… bank.

Later versions of such ferries were … cable and, better still, by chain, which… in use lay flat on the river bed; the ch… up and round a drum on the side o… which, when turned in the appropriat… with the wheel provided, moved the f… the desired direction. Rope-opera… tended to provide a hazard for passin… to the rope floating near the surface)… some readers can recall catching thei… in the rope at Bablock Hythe before t… withdrawn from service in the late 19… useful life of some 700 years.

Passenger ferryboats, other than … usually a wherry, or a rowing boa… proportions: craft that would be e… under adverse conditions, whilst be… to have good stability when carryir… of people. In the late 17th centur…

A Thames ferry, from a wood engraving by H.R. Robertson and W.J. Palmer.

Parliament was passed, with a view to ensuring that ferryboats were built to a suitable standard:

That if any person or persons whatsoever, from henceforth do, or shall make any wherry or boat, to the intent commonly to use rowing and carrying people upon the river Thames, which shall not be 22 ft. 6 inches in length, and 4 ft. 6 inches broad in the midship or which shall not be substantially and well able and sufficient to carry two passengers on either side (on bench seats), built according to the old rules for scantlings (i.e. size to which wood is cut) thickness of cladding, and good proportions to the boat, then the said boat is liable to be forfeited to the King and Queen.

Their majesties referred to would have been William and Mary.

Most of our 'accommodation ferries', that is, ones that connected with roads or adjacent villages, pre-dated many of the oldest bridges; whereas the 'roving' or 'navigation' ferries of the later 18th century came with the advent of horse-drawn barges; as horse towing paths were built, there arose the need to ferry horses across the river at points where the towpath changed banks. This resulted in an upsurge in the number of ferries upon the river.

But back to the accommodation ferries; not all of these were displaced by bridges, and in fact the only one still running (by statute) is at Hampton. It goes back to Domesday and in 1606 the tenants, Greensmith, Crane and Budbroke, also ran Hampton Court Ferry. Lord George Sanger in his circus biography gives a lively account during the 1880s of a fight between two rival groups of gipsies on the ferry landing; police intervened and both lots of gipsies turned on the police; the ferryboats laden with fugitives sank and threw their freight of frightened and wounded men into the river, which luckily was shallow at this point. It should be noted that in the days before Hurst Park Racecourse (which came to an end in 1960), Moulsey (original spelling) Hurst was the scene of Happy Hampton races, cricket matches, fairs with prize fight-

ing, and the annual circus. Not only was the statutory ferry kept busy, but on these special occasions watermen were allowed to ply for hire and take passengers across the river from any of the public landing places in Hampton. The number of passengers per wherry was limited to twelve, but the writer can recall the days of race meetings at Hurst Park, when the waterman was either poor sighted or found counting rather difficult! Hampton is one of those ferries that under an Act of 1659 is forbidden to work between sunset and sunrise without a special licence. This presumably is in the interests of safety. In the half-tidal reach that lies between Teddington and Richmond, at the tail of Eel Pie Island is Twickenham Ferry. At the beginning of the century this was very much in the news, when Hammerton's set up a new ferry a little further downstream. Earl Dysart, owner of Twickenham Ferry, instituted action against Messrs Hammerton and Co., the earl claiming the monopoly of ferrying from any point in Twickenham to any point in Ham. After six years the case ended in the House of Lords in favour of the new venture. In July 1915, to celebrate their success, Hammerton's had published by Dimbleby and Son a song in commemoration of their victory in the House of Lords. It was entitled *Hammerton's Ferry — the Ferry to Fairyland*, and cost 2d. (old pence).

Swinford Ferry was in business long, long before the building of the Toll Bridge (which opened August 4th, 1769); in 1636 it was in grievous trouble, when on one winter's day several passengers were drowned. One of the most interesting of our former ferries was at Medmenham. It was used by King Charles II in 1678, or thereabouts, and further patronized by royalty in 1905 when Edward VII made a crossing. In 1911 it was used by King George V and Queen Mary, accompanied by Edward, Prince of Wales, and Prince Albert, later George VI. A milestone in the history of the ferry was reached on March 28th, 1889, when a court of appeal decided that the Medmenham Ferry was public (i.e. could be used by others than those engaged in towing). A monument to commemorate the successful action stands nearby.

Tims Ferry, Staines, in the 1920s used for carrying pedestrians. Would be regarded as a 'vil to vil' (or accomm
Note the vast number of punts moored end on along the downstream bank and the large number of skiffs
remainder of the frontage.

So much for the old ferries and on to the recent 'navigation' ferries that came into being, as already mentioned, in the 18th century with the making of good horse towing paths, sometimes termed 'bargewalks'. Whenever the bargewalk changed banks there would be a ferry to transfer the horses; remember that on an upstream trip with a heavy barge, a dozen horses could quite easily be involved. The minutes of the one-time Thames Commissioners make interesting reading; for example, at a meeting on August 31st, 1771, it was 'reported from a meeting held for the third District this day in Henley that until such time as horses are provided to take barges from Soloman's Hatch the Horse Towing Path be on the Oxford side of the river from the Wharf to Chipp's Mills. Ordered that the said Report be confirmed and carried into execution as soon as conveniently maybe.' Then on the 14th of the following month it was ordered 'that as soon as the horse towing path be finished and opened between Windsor Bridge and Maidenhead Bridge a toll be taken at Windsor Bridge of 3d. per ton for every voyage of every barge passing through the said bridge and if any such barge shall pass through said Windsor Bridge only once and not return in that case 1½d. per ton

be taken for the passage of suc
August 1772 the commissioners n
ments with a Mr James King to
horses in a ferryboat from Cook'
Oak. In July 1776 the commissi
that a chain, about 2 fathoms
should be put to each end of the l
(note old spelling) Ferry and that a
house be built there for the ferrym
summer of 1780 it was decreed
boat at Lashbrook be replaced
one at Bolney be repaired, 'bein
condition and even dangerous.'
ferry was proposed in 1787 and
that the ferryman take horses
1½d. per horse. Soon after this it
monthly meeting (September 8
'Ferry with boat and proper tacl
at Chalmore Hole for carrying
the river.' Next spring R. Chil
ferryman at 3/6 per week and
be made for each horse. In June
was appointed ferryman and t
a rood of land was purchased
ing a ferryman's house.

In the summer of 1798, t
made a bold move and subs

My Lady Ferry, Cliveden reach, in the 1880s. This was a 'navigation' ferry for conveying horses where the towpath changed banks.

ropes; the decision was arrived at after, it seems, somewhat lengthy discussions over the short life of ropes and the heavy and recurring expense of replacing them. Keen Edge Ferry at Shillingford, so beautifully delineated by J.T. Serres (whose painting can be seen in the National Maritime Museum) was first mentioned in July 1798 when the tolls were about 10/- monthly. In 1814 a new ferryboat was provided subject to material from the old one being used 'in the repair of the navigation'.

As steam tugs began to show their power, many old bargees, naturally resentful of change, were worried about competition; these fears no doubt influenced members of the commission at their meeting of July 1st, 1848, when it was decided that 'Bargemen and Horses to go free on all ferries run by the Commissioners'. This really spelt the end of barge traffic, but oddly enough one of the ferries established by the commissioners, My Lady Ferry, at Cliveden, was the last to be closed by the old Thames Conservancy, after their decision of 1953 to gradually close the remaining 19 navigation ferries at various points where the towpath changed to the opposite side of the river. The decision was reached at a board meeting, somewhat regret-

fully, owing to the virtual non-existence of horse towing, changes in public customs, and the fact that Thames ferries ceased to be used by the public as much as they had been in former times; the revenue from them was a pittance compared with the very heavy operating costs.

Benson ferry, at one time worked by the lock-keeper, was nearly the last to give service to those exploring the river by walking the tow-path; this service ended about two decades back. Other ferries closed prior to My Lady were: Bloomer's Hole (upstream of Buscot), Rushey, Shifford, Abingdon, Day's, Keen Edge, Chalmore Hole, Gatehampton, Mapledurham, Roebuck, Lashbrook, Harpsden, Aston, Temple, Spade Oak, Cookham Upper and Cookham Lower.

Bridges

As I write this chapter, it has just been announced that archaeologists digging in the City of London are 99 per cent certain they have found the first structural evidence of the Roman bridge that spanned the Thames. In contrast, 1,900 years later, the great eight-lane motorway bridge at Runnymede is nearing completion, which when opened will be the widest Thames Bridge. Such progress would surely have been applauded by Roman engineers!

But from these superlatives to more humble – but often very beautiful – bridges. If we work our way downstream: the bridges above Lechlade are of no special merit, the majority being small and of varied construction. The one at Cricklade has projecting keystones (central stones of the arch), which feature was quite common at the end of the 18th century; the bridges at Waterhay and Castle Eaton are of modern girder construction, the latter replacing an earlier arched bridge. In the 'Red Lion' pub at Castle Eaton there is a picture of this bridge as it stood when commercial craft used this part of the river. Hannington Bridge, the last before Lechlade, was built in the early 1840s.

'Halfpenny Bridge', so well known for its former toll to all who make the pilgrimage to Lechlade, was built under an Act of Parliament passed in the year 1792; during the last war it bore the weight of heavy military vehicles trundling through Lechlade, without any embarrassment to the highway authority. After the war, when a detailed survey of the structure was carried out, it was revealed that the footings for the abutments were laid on mattresses made of withies, or slender branches of willow. A little downstream of this we come to St John's Bridge, Lechlade, built in 1884 on the site of earlier structures dating back to 1337. At Radcot there are two bridges, the one under which the present navigation passes and the other across the former main stream. The latter is the oldest surviving bridge over the Thames, dating back to the year 1200. The former was built in 1787 to cross the new channel dug in that year, which was planned to take the anticipated extra barge traffic with the opening of the Thames–Severn Canal.

Old Radcot Bridge is, not surprisingly, built of Taynton stone, about which more will be said in the chapter on Barge Traffic. Tadpole Bridge is the next crossing; built in 1802, it is of pleasing appearance, but with no outstanding features. As with many river crossings, there was at one time a small wharf close by; it still boasts another feature of river crossings – a hostelry,

for the delightful little 'Trout' inn sta by. Newbridge with its 'six great arche (as referred to by Leland, Henry VIII's was 'broken' in 1644 by Parliamenta Swinford, otherwise known as Eynsha is a fine and noble structure built in 1 Earl of Abingdon and is one of the tv ing toll bridges on the river, the oth Whitchurch. Godstow Bridge, of me dates from the cutting of the present channel in 1780. The other two brid stow cross the Weir Stream and Seac respectively. The arches have brick are faced with stone, in common bridges built in the late 1700s.

The bridge at Osney, at one time is an ugly affair of steel and has the room of any bridge on the Th opened for traffic in January replaced an earlier stone bridge. which were said to be massive. Fo home of Salter's steamers and the waterborne holidaymaker, gain name in about 1650, formerly b 'Grauntpount' Bridge. The pres built in 1825; according to Wa the 19th century historian, there this site in A.D. 871, although th which there was definite know about 1085. The bridge at Abing replace a ford and dates from 14 in two sections, with an island i section on the Berkshire bar Abingdon Bridge, whilst th rejoices in the name of Burfor don Bridge was widened on th 1828 with semi-circular arche underwent alterations and 1927 when it was found that arch over the navigation char was unsound. The alterations the widening of the bridge it the width of the navigation three of the small 15th cent

Culham Bridge is as old a like the channel beneath it, bridge is closed to traffic. A insignificant bridge spans t upstream of the old one. The Swift Ditch is the former navigation channel. A comparative newcomer to the scene is Sutton Bridge which was built at the tail of Culham Lock in 1807. The next bridge, Clifton Hampden, belies its slightly mediaeval atmosphere with its four centre arches decorated in a ribbed style, for it was only built in 1864, whilst Shillingford Bridge was built in 1827 to replace a rather light wooden structure on stone piers built in 1784 to replace a ferry, which succeeded an even earlier ford, although there is a possibility that a bridge of rudimentary form may have existed on the site as early as 1300.

According to tradition, Wallingford had its first bridge in A.D. 600, and documentary evidence of a bridge dates back to 1141. The bridge was plagued with problems; apparently it was in a bad state of repair in the 14th century, for a grant of pontage was made by Edward III in 1344. Another grant was made in 1383 and a third one in 1407. The repairs under these grants were apparently poorly executed and a further grant for two years was made in 1429 when it was said that the bridge was so ruinous that many accidents occurred to people, horses and carts crossing same. Still the problems continued: a further grant was made in 1433; five of the land arches were rebuilt in 1530, and in 1646

four river arches were removed and replaced with wooden drawbridges during the defence of the town by Colonel Blagge. These arches were replaced with brick and stone in 1751. The central river arches were damaged by floods in 1809 and were replaced by the three existing elliptical arches.

The present bridge at Streatley replaces the original one built of timber in 1837, like its older cousin at Whitchurch, which was built in 1792. This bridge lasted until the latter part of the last century, when it was replaced by the bridge which is in use today, and enjoys the privilege of being the second of the two toll bridges over the Thames.

Caversham Bridge dates from the 13th century. In 1314 there was a chapel on the bridge to which many references are made; this bridge did great and heroic service until 1869 when it was taken down with the opening of the new bridge built of wrought and cast iron with latticework girders. This bridge, however, only lasted until 1926 in which year the present ferro-concrete structure was opened.

Reading Bridge, also of concrete, was built soon after World War I. Sonning (originally spelt, and still pronounced, Sunning) has a fine brick bridge which is an excellent example of 18th century craftmanship. Earlier bridges on

The present Reading Bridge, which was built very soon after the first war, in 1923. At the time it was a civil engineering achievement, with its great concrete arch spanning 60 yards. Note steamer passing under the lofty arch without the need to lower her funnel; also the collection of narrow boats against the far bank.

the site were of timber and probably date back to 1125. The present Henley Bridge, of Headington Stone – the Headington quarries being near Oxford – was built in 1786; the sculptured heads of Isis and Father Thames were the work of the Hon. Mrs Damer in 1786. This bridge replaced the one carried away by the great flood of 1774. It appears that the earliest record of a bridge at Henley goes back to the early 13th century.

The present Marlow Bridge, which in recent years had an extensive re-fit, was opened in 1835, having been built to a design by W. Tierny Clark, who was a pupil of that great engineer, Telford. Tierny Clark became famous for his bridge across the Danube at Budapest, which is almost a largescale version of the Marlow Bridge, and Marlow is sometimes thought of as the prototype for Budapest. Bridges at Marlow date back to 1300; in 1530 there was a timber bridge which was partly destroyed in 1642. A new bridge was opened in 1789, having been

built as the result of a public subscrip of timber and sited downstream of bridge. A little timber bridge was Cookham in 1840 but after a shor replaced with the present iron bridg

Maidenhead Bridge dates from th ter of the 13th century. Not surprisin of timber construction; whilst the was planned in 1772, there was so carrying out the actual constructior

There are early references, 13th fact, to oaks from Windsor Forest b the repair of Windsor Bridge; tol barges passing under the bridge wer a popular feature, nor were the to from those using the bridge itself co acceptable. The present bridge, of granite piers, was built in 1824, a stream of its predecessor. The si bridge abutments on the Eton public landing area, whilst the brid forms a superb pedestrian prome

Current Staines Bridge circa 1907. The bridge opened in April 1832. The steam launch in the foreground w who was a local brewer and banker, by Tom Taylor of Staines, previously of Chertsey – just upstrear corrugated roof covers a slipway which was removed in the 1970s. The boathouse and yard seen throug over by Biffens and is now the extensive yard of Cheesman, Rollo and Company.

been closed to vehicular traffic in the early 1970s due to weakness in the structure, no doubt accelerated by the action of floods and fast winter currents, for on the downstream side of the bridge the river is about 30 feet deep, with resultant turbulence, as anyone who has taken a large craft upstream under adverse conditions will know.

The next two bridges are the Victoria and the Albert respectively; they were opened in 1851, prior to which there was a bridge at Datchet. In the time of Edward III there was a ferry at Datchet; then in 1706 Queen Anne built a bridge on this crossing; this bridge was re-built in 1770, but it collapsed in 1793 so the ferry was re-instated until the building of another in 1812.

The present Staines Bridge was built by Rennie and opened by King William and Queen Adelaide in 1832. It stands slightly upstream of its immediate predecessor. The previous Staines bridges, excluding anything of the Roman period, were as follows: the old timber bridge

which remained in use until 1796, in which year a stone bridge was erected alongside, on the downstream side. However the arch cracked shortly after opening and the old timber bridge went back into service until the third bridge, which was constructed of iron, was opened to traffic in 1807, whereupon the old wooden bridge was at last pulled down.

The present Chertsey Bridge was built in 1785; there is little information on the earlier bridges except that John de Rutherwyke, Abbot of Chertsey, 1307–46, was credited with being an excellent builder of bridges, so we assume he was responsible for an early bridge. Walton, like other river crossings, has had its share of bridges. The first one, built in 1750, was unique in design, its appearance being slightly oriental due to the lattice timber work, arranged so that the replacement of damaged timbers could, theoretically, be made with ease. The piers were of stone, which were later used to carry the brick arches of the succeeding bridge. In August 1859,

Hampton Court Bridge, 1790, from proof No 7. of Thomas Rowlandson's print. The building on the far left is the 'Toy' Inn, much patronized by William III. In foreground are a Peterboat, a couple of punts and two small West Country barges.

the centre arch collapsed and it was not until 1864 that the present iron bridge, currently closed to traffic because of weakness, was built. As the years slip by it seems that the present temporary bridge – erected in 1954 – has become a fixture. At least the emergency bridge built at Staines in the last war, as a standby in case the main bridge was bombed, was dismantled as soon as possible after the cessation of hostilities.

As the writing of this chapter nears completion, so the building of a permanent bridge over to Tagg's Island, from the Middlesex or North Bank, has begun. This structure will be able to take a 32-ton vehicle and will replace the Bailey Bridge, situated a short distance downstream, which was a wartime expedient to maintain supplies for several factories on the island. These factories were established by converting the covered tennis courts that dated from days.

The first bridge to be erected at Court was a timber affair, opened although it was intended to replace which was of ancient origin, the ferr tinued to ply his trade for some co time after the bridge was in use. In bridge was replaced with an ele timber structure; this lasted until the a very ugly iron bridge in 1866. Ham Bridge was freed of tolls in 1876; cast-iron pillars that formed the ent side of the old toll house have, since mounted the flight of steps leadin entrance of Hampton Church at a commands a fine view of the river. very beautiful bridge, designed b Lutyens, was opened in 1933.

The Hampton Court Bridge of 1866–1933 pictured circa 1930. The steamer is the *Viscount*, built in 1908 of Richmond, used principally in the Richmond–Hampton Court tourist trade. The foreshore where pu originally Harry Tagg's boatyard, birthplace of many a fine steamer.

The original Kingston Bridge was built in the 13th century and until the 18th century was the second Thames bridge from the sea. By the 14th century the bridge was in a poor state of repair — complaints about it were made with monotonous regularity. In 1377 Edward III by letters patent gave authority for tolls to be levied on craft passing beneath the bridge, in addition to traffic crossing over it. In the civil war the bridge was modified to receive drawbridges, which not surprisingly weakened the old and somewhat narrow structure. In the last decade of the 18th century a few improvements were carried out, including the widening of the north, or Middlesex end. In 1814 part of the bridge collapsed; it was closed for several weeks and the design and building of a new bridge came into being in 1828. In July of that year it was officially opened by the then Duchess of Clarence, later to become Queen Adelaide. At the beginning of this century it was found that with the coming of trams and increase in traffic, the carriageway was not wide enough, so the bridge was widened on the downstream side by 30 feet. The widened structure was reopened in 1914 and great credit is due to the designers and builders for retaining the original appearance, other than the removal of the toll houses.

Footbridges are very limited in number; apart from the few mentioned upstream of Oxford, the rest are either across lock cuts or providing access to islands. There is an unusual footbridge across the navigation at Oxford, where the bridge built in 1882 that once carried supplies to the old gas works has been relegated to pedestrian use only. Oxford also boasts the Free Ferry Footbridge built by the Oxford Corporation in 1949 to link Iffley with South Hinksey; the single span is 125 feet, with 25 foot headroom at the centre.

Railway bridges hardly come within the scope of this book, for they are surely the preserve of the train enthusiast. However, mention must be made of Brunel's masterpiece at Maidenhead. It was the third of his designs, which, to conform with the then Thames Commissioner's stipulations and railway requirements, presented a special engineering challenge; the result is a bridge with the largest and flattest arch ever built in brick. The bridge had important links with the original broad-gauge Great Western Railway, since some of the locomotives built in the north had to be brought upriver by barge, whence they were lifted by crane on to the rails.

Wharves

Apart from the many commercial wharves that once existed in plenty, every Thames town and village, as well as a river crossing, had its public wharf, known variously as a 'hythe', 'hithe', 'hard', 'drawdock' or 'parish wharf'. Some were elaborate affairs of masonry, some a length of timber campshedding with consolidated ground behind, whilst others were just a cleared section of bank with mooring piles, and ashore some stacking space with turning room for horses and carts. Then there were the grand ones, such as at Folly Bridge, where excellent warehouses dominated the scene; these buildings are now part of the popular 'Head of the River' public house. Some wharves were in the form of docks and quays built at right angles to the river, a good example being at Lechlade directly upstream of, and almost alongside, Halfpenny Bridge. As will be described in the chapter on Barge Traffic, the wharves by Radcot Bridge are just discernible; a large dock once existed at Remenham just downstream of Henley Bridge, and Bray had a useful one which was at the back of the 'Albion' pub. Many, many wharves are lost to oblivion, a few are still usable and a very small number still used; a fair number have been converted, quite commendably, by local authorities into landscaped open spaces; but woe betide the boatowner who tries to exercise his right in using such a wharf — if a park attendant is around, the skipper of a boat is liable to be treated as if he were a juvenile delinquent. It is high time that all our existing wharves were maintained for mooring as well as for their original purpose. They are as important to a riparian town as a car park is to a shopping precinct.

Many a Thames-side town has a lane, road or alley delighting in the name 'Ropewalk'; very often such a thoroughfare is in the vicinity of a former 'hard'. In those far-off days of towing, ropes were in great demand, which gave rise to an important and lucrative local industry of rope making; this was situated in the 'Ropewalk'.

To conclude the story of Thames bridges, there are some seven new ones that built since the last war, most of whic motorway bridges or by-pass/motc nections: Oxford (2), Marlow, Bray Runnymede and Chertsey.

No doubt the heading of this chapter conjures up pictures of wildlife, shafts of sunlight sparkling on the gravel bed beneath a vast willow, or a great splash of colour where purple loosestrife is clinging to the inboard edge of an eroded bank; well, all in good time, but for starters the uncomfortable side of nature must be considered – that is, floods, droughts and frosts!

Floods

Floods in the past were generally more serious than those of today, for now more dredging takes place, weirs are larger, more efficient and easier means of control are available; however, that does not mean that riparian owners can live in a fool's paradise. In spite of modern engineering techniques and improved methods of river management and control, nature always holds the whip hand! A very rapid thaw, coupled with heavy rainfall, spring tides and north easterly gales, could make life throughout the Thames Valley very uncomfortable indeed. And this of course is precisely what happened in the past, bringing with it great hardship: in particular, barge traffic was often brought to a halt, which meant not only lack of work with the resultant problems but also shortage of supplies such as coal, grain, animal feedingstuffs and so on. Fishermen were quite often hit by loss of tackle and therefore there was a shortage of fish; mill-owners had to face their share of troubles with

stocks of corn left unground, as barges were unable to collect flour.

The earliest recorded flood on the Thames is that of A.D. 9; in A.D. 48 the flood waters of the Thames extended through 4 counties and it is said that 10,000 people were drowned. From then until the great flood of 1894 there is information – often very scanty – on no less than 31 Thames floods. Here are some of the dates – years which our forefathers talked about with bated breath for many winters afterwards:

1099 'Thames much flooded on festival of St. Martin'

1555 'September 21st. Westminster Hall flooded'

1660 'November 11th great floods'

1680 'June, great floods at Oxford'

1763 'Vast extent of meadows from source of the Thames to the sea covered with water'

1764 'Long Wittenham, January 14th. Greatest flood for 30 years'

1764 'Great distress prevailed amongst the bargemen as they had not been able to work for two months by reason of the floods'

1768 'Long Wittenham, 7' 7" rise December 3rd. Rapid thaw after snow – greatest flood for 80 years'

1774 March 10th. 8' 1" rise – greatest flood for a century – Henley Bridge carried away'

1795 'In this year of terror of the French Revolution there was a heavy flood in mid-February. At Staines the Southampton coach was upset passing through deep flood water'

1809 'King George III had to remain at Windsor as the Ford at Datchet was impassable and Eton bridge had been carried away on the rising waters. In the same year — evidently a bad one — there was further flooding, in April, on the 26th of the month the road through Slough was flooded and the King had to go to London through Egham and Staines'

1823 'A sudden flood in early November, many sheep drowned'

1852 'November 17th was named the "Duke of Wellington's flood" for on the occasion of his funeral, the hearse and horses were upset in the flooded Bath Road at Maidenhead'

1875 'November 10th–17th was another week of severe flood'

It is interesting to note the exact dates of the last two floods, for the greatest Thames flood of all time — the one of 1894 — reached its terrible peak also on November 17th.

Some of the bad floods were of course aggravated by unofficial weirs and structures in the course of the river and some claim that the old London Bridge (pulled down in 1831) acted as a dam and so impeded the exodus of landwater to the sea, but on the other hand that self-same bridge played a useful part in checking the flow of tides upriver.

Way back in 1777, the dear old Thames Commissioners, who were then caring for the river, called a special meeting on December 27th of that year ordering that a bill to amend the Act of George III of 1768 be presented to Parliament to help them alleviate floods. At a meeting of February 5th, 1828, the general surveyor delivered, in conformity with the order of the last meeting, a report upon the cause of the late increase of floods in the neighbourhood of Iffley, and upon the most advisable mode of relieving them, 'and the General Clerk is thereupon

directed to write to Mr. Swann to re
obstacle therein complained of . . .'

At a meeting of the Commissione
December 29th, 1849, we read that: '
having complained on the part of th
Oxford of the flooding in and in the r
hood of the city of Oxford arising a
posed from the water ways at Iffley
ford being impeded, the Committee re
that a sub-Committee be appointed
deputation from the City to confer
subject.' Then, as now, meetings ar
dissertations were, seemingly, the or
day. However the minutes of a mee
July 20th, 1799, were concise: 'No cc
locks owing to great and long flood
surely proves that wet summers are r
rogative of the space age!

The great flood of 1894 was due to
ally heavy rainfall during a limited p
amount of rain that fell in the 26 day
the peak period of the flood on Nove
was almost one third of the total ann
for the area — over 8 inches of rain. Ar
of the immensity of the great flood is
brief list of locks and height of the fl
(in each case at the head of the l
normal summer level.

Hambleden	5' 2"	Boveney
Marlow	5' 9"	Sunbury
Bray	8' 3"	Temple
Old Windsor	8'	Boulter's
Hurley	3' 4"	Romney
Cookham	5' 10"	Molesey

At Cookham the flood was from 6
higher than in 1852, and the follc
extract from a report by that once
Bourne End boatbuilder, Eric Tow

We had 4' 6" of water in the
rooms at our boatyard and as nea
tell it was 3' 6" above the towing
the opposite side of the river. It is
est flood known by anyone livi
here. Traffic was stopped on the
branch line owing to the depth of

the metals. At Cookham the flood was 9″ above any existing record at 4 a.m. on November 17th. Whilst at Boulter's Lock it appears the flood reached its zenith at 2.15 a.m. on that day.

At Eton the playing fields were submerged and rooms of masters' houses inundated; the boys rejoiced for they were given ten days' holiday. Wood paving in the road at Eton was washed away, and the London and County Bank, which had been built above flood levels in accordance with bye laws, had 4 feet of water over the ground floor. Her Majesty Queen Victoria, then 75 years old, showed much concern over the flood. Not only did she head the subscription list to the fund, but put all the wagons, traps and water carts of the royal estate at Windsor at the disposal of the relief committee. Furthermore she visited scenes of devastation and witnessed the plight of her peoples; her greatest concern seemed to centre round adequate supplies of fresh water for drinking purposes, which was the reason for allowing H.M. water carts to be put into general service. As Eton college was closed, the school food supplies were used for the general public. In Datchet, as in many other towns, tradesmen delivered goods with the aid of punts. Train services between Staines and Windsor were suspended due to the permanent way being damaged whilst at Datchet station the water flowed up to the platform.

An enterprising Surrey photographer produced an interesting booklet entitled *Souvenir of the Thames & Mole Floods, East Molesey, 1894*. At the peak of this flood the writer's father took his canoe across Molesey weir and lock without seeing a vestige of either! When the flood subsided it was found that the eddy at the tail of the lock had made a crater between the bank and the road large enough to take a coach and horses.

Although there have been serious floods since 1894, none has been of such magnitude over such a wide area. This has of course, been largely due to the long-term work of the former Thames Conservancy; one of their major engineering works was the construction of the new channel by-passing the Halliford bend, now known as the Desborough Cut, for it was officially opened by the Conservators' most distinguished Chairman, Lord Desborough, in 1935. Now we have the Thames Water Authority maintaining the good work.

He or she who only uses, or enjoys, the river in the fine days of summer is probably unaware of the gradient occasioned at the time of a main flood; over a distance of 4 miles from a main weir the gradient can be as much as 1 foot in 4 feet. Another facet of flooding is that summer floods are invariably short and sharp, due not just to subsequent fine weather and/or good rates of evaporation, but also to the transpiration rate of trees when in full leaf being very high. A really large Huntingdon Willow, a fully grown plane or a massive oak will draw as much as 1,500 gallons of water a day; every drop of which will be exhaled into the atmosphere from its foliage.

Droughts

In the present age droughts are pretty well unheard of, for, even in the long hot summer of 1976, navigation was not impeded, though water had to be pumped back upstream at Molesey Weir; the real difficulty was in the abstraction of water for domestic and industrial use. The last severe drought to affect navigation was in 1921, when levels dropped in every reach to an all-time low. But in the past flash locks and somewhat elementary water control, combined with extensive shoals due to lack of dredging, sorely affected navigation; this caused hardship amongst bargemen and shortage of supplies to riverside towns. For instance in August 1825 the draught of barges passing pound locks was restricted to 3 feet 3 inches for two months because of severe drought. To the reader who slips upriver in his motor cruiser for a short break, spare a thought for the bargemen of the 18th century, when in times of drought it could take as long as three weeks to tow a laden barge from Kingston to Reading, due to waiting for a 'flash' of water to help them through shallows.

Romney Weir at the start of the great freeze, winter 1962–3.

Frosts

The last (or first according to preference) of the
three evils of nature must surely be frosts. The
last great frost, when almost the whole river was
frozen over, was in 1963. Although in many
areas the ice was thick enough for light vehicles
to travel safely upon it, there were isolated reg-
ions where no ice formed at all, this phenomenon being due to springs in the river bed; most of
them were orientated towards the north bank of
the river and in many instances indicated points
where subterranean streams join the Thames.
Due to the falling off of commercial traffic upon
the river, this great frost did not cause the hard-
ships endured in years gone by. The previous
great frost was in 1895; although this caused
some problems, much fun was had skating,
including some long-distance (i.e. lock to lock)
runs as well as frost fairs and roasting of oxen on
the ice. The latter would have been an event
comparable to our present day 'barbecues'.

Frost fairs or 'fayres' were in the old
ized by watermen and bargen
endeavour to support their families
barges and boats were frozen in.

Apparently the earliest recorded
the Thames was in A.D. 220 whe
endured a frost which lasted for 5 m
in the year 250 the river was frozen f
this record was beaten in 923 when t
frozen for 13 weeks; only to be bette
when ice remained on the Thames fc
It is hard to realize what the river
1795, for January 25th of that year is
the coldest day ever known in th
although apparently the river was nc
such a long period as in the winter c
when the ice remained for nearly 3

Flora and fauna

Let us now turn away from the act
which cause concern to those of us

the river for our livelihood, and concentrate on the beautiful flora and fauna which abound for all to cherish and enjoy. 1970 was Conservation Year, which sparked off many good ideas, although, alas, as the decades pass enthusiasm in certain quarters wanes. Of course, conservation on the Thames wasn't anything new: way back in 1884 the House of Commons appointed a Select Committee to enquire into the operation of 'the Acts for the Preservation of the Thames, and the steps which are necessary to secure the enjoyment of the River as a place of Recreation.' One of the many subjects raised concerned steam launches: 'It is also urged that the presence of steam launches, of late years in increased numbers on the river adds greatly to the wear of the banks, and therewith to the destruction of the water plants that edge the river.' That committee was very far-sighted; the amount of damage caused by steam launches was negligible, but the steam launch was the forerunner of the motor boat in its many and various forms, which has been responsible for the diminution of many of our riverbank plants, as well as aquatic specimens. For instance, the lovely white water lily, *Nymphaea alba* is quite rare and has disappeared from sites where once it grew in profusion. The coarse leaved, yellow flowered *Nuphar lutea* or 'Brandy Bottle' still thrives fairly well, due to its growing in muddy bottomed shallow water – conditions often found in small neglected backwaters and other corners that are rarely dredged. The Loddon Lily, *Leucojum aestivum*, is a flower of great charm and grace that once adorned riverside meadows in gay abandon; fortunately there are still large groups of this lovely plant on several islands and in a few isolated spots. *Myosotis scorpioides*, the bright blue forget-me-not is not so prevalent as in the past; the same applies to the orange balsam, *Impatiens capensis*; this attractive plant is really a native of North America, but became established on the banks of the Thames so long ago that it is considered by most as one of our plants. The flowering rush, *Butomus umbellatus*, is a gay, colourful character unrelated to the common rush, *Juncus conglomeratus*. Yellow flag, *Iris pseudacorus*, is *the*

flower that heralds early summer upon the river. *Acorus calamus*, the sweet flag, is so called because when the foliage is bruised an aromatic scent pervades the air, which is one of the joys that assails the nostrils when the river is free from the disturbance of powered craft. Lovely as it is, sweet flag should be planted with forethought, inasmuch as it can cause silting under favourable circumstances: not surprising, for this plant is not a native, having been naturalized on the Thames from Asia in 1660. It seems that plants – like animals – introduced from foreign lands either struggle to survive or monopolize the scene!

Other wild plants adding to the joy of the Thames's bank are water figwort, willow herb (a terrible weed if it invades the garden), purple loosestrife, comfrey, ladies' smock, water mint with mauve/grey flowerheads, dewberry with white flowers followed by luscious little fruits, and clumps of meadow-sweet with great heads of creamy white flowers. Out in fairly deep water grows eelgrass, which is enjoyed by duck and waterfowl, but should be avoided by skippers of powered craft, for the growth is of such length that it can get tangled with a propeller and jam up the works.

Please do not be tempted to pick the flowers or disturb the roots of any of the plants growing along the riverside. Some are rare, and each and every one of us must help with conservation. Should you require some of these delightful plants for your garden, remember specialist bulb merchants can supply Loddon lilies and snake's head fritillaries, whilst native aquatics and wild flower seed can be obtained without too much difficulty.

Of our riverside trees, willow and alder proliferate; of the former there are literally countless varieties, some being native and others with worldwide distribution and, as mentioned in the first chapter, willow is as old as any of the earliest recorded plants and is of pre-Ice Age origin. Many non-gardeners think of willows as weeping trees, which of course is far from the truth. That popular weeping willow, *Salix babylonica*, is not, as its name suggests, a native of the Euphrates but of China, whence it was brought

A heron in flight.

to England and the first one planted by the Thames at Twickenham in about 1730.

Trees not only lend beauty to the riverside, but their roots help to stabilize the soil, so holding river banks together; another important point is that when in full leaf, trees transpire (draw up by their roots and breathe out through their leaves) a fantastic quantity of water, which can be of inestimable value in time of summer floods. Trees and bushes have another function, in providing cover for the fascinating wildlife which abounds on a fine, full bodied river.

To the author, there is only one way of being united with nature and watching the movements of small animals and birds, and that is to enjoy the freedom of sleeping beneath the stars; the happenings of really late evening and very early morning are truly captivating. The recommendations are, rather than spend a lot of money on field glasses and special equipment, invest in a really high quality down-filled bag; in such a bag you will be comfortable regardless of the outside temperature. How lovely it is to wake up to spot a kingfisher perched on a branch but a few yards away, then to watch him make three or four successive dives to catch the prey he has spotted, by spearing it with his bill with unerring accuracy. The speed with which he acts and repeats his performance is incredible.

The stately heron, who seemingl[y] slow motion, is really no sluggard. fishes in shallow waters, standing m[o] the bank or foreshore until an unwar[y] by. Then the heron shoots his head f[o] with perfect aim captures the fish, [c] death, and swallows it head first. If [h] in deeper water, his large wings — ne[a] which make him look like an old ge[ntleman's] coat tails — trap air which enables hi[m] at lightning rate after catching the choice. Herons are large birds with [a] of about $4\frac{1}{2}$ feet. They nest at the top great colonies and use the same trees the same nests with a bit of titivating year until the trees die from the over of herons. The nests are about 3 feet at nesting time the female sits for ab[out] on the eggs, all the time being fed by h[er]

Wild duck (mallard) now abou[nd] numbers, and over the years have be[come] tame and companionable; the ter[m] was in old sporting language the mal[e] duck, however that goes back to the duck shooting was commonplace a[nd] in question, quite naturally, were ver[y] of man. Little grebes, otherwise kno[wn] chicks', are fun to watch, being grea[t] capable of popping down to the de[pths] rate of ten times a minute to catch small fry, larvae of the may-fly and water shrimps, for example. The moor-hen is one of our commonest water birds; it's rather poor at flying, and looks ungainly, when airborne, with its feet hanging down. This bird lives on land as much as water and its feet are not webbed; it fights bravely for its home and the parents are wonderful at guarding their eggs. The coot is similar in many ways, but not quite so plentiful; it is a wary bird and readily gives warning of danger to its feathered friends; coots incidentally are excellent divers. The main food of these birds is water snails, aquatic insects and water plants, besides worms, slugs and snails on land. The coot for all its silly ways is no fool and something of a traveller; only recently, the ring on a coot examined at Shiplake showed that the bird had flown across from Scandinavia.

It is only since the great freeze up of 1963 that Canada Geese seem to have multiplied at an alarming rate; they are intelligent and beautiful birds but something of a problem for farmers when it is realized that a goose can eat more grass in a day than a sheep.

Another fellow making himself very much at home on the upper Thames is the great crested grebe, who not so many years ago was just a rare visitor; talking of visitors, in winter time cormorants seem to be taking rather more interest in the upper river than in the past, no doubt because the fishing is so good that regular meals can be assured.

Birds are fascinating, but the real pets of the river bank are the small animals that live such a busy life foraging for food, building homes and raising families. The water shrew is an adorable bankside inhabitant; only about 3 to $3\frac{1}{4}$ inches long, plus a tail of about 2 inches, it rarely swims far out from the bank and looks most attractive swimming under water, for its fur holds much air, giving the submerged body a silvery appearance; sometimes it routs on the bottom for caddis worms and other larvae or chases watergnats or whirligig beetles on the surface. It burrows into banks and lines its chamber with moss. In May the female weaves a nest of grass and leaves within the burrow where she brings forth her litter of up to 8 minute youngsters.

The most popular, albeit fictitious character, of the river bank is the water-rat. The word 'fictitious' is used advisedly, because there is no

Water voles; being mainly vegetarian they enjoy nibbling reeds and rushes.

such animal as a water-rat; it is the folk name given to the water-vole, which is neither a rat, nor is it of a rat-like nature. The water-vole is a delightful chap, quite heavily built with a rounded face and short thickish head. When swimming, his body is about two thirds submerged and from a distance looks like a large twig on the surface. The water-vole is a swimmer and diver par excellence. He feeds on bankside herbage as well as on grubs from the river bed. He does not hibernate but often lays up a store in order to have reserve supplies for the winter. The water-vole is a very clean animal and quite inoffensive. The only nuisance he causes is when he burrows into the banks of artificial watercourses, so causing leaks, which in some circumstances can turn into breaches. The female, with the help of her mate, makes a most beautiful nest in which to rear her young, there being about 5 to a litter. The name water-rat is sometimes given erroneously to the brown rat, which is a good swimmer and under certain conditions will choose to live near the river.

Those shy creatures with nocturnal habits, otters, were once very plentiful until their numbers dwindled due to otter hunting; this was originally practised because otters were competing with the livelihood of professional fishermen. The scarcity of otters has received – quite rightly – much national publicity; however it is good to know that their numbers are now increasing on the Thames.

The sight of baby otters playing is an unforgettable pleasure and experience; otters are very shy but also extremely inquisitive; the cubs, like all youngsters, love to tumble and play, and on the upper river several slides have been located where playful young ones 'whoosh' into the river, often to receive swimming lessons from their parents. But otters are not just confined to the upper reaches; with patience and an observant eye they can be seen throughout the length of the non-tidal Thames. Why not? They have good clean flowing water with an abundance of fish, man no longer hunts them, so it is quite possible that they are getting used to boats and civilization in the same way that the fox is accepting urban surroundings. A word of advice

to the aspiring naturalist: do not knowledge on the media – start exp river bank!

No chapter on nature would be com out mentioning that regal bird, the (Cygnus olor), which in the eyes o almost synonymous with the very nam Although swans are virtually wild differ from most of our feathered fri much as their forebears of three or fo years ago were domestic, or semi stock. According to certain schools they were always an indigenous spe country; on the other hand they coulc brought in from Europe or fore Romantic legend has it that Ri Lionheart brought the first swans in from Cyprus. Swan was at one time an excellent game bird for table use purpose its demise only came abou introduction of the turkey for culinar Swan owning was a privilege gran Crown, and, apart from the royal b only given to City Livery Companies nobility who resided by, or near the

Nowadays there are but three ow Thames: Her Majesty the Queen, th Company and the Dyers' Company tion of Royal Swan Keeper goes back the very least, and at present the pos by John Turk of Cookham, who too his father Frederick in 1963. The o swans is established by marking: roy unmarked, whilst those of the Vint mark each side of the mandible as op Dyers which have one mark only. Th made by making a small cut in the up mandible; if there is any tendency bleeding it is stopped with pitch.

Marking of swans is carried out the third week of July, by which time old enough to be handled: John Tur who organizes this operation – th of his job – which is termed 'sw although at one time it was often ping'. He is assisted by the swan kee the Vintners' and the Dyers' Con cousin, Michael Turk of Kingsto

Swan upping: note crook in foreground for catching birds. Dyers Company boat is on the left, Vintners to the right and the Queen's in the background.

former position until recently. The boats are crewed by watermen who assist with the catching and marking of birds. For the job they use double sculling skiffs, except John Turk, who uses his randan (see Traditional Thames Craft). At this very time (winter 1981) he is building a replacement randan in the workshops of his old-established family business, Turk and Sons of Cookham. The annual swan-upping trip upriver to Henley, which is the upper limit of the Swan Keeper's jurisdiction, is a very colourful and jolly event, throughout which much beer is consumed.

Although swans are strong and powerful birds, they soon shy away if splashed with water, just as though it was some noxious substance with which they are not familiar. At present there is a dearth of swans due to lead poisoning, brought about by the birds swallowing lead shot that is left around on the banks by fishermen, or caught up in growth on the far bank due to long-distance casting. The matter is receiving serious attention and just recently a Maidenhead veterinary surgeon has come up with a method of restoring the birds to normal health; however that is not eradicating the source of the trouble, which must be dealt with as expeditiously as possible. Since writing the above, a swan which habitually visited Chaplin's workboat moorings at Hampton has just been killed (December 1981) by a fox, for whom it provided several good square meals during the pre-Christmas freeze-up and heavy fall of snow.

Fishing

Fishing as a profession has been important since man first lived by the banks of the Thames; the catching of fish in quantity for a local population was usually performed by erectir hedges'; these really were a form of tr weir set athwart the current and above the water; being of a tempor they were put up as and where requ

TO-MORROW WILL BE FRIDAY, WE'VE CAUGHT RHEUMATISM TO-DAY.

This picture is from a postcard by Louis Wain, who was a very popular 'cat' painter and often used river settings (born 1860, died 1939). He designed some 500 postcards. His cards are currently worth up to £10–£12 ap

Two well known Thames fish – a perch and a gudgeon.

crayfish population seems to be pretty large on that fine Thames tributary, the Kennet.

Another form of trap was the 'grig-' or 'ground-weel', for the catching of small eels, which on the Thames were called 'grigs'. The weels were roughly cigar-shaped, with a flat underside which rested on the river bed; they were made from willow rods to form a chamber with an entrance narrowing inward. Bait was placed in the chamber and as the eel wriggled up the entrance the force of his body pushed the rods aside; however, once in the trap, the rods sprang back into place sealing off any return route. Grig-weels were generally laid with the opening facing downstream and kept in place by weighting with stones; a fisherman would usu-

A fisherman mending his hoop-nets, which are hung out to dry. In the foreground is a typical fishing punt. Note early-style timber campshedding on extreme right foreground of picture.

tures of a more permanent type were 'kidels' which caused a shallow to build up on their downstream side for the sole purpose of catching lampreys, which thrive in the soft mud of shallows. At one time the catching of crayfish (small freshwater lobsters) was an all-consuming job; from Cricklade down to Shepperton the typical holes in the bank, denoting the whereabouts of crayfish, were very numerous. They were caught in 'crayfish pots' made from withy rods, which, suitably baited, were placed on the river bed near the holes of an evening. There was an excellent market for crayfish, particularly at Oxford. Unfortunately at the end of last century a disease killing off crayfish broke out at Staines and steadily spread along the river. Today the

Another popular fish – the chub.

ally set down about a dozen or a dozen and a half traps in one area at dusk and pick them up, with the aid of a boathook, early the following morning. A wooden stopper in the head of the grig-wheel facilitated release of the catch; as well as eels, the odd fish would sometimes be caught. Individual fishermen had their own techniques for identifying the spot where they had laid their traps. In the Oxford area grigs were mostly referred to as 'grits' or 'gluts', whilst on most parts of the river the popular term for catching young eels was 'to go a-gregging'.

Hoop-nets had a vague similarity to grig-weels but were used to catch fish; they were made of string as opposed to osier rods, furthermore they had a very large opening; the size of the mesh was 2 inches, a smaller size being illegal. The nets were laid of an evening with the large open end facing downstream so that fish on the move during the small hours worked their way into the small chamber, like eels in a grig-weel. A wide variety of fish were caught, such as chub, dace, jack and roach. The nets were weighted down

with large stones; these were ofte shaped and generally had a hole thro that they could be attached to the n dage.

Another queer appliance for catch the eel-buck; like the grig-weel, it from willow rods, but of heavier sec bucks were large, being 9 to 10 feet in a timber frame side by side, to forn eel-bucks. There would be about h bucks to a stage, which would be se river at a point where the current wa away from the navigation channel. the opposite direction to grig-wee catch the large eels on their migra stream, whereas the weels were t small eels on their way upstream. T were so arranged that they could b lowered in a similar manner to a sluic a popular food and in much deman from a set of 6 bucks would be abou one night's catch. Up till the latter century, eel fairs used to be held

Eel bucks being lowered into position.

Fish ladder (to left of picture) which enabled salmon to negotiate Molesey Weir (1864).

when eels were travelling upriver in great numbers. Eels were also netted by fishermen using 'Peterboats', which craft are described in the Traditional Craft chapter; from these craft a wide range of fish were caught, including salmon and trout.

To help the salmon on their way upstream for spawning, there existed in 1865 at Molesey Weir a fish ladder. The subsequent demise of salmon on the Thames was due to the pollution of the tidal river. In the same year the Thames Angling Preservation Society founded breeding ponds at Pecker's Ait, downstream of Sunbury Lock, long since obliterated by the construction of reservoirs. The Thames Angling Preservation Society was formed in March 1838, the inaugural meeting being at the Bell Hotel, Hampton. Angling is, and always has been, a very popular pastime, carefully supervised to protect stocks. This is not surprising considering the wide variety of species in the Thames and the fact that it is the country's finest coarse-fishing river abounding in bream, barbel, chub, dace, gudgeon, carp, perch, bleak, rudd, roach, pike, ruffe, grayling and eels. Trout are around and in the summer of 1981 a salmon was located at Reading. From the 13th century 'deeps', that is areas in the river 200–300 yards in extent, were granted by the Corporation of the City of London to towns and villages between Staines and Richmond to be preserved exclusively for angling (no net or 'engine' being allowed). A deep was granted to the village against which it lay and attracted many visitors during the fishing season. Deeps are in some cases a natural phenomenon, in others, where there has been a good bed of gravel, it has been ballasted for building purposes, so leaving a large hollow. Ballasting is, of course, the old Thames term for dredging.

Willow growing

A local trade that is possibly as old as fishing itself and still continues to a limited extent, is the growing of willows in various forms and in numerous varieties for a multitude of purposes from fencing to baskets. Large areas were at one time devoted to their cultivation, including the rich alluvial deposits found on the abundance of aits or eyots (small islands) scattered throughout the length of the Thames. Willow provides excel-

Pollarding willows in winter. The following spring new 'breaks' (shoots) will grow from the stubs that have been left.

lent timber for fencing, gate-hurdles and numerous other jobs around the farm; to produce the correct type of wood, trees are pollarded, that is, the crown is cut off so that many branches are thrown up in a tight cluster; when grown to the required size they are removed in winter time, allowing fresh 'breaks' to appear the following spring which will produce a further crop for cutting in 5 to 6 years' time.

Popular varieties for producing poles are *Salix vitellina, Salix alba* (the Huntingdon Willow), *Salix chrysostella* and many others. *Salix Coerulea* (the bat willow) is grown for producing cricket bats, so it is not pollarded but grown as a standard tree with a good straight knot-free trunk. Willow, besides producing wood for cricket bats, has properties which make it excellent for paddles of watermills and paddle steamers; other uses are the making of shoemakers' lasts, hay rakes, ladders, gun stocks and innumerable other items, including packing crates used for

the export of large and heavy objec veneer can be bent at right angles so admirable for forming into various s sizes to produce punnets, chip baskets The bitter white substance, salicin from the willow bark is the natura acetyl-salicylic acid so well known killing tablets; it is not surprising, th find elderly animals suffering fron nibbling the bark of willow trees. Anc willow bark is in tanning, it being use ence to oak for Russian leather.

The names 'willow', 'withy' and bandied about with resultant confusi is straightforward (meaning the tree 'withy' really applies to the thin whip cut from willows for making ties; 'o from the Latin 'ausaria' which litera 'willow bed'. Varieties of willow, su *viminalis* and *Salix purpurea* are suitable for producing rods for basket

A 'holt', or bed, of osiers being cut and tied into bolts.

Osier rods being peeled by pulling them through iron 'breaks' which are secured to a solid timber frame.

the passage of time trees coppiced for rods for basket-making (i.e. cut down to the ground and allowed to shoot again) tended to be referred to as 'osiers' as opposed to pollarded willows, which often enjoyed the simple name 'pollards'. The aforementioned osiers are grown in beds or 'holts'; they are planted close together, and, to obtain maximum long straight rods, low willow stools providing plenty of 'leaders' are used. Osier-cutting, or harvesting, was an important task requiring knowledge of grading the rods according to quality and size: they were sorted into 4 different groups: Luke, Threepenny, Middleborough and Great. After sorting and grading, they were tied into bundles of 40 inches circumference, these bundles being referred to as 'bolts'. After grading, the osiers had to be prepared for their ultimate use: eel and fish traps, basket-making, market containers of numerous shapes and sizes for growers and farmers, sundry domestic items, reinforcement for mud or plaster walls and gabions for bridge footings and river bank retention, whilst the thinnest and finest quality rods were used for making corn sieves.

On completion of the sorting, the bolts had to be laid up in stacks and allowed to dry, care being a requisite in stacking, for they were liable to become heated if packed too closely when still green. In due course these rods were peeled by pulling them through a wrought-iron device known as a 'break', after immersion in hot water, or being exposed to steam; this not only made the task of peeling easier but gave the rods a distinctive tan colour, and this treatment was said to improve the quality. White rods were obtained by standing the bolts in trenches – termed 'pits' – with their butt ends in about 6 inches of water. With the arrival of spring, sap started to rise in these rods, which was the time to lift them and pull them through the 'break', for the rising sap enabled the bark to fall away easily, so revealing clean white wands. All these operations took place near the growing area.

Cutting reeds. Top quality reeds are used for thatching; lower grade reeds were once in much demand for

Whippy wands that had not reached maturity were cut as withies; being flexible and strong, they made excellent bonds for tying purposes.

Thames aits are no longer used for the growing of osiers, but thank goodness most of them are still a haven for wild life. Some islands have residences upon them, often weekend chalets, which owe their origins to the willow producers' seasonal headquarters; a few have hotels on them, whilst several are occupied by well known boatyards. De Montefort Island, Reading, is unique in having a very fine bowling green; in addition there are moorings for members' boats.

Milling

Another very important trade was milling. Prior to the Industrial Revolution, water was the main method of power, and the river the main method of transport. The principal commodity for grinding was cereals; however, as time went on more powerful mills were developed for paper-making, fulling (cleaning and thickening cloth),

and the manufacture of copper pots the last case the waterwheel powe hammers, flat-rollers and other in required for repetitive metal fo Ancient Greeks are commonly c developing the use of water power course, the Romans were not far be to them that in all probability we o duction of water power to this co ever, it is doubtful if the Romans we with developing mills due to the al ply of slave labour for working quern stones — hard labour indeed that the widespread building of m way in Saxon times.

The earliest mills presented qui picture from the chocolate-box which we are all so familiar; the ve had the wheel in a horizontal plar situated in line with the surface Such watermills were called 'Nors mills due to their popularity in the

The mills introduced to England by the Romans were undoubtedly the 'Greek' type, although a Roman architect and engineer, Vitruvius, was possibly the inventor of the mill as we know it with its vertical wheel and cogged gearing.

There are three main types of waterwheel to suit varying local conditions and water supply. They are known as 'undershot', 'overshot', and 'breast' wheels; the names refer to the way in which the water hits the paddles of the wheel. The earliest waterwheels were constructed of timber throughout, but as early as the 17th century iron began to take the place of timber for certain components. The gear wheels used in transmitting the power from the waterwheel to the stones were invariably of wood with replaceable cogs of hornbeam, with the grain running from top to base. Hornbeam was preferable to oak or apple for this purpose, although the latter wood was sometimes used for bearings. Willow was used for the paddles of the waterwheel whilst timber used for other items was beech, whitethorn, acacia, holly and sometimes ash. Cast-iron gearing gradually moved onto the scene after Abraham Darby set up his blast furnace at Coalbrookdale, on the Severn, in 1708.

The stones used for grinding came from a limited number of quarries. Derby Peak was one of the most common, whilst the imported French Burr was greatly favoured. Millstones also came from Sussex, Nottinghamshire and Monmouthshire. Different types of stone were used according to the material being ground – flour would be different from animal feedingstuffs, for example. The stones had varying dimensions, the average being about 4 feet in diameter with a thickness of 4–5 inches, whilst grooves chased on the flat surface had a depth of about one inch.

By the time the Domesday Survey was carried out, over 5,500 watermills were recorded throughout Great Britain, the River Thames with its attendant tributaries accounting for a

Mapledurham Mill in about 1902. The outboard waterwheel was removed in 1922 and replaced with a water turbine designed and manufactured by Gilkes of Kendal. This new unit pumped water and powered a generator.

goodly share; by the 18th century the number of mills had increased almost threefold, but by the 19th century the decline had started, and now we have only a few intact mills left. The oldest surviving mill is Mapledurham, which is also one of the finest; it has been restored and is now in working order; on certain days during the season visitors are allowed to tour the mill and witness corn being ground; furthermore, at the end of their visit they have the opportunity of buying stone ground flour, from wheat grown on the Mapledurham Estate. The varieties proving best for old-fashioned grinding are at the present time 'Bounty' and 'Armada'. Bringing an old mill, such as Mapledurham, back to life is a mammoth task, costly too! The very first job was to clear the vast quantity of debris that had collected over a long period of time, blocking all channels; the next task was to make and fit new sluices. Making and fitting was one thing, but removing the old sluices, which were within the mill building, was a difficult and delicate operation due to the tender condition of the mill fabric and lack of space for modern tackle. The new waterwheel was built under the guidance of David Nicholls who is the miller at Mapledurham; he is a millwright of no mean ability. On the far side of the mill there is an early water turbine which was very compact and far more powerful than the conventional wheel, built by Gilkes of Kendal. It is hoped that this will also be restored in due course. In its prime Mapledurham Mill was multi-functional: it pumped water and generated electricity for Mapledurham House as well as grinding wheat.

The mill at Cookham was last used at the turn of the century for preparing animal feeding-stuffs; a few years ago it was converted into a recording studio, whilst its exterior appearance was not only maintained but enhanced. Cleeve Mill has been renovated and modified by its present owner so that it now supplies him with his basic electricity. One of England's oldest mills is the Abbey Mill at Abingdon which at its zenith kept seven pairs of millstones turning from two waterwheels. Abingdon was endowed with several mills using the power of the Thames and the adjacent tributary, the Ock. In the early

part of last century Abingdon must] very important centre with the ope Wilts and Berks Canal (22/9/181(route to the Kennet and Avon Canal ton with branches to Swindon, Caln(penham, which enabled grain to be Abingdon from a very wide agricul(

The sire of Marlow Mills has developed as a residential area; hc architect designed the new dwellings timber-clad mill buildings. The resul of personal opinion, but one link w remains, the mill 'thorough', throug] water rushes in an impatient manner nal mills consisted of several units, the grinding of corn, although one w extracting oil from rape, whilst the s was, from the beginning of the 18 engaged in the production of thimb] ally Marlow Mills turned over to the of paper.

At Eton, the former Tangier Mil famed for its production of high c smoking pipes, whilst Hambleden n of the best known mills on the Tham by the times it has been painted photographed, filmed and used as a b for advertising and publicity stunts was recorded in the Domesday surv 1235 it was granted to Keynsham / mill ceased working in 1958, havin last two decades of its life grinding power supplied by a water-driven tur replaced the old waterwheel.

Upstream of Marlow were the gr Mills, which take their name from t Templar who held the Bisham Esta(12th century; they were followed by tine monks, at which time grindi(would have been the sole function of the beginning of the 18th century th converted to the production of copp the waterwheel providing the motiv(drop hammers. In 1788 the mill was (a Thomas Williams who had minir and also a smelting works in Sor amongst other things he was M.P. fc where he built a very luxurious man:

same time he commissioned the architect, Samuel Wyatt, to design additions for the existing mill buildings. With the opening of the Thames–Severn Canal in 1789 copper ingots were shipped from Swansea in Severn trows; at Brimscombe Port they were trans-shipped into West Country barges for the second stage of the journey through to Temple. At this mill both copper sheathing and bolts were turned out for the Admiralty; domestic equipment was made in great quantities, both for the home market and export. One of the wheels at this mill, capable of generating 100 h.p., was claimed to be the biggest on the Thames.

The decline of the Thames–Severn Canal gave rise to problems in supplying Temple Mills with raw materials, and the mill changed hands. It was acquired by a firm by the name of Weedon and Sons, who, after carrying out various modifications to the buildings and layout, went into the manufacture of brown paper. It continued to be run as a paper factory; then in the 1980s the mill area and adjacent Temple Island, were, like the site of Tangier Mill at Eton, redeveloped as an exclusive residential estate.

At Sonning, the fine old mill building has been re-clad in top grade western red cedar, which upon weathering gives a most charming appearance. Inside, the building is being converted for recreational purposes, which should give great pleasure to travellers by water, for moorings are being provided. This mill dates back to about late 17th century and in latter days it was operated by two wheels housed within the building and also a turbine; working of the mill ended in 1963.

Marsh Mills, just above Henley, was equipped with two undershot cast-iron wheels which worked the mill until electric power competely took over in the 1960s. It was one of the last mills on the Thames to receive deliveries of grain by water, this being carried in the narrow boats of the Willow Wren Company. The mill came to an end in 1970, with again, residential redevelopment.

Sandford Mill still produces paper, but, alas, no longer by water power, for steam took over in the 1930s; this mill dates back to the 13th century, the original being built by the Knights Templar.

As mentioned in an earlier chapter, millers, bargemasters and fishermen vied with each other for control of water for their respective trades; battles and wrangles often ensued and the law had to be laid down by the Thames Commissioners, as can be observed from the following two abstracts, taken at random from their minutes:

16th. June 1815. The Committee being informed that there is an obstruction to the navigation at New Mills Marsh notwithstanding the Surveyor has forced a passage according to the orders of the Committee Ordered that the Bargemasters be informed by the Surveyor that if they force the passage for the Horses towing there the Commissioners will indemnify them from any action that may be brought against them for so doing and that in the meantime the General Clerk do bring action against Mr. Ellsee for obstructing the navigation by shutting up the towpath.

Then another minute, dated January 1st, 1853, at a meeting held in the Town Hall, Oxford, reads as follows:

Resolved that the General Clerk do serve notice upon the owner of Sandford Mills near Oxford requesting them to reinstate the water course to the same level as when the mill was converted from corn to a paper mill and also to open the various sluices and remove all obstructions which now holds up the water in flood and at other times to the injury of the Navigation and landowners in vicinity of the river. And that the General Committee be empowered to watch over the same to see it efficiently executed . . .

To give details of each and every mill upon the Thames, and its tributaries, would result in producing a complete book on the subject; however it is hoped that the information in this chapter will not only give an insight into mills and milling, but stimulate further interest. With the present demand for stone ground flour and various health foods, it is conceivable that other mills may be restored, like Mapledurham, to produce these excellent items but to de a tourist attraction.

7

Commercial traffic upon the non-tidal Thames is, alas, almost past history. However it is heartening to know that at the time of writing grain traffic from London to Cox's Lock Mill, on the Wey Navigation, has re-commenced. Other than this, the only traffic encountered nowadays is the piling rigs, barges and waterborne equipment of both the Thames Water Authority and riparian contractors, whilst the odd narrow boat makes an occasional visit to the Thames, selling to householders coal that has been brought direct from a canalside coal mine – shades of the past! I also understand that arrangements are proposed for the running of a powered tanker barge for bulk deliveries of diesel fuel to boatyards and hire cruiser bases, whilst a 300-ton coaster has started bringing general cargoes to Kingston for distribution by lorry.

As mentioned in the previous chapter, hauling laden barges upriver, or for that matter navigating them downstream, was no easy task until the late 18th or early 19th centuries due to the preponderance of shallows. It was hardly surprising, therefore, that in the reign of George III, under an Act dated May 10th, 1768, there is a reference to the draught of barges, which reads as follows: 'And be it enacted by the Authority aforesaid, that no barge, boat or vessel, shall draw more than three feet of water; which depth shall be ascertained by a strait white line, one

be) to the Owner, after the Charges attending such Distress and Sale shall be deducted.

Provided always, That nothing relating to the Draught of Water that such Barges, Boats, or Vessels, are to Draw, or the Mark of any Line on such Barge, Boat, or Vessel, shall extend, or be construed to extend, to any Barge, Boat, or Vessel, that shall not be navigated beyond the Flux of the Tide.

Not to extend to Barges, &c. not navigated beyond the Flux of the Tide.

And be it further enacted by the Authority aforesaid, That all the Orders of the said Commissioners shall be signed by such Number of Commissioners as are herein

Commissioners Orders how to be signed.

Part of a page from the Act of George III regarding the draught of barges.

inch broad, extending from head to stern, on each side of every Barge, Boat or Vessel . . . Not to extend to Barge, Boat or Vessel *not* navigated beyond THE FLUX OF THE TIDE.'

West Country barges and boatmen

To most watermen, 'travelling beyond the flux of the tide' was not, according to our present jargon, 'going upriver', but termed 'travelling West Country'. This of course gave rise to the traditional upriver Thames trading boats being called 'West Country barges'. The term West Country was also applied to the boatmen handling these barges; these West Country boatmen held a special concession inasmuch as they were allowed to navigate through the Pool of London without the compulsory use of a licensed waterman or lighterman. The concession was originally granted in gratitude of the West Country boatmen's gallantry in providing essential victuals for the City of London during the Great

Plague of 1665. Mind you, the old-ti̶ men did not like venturing down to L fear of the press gang: good Thames much sought after by the Navy. A ski̶ a cargo down from the West Cou̶ invariably hand his boat over to an ol̶ skipper when he had got down as far a or thereabouts; he would then wor̶ upstream on another craft so as to ke the press gangs!

Cargoes consisted of bricks, ceme malt, grain, flour, general mixed manufactured items, and on the d̶ run prodigious quantities of hay fo̶ horses, besides cheeses, paper f̶ Wycombe and general produce. Fu modities were added to the list with t of the canal system. West Country b flat bottomed with a hard chine, i̶ sides set at right angles to the bottom. swim-headed, that is they sloped up̶ punt; they generally had a transom

A pair of 'wussers' (small barges) off St Nicholas, or Church, wharf at Shepperton.

Windsor Bridge in the 1780s. To the right is a West Country barge moving up to Jenning's Wharf. In the foreground is a heavy version of a randan, whilst to the extreme left is a Peterboat. The sailing barge in the centre is preparing to lower the mast before shooting the bridge.

flat stern, from which hung a large rudder; the transom was usually set across the upper part of the 'huff', that is the upward slope of the hull at the stern. This type of construction at the after end was known as a 'Budgett' stern, although some West Country barges had a complete transom stern.

The barges were built according to the requirements of the owner and varied in size from 25 to 200 tons; the former were often known as 'worsers' or 'wussers'; this was also a Thames term for a narrow boat. The latter must have been massive brutes; they were often built not in a covered yard, but on the river bank, and quite often were launched sideways. This practice was perpetuated by William Stevens, who built his barges on the River Wey, as well as by firms building trading narrow boats on the canal system. Information on West Country barges is very scant and it is a great pity that there is not a surviving, or preserved example of one. It is

highly probable that many of these craft, like steamers of later generations, were made by itinerant boatbuilders. West Country barges were, by their very concept, of shallow draught; however, the 200 tonners fell foul of the Act of 1768 owing to their draught being 4 feet. Fortunately this Act was amended after a few years to allow a draught of 3 feet 10 inches; no doubt a blind eye was turned on the odd 2 inches!

According to contemporary reports it took gangs of from 50 to 80 men to haul a 200-ton barge upstream or, if horses were available, a team of 12 or 14 would be required. On the trip downstream they relied on the force of the current to a very large extent, which at times could be a dangerous torrent. A large barge, with suitable tow and under favourable conditions, could travel about 25 miles a day in an upstream direction, and again according to conditions, as much as 35 miles a day downstream, particularly when an old flash lock with a 4 or 5 foot head of water was unpenned, forming a miniature tidal wave. Gangs of men employed on towing were known as 'halers' (i.e. 'haulers'). It is not generally appreciated that horse towing did not become widespread until the late 18th century. Sometimes the smaller boats would be poled, or 'quanted' with long shafts and, if they were in a favourable reach with a following wind, a square sail would be bent to a small mast stepped well forward and supported by three shrouds.

A bye law of 1832 decreed that no barge should be towed other than from its mast. As old hands who have 'bow hauled' a skiff or punt from the towpath (often called the 'bargewalk' by earlier generations) will know, a tow rope made fast to the bows will pull a boat into the bank; conversely, if too far aft, the bows tend to sheer out. The ideal point for towing is usually just abaft the bows, and a mast not only provides a good towing point but keeps the line above reeds and other obstructions.

In the 18th century there were along the towpath at various points paygates, for example at Twickenham, Hampton Wick, Kingston, Abbs Court (opposite Sunbury Village) and Laleham. The most upstream paygate was at a point called Neville's Bridge, at Old Windsor. This bridge was presumably one over a small watercourse that joins the river a little below Old Windsor Lock. These days it is invariably dry, but was once a full bodied stream. Shortly after the last war an archaeological 'dig' was held in this area and it was considered that in Anglo-Saxon times the stream had been opened up to form a canal running into Old Windsor, which at that time and until the 11th century was considered great and glorious. It was here betwixt the river and the church that Edward the Confessor built his palace. In modern times the late ex-King Farouk built his English home here; the last vestiges of his royal possessions were the beautiful lion's head mooring rings set into the walls of the boathouse and the wet dock.

In the 1770s the toll at Laleham Upper Paygate was 2d. per horse, at Abb's Court it was 3d. per horse, and the same amount was levied at Kingston. The dues collected went towards the upkeep of the towpath. If the water level was

well down, tolls would sometimes be the horses by-passing the towpath a along the foreshore, where there w hard gravel bed. The change-over f power to horse towing in the 18th ce have been a great step forward; how little to reduce many of the hazard ample, when travelling downstrear depended on the horse or horses mai faster speed than the current of the ri of flood the whole procedure could be hazardous. A very dangerous point u conditions was where a weir chanı course away from the towpath with th the horse to cross to the other ba navigation or roving bridge, and be in to take up the slack in the tow rope to boat shooting on.

Horses for towing were sturdy f adept at being able to 'hang in the coll get a boat under way. Horses are g mers and the odd dunking was not u in addition to which there were situa as at Windsor, where at the head of (in those days it extended muc upstream), horses had to plunge into with tow lines attached and swim to just below the bridge on the Eton shor prior to 1824 when the present bridge which is a little downstream of its p The horses on reaching *terra firma* ha lines transferred to a winch for pulling up to the bridge, in order that tov again proceed. Incidentally, the site o ments of the old bridge is now a pub for those wishing to visit Eton.

In the old days life must have bee both man and beast. In mitigation from the *Windsor and Eton Express* worthy of being quoted:

A horse, the property of the Navigation Company, which fr hauled barges up and down the and Eton towpaths has died at mendous age of 52. It is believed t of the greatest ages reached by shire horse in the country. Only time ago the old horse was freed from further labour on the barges and put out to grass for the remainder of his life. He certainly earned his short lived retirement.

The horses were usually resplendent with brass ornaments on their leather tackle; the wooden bobbins (often brightly painted) on their traces were to prevent chafing. Before a parliamentary committee in 1793, evidence was put forward with regard to the number of horses required to tow a seventy-ton barge against the current over different reaches of the river. Herewith a few examples:

Windsor to Amerden Bank [just below the present Bray Lock] 8. To Boulter's 10 or 12. To Spade Oak 8. To Henley 5 or 6. To Gatehampton 10. To above Abingdon 10 or sometimes 12. In the 1790s when the Corporation of the City of London took over the responsibility of Paygates and levied a toll on barge tonnage with the result that bargemasters tended to employ more horses than previously. An enquiry into the matter in 1795 showed that a 130 ton barge that was pulled by 7 horses was now using 10, a 90 ton barge using 8 instead of 5, a 45 ton barge 6 instead of 3.

The Thames lighter

The Thames lighter originated in the days before docks were built in London. Ships had to moor out in the stream and unload their cargoes into lighters which, at low tide, could lie alongside the wharves. These lighters or 'dumb' barges date from the 17th century and, with the exception that all modern lighters are built of steel, the basic design has remained unaltered. They have

A timber-built Thames lighter with an early-style Thames sailing barge alongside. Not only does this illustrate the ancestry but shows the sprit running diagonally from the mast to the peak of the sail (circa 1880).

flat bottoms, square chine at the bilge with straight – almost punt-like – overhanging bow and stern, being referred to as 'swim-headed'. Typical measurements of a 75-tonner are 63 feet long with a beam of 17 feet. A lighter, unlike a barge, does not have a rudder; also it has far greater freeboard (the side of the vessel above water level) than a West Country barge. Lighters were never a common sight on the upper river and the last to be seen as regular traffic were those carrying coal to the waterworks at both Hampton and Abbs Court (just below Sunbury Lock), which trade ceased in March 1968. These lighters were towed by tugs but in tidal waters it is common practice for a lighterman to move his craft around on the tide with a sweep (a single oar with a long straight blade and very long shaft).

The Thames sailing barge

The well known Thames sailing barge was evolved from the dumb barge or lighter; it had leeboards, which are large pear-shaped wooden appendages, pivoted and suspended over either side of a flat bottomed boat. The lee one would be lowered to reduce leeway in a wind. (Leeway is the amount that a boat is driven to leeward off course by the wind.) They carried a square sail. The now famous spritsail rig, that is the fore-and-aft sail that is supported and extended by a sprit (a spar set diagonally across the sail from the mast up to the peak, which is the upper after corner of the sail) was not developed until the 18th century and it was not until well into the 19th century that the hull took on its better known form with rounded bow and vertical stem, which is the massive piece of timber rising up from the keel and into which the planks form-ing the sides of the barge are butted after follow-ing round in a fairly sharp curve, which gives a bluff appearance. Cargoes carried by these large craft were much the same as aboard the West Country barges, with the addition of Newcastle coal brought to London by colliers. They navi-gated high upstream, trading as far as Shilling-ford and possibly Abingdon. A variation of the spritsail barge, known as a 'stumpie', was far

Thames sailing barges at Kingston Bridge cir

more popular for upriver work and narrow reaches. The saving of time m reduced cargo: it was slightly smaller, topmast and was easier for shooting landsman's language 'passing under some resemblance to a West Countr

The 'chalk barge' was a specialized these craft, of about 40 tons capacity, name implies, was used in the agricul to supply farmers and growers with lime for their land, and also to suppl tors and builders who needed quantiti for foundations and lime for mort barges were worked by a crew of two, living space was quite generous – beneath the aft deck, entered via a sli and a companion way (flight of step were bunks, a bench with lockers, a most important of all a stove for co that very essential duty 'brewing up' quite luxurious compared with the V try barge, whose crew lived under a stretched over hoops, which made the the craft look like an American wagon.

It was really remarkable how th barges managed to navigate the uj where they traded regularly. Shooti with a spritsail barge meant lowerin sail, but also rigging and mast; the latt anything up to 40 feet in length! Once through the bridge the mast had to be raised smartly and sails set; all with a crew of two – that is a skipper and his mate. On a large barge the sail area could be around 280 square feet, so giving good 'windpower', not forgetting that when beating to windward, or tacking, the skipper would in a narrow or sheltered reach be forever 'going about'. In very difficult or extremely narrow channels the barges would be quanted rather than sailed – that is, pushed along with poles, akin to punting, except that a 'quant' or 'barge pole' was often fitted with a disc or button at the top so as to give extra power when the bargeman literally 'put his shoulder to the quant'. Facing aft, he would steadily walk along the side deck with all his weight on the quant so as to push the barge forward. Stumpies, as already mentioned, had no top mast and could pass under some bridges without lowering the mast. A further variation, the 'luff barge', was slightly smaller, had sharper bows and less freeboard; it was essentially a craft for confined spaces and uppermost reaches of the river.

That very fine painting 'Keen Edge Ferry' (upstream of Shillingford Bridge) by J. T. Serres, which is reproduced on the jacket of this book, must have been painted for posterity, because in the scene are a West Country barge, a stumpie, a chalk barge and a Peterboat – all clearly delineated. The Peterboat is the oldest known Thames craft. These boats were designed and used for fishing and no doubt their name is taken from the patron saint of fishermen; they were double ended boats of clincher construction, generally decked at each end and with rowlocks set into the top strake, which gave a flush gunwale with no projections to catch in the nets. They had a wet well for the catch and were about 22 feet long with smaller 12 foot versions for use right upriver; they were very beamy in relation to their length and their method of construction, also double ended design, suggest they may have been developed from Viking craft. The last surviving example lay rotting away at Putney, around 1927, in the days before 'conservation' had really caught on.

Wharves

At the peak of waterborne trading, when 69,000 tons of merchandise a year was transported on the upper river, pretty well every Thames-side town, village and hamlet had its public wharf, known variously as 'the hard', 'the parish drawdock' or 'the hythe'; in addition there were the wharves of various merchants dealing in their respective wares, such as timber, animal feeding-stuffs, bricks and so on. As time progressed wharves were set up for bringing coal to gas works, water pumping stations and other undertakings.

Reading was a busy centre for waterborne trade, especially with the opening of the Kennet navigation in 1723; in the 19th century large export orders for both Huntley and Palmers' biscuits and Simmonds' India pale ale increased the traffic in those products conveyed by barge to the London Docks.

The smallest wharf was the furthest upstream – at Waterhay Bridge, which is upstream of Cricklade; only small barges could penetrate so far upstream, but they were vital to the economy in providing safe and reliable transport. The writer once had the pleasure of hearing first hand how the channel used to be kept clear of silt and weed growth with the aid of a team of horses and a drag when the water was really low in a very dry summer.

Typical of the many busy wharves throughout the length of the Thames was Lechlade, which really came into its own with the opening of the Thames–Severn Canal in 1789, which joined the Thames at Inglesham about half a mile above Lechlade. Along its route came salt from Droitwich, copper from Swansea, fruit from Evesham and coal from Staffordshire, with the opening of such canals as the Staffordshire and Worcester (1776), the Droitwich (1771), the Worcester and Birmingham (1816), as well as navigational improvements to the Lower Avon, which was first navigable in 1640.

Mention must be made of Buscot, where there was a short canal, known as 'Buscot Pill', which gave waterborne access to a small brick and tile works on the great Buscot Park Estate, now

National Trust property. This estate was acquired in 1859 by Robert Campbell who modernized and mechanized his farms, and installed irrigation systems fed by a waterwheel-driven pump at Buscot, and another pump at Eaton Hastings Weir, powered by twin waterwheels; he also built a distillery on the island against Buscot Lock, which gained it the name of 'Brandy Island'. The spirit, which was distilled from the vast acreages of beet grown on his estate, formed an important London-bound cargo, much of which was trans-shipped to France. Even at a remote spot such as Tadpole Bridge there was a small wharf hard by the 'Trout' public house; no doubt this would have served Buckland and other villages.

Stone from the quarries at Taynton, situated some 12 miles north of Radcot, and reasonably near the River Windrush, was shipped in West Country barges to London and other riverside towns in prodigious quantities from in all probability the 10th century. Taynton stone was used in the re-building of St Paul's Cathedral and perhaps it was no coincidence that Thomas Strong, one of Wren's master masons, was at one time owner of Taynton Quarry. This quarry was apparently being worked well before Domesday and some of its stone, after the long journey downriver, was trans-shipped to France. The principal place for loading this stone was at Radcot, where at one time there were a number of wharves; the material was brought down from the quarries by horse and cart, and, due to the condition of the roads in winter, it appears that much stone was stockpiled at the wharves in summer time; barges could take plenty of this away during the winter when they had strong currents – and sometimes floods – to speed them on their way. At times Taynton stone was also carted to the wharf at Eynsham; a certain amount was taken on horse-drawn skids through the woods to the River Windrush at Little Barrington, where it was loaded on to rafts or flats from a wharf near the present 'Fox' Inn. The flats would be poled or quanted down river to Newbridge, where the stone would be transferred into barges for its main journey on the Thames. Another quarry was at Burford; it was

known as Kit's Quarry, after its Kempster, who was also a master m Paul's. This produced a much softer Taynton. It was used for interior apparently was never very satisfact

At Oxford, directly below Folly opposite Salter's, was a very large w time the warehouses at the back we storing sugar that had been brou from the London refineries. These have now been converted into a p bearing the sign 'Head of the River'. saw its fair share of waterborne tr down by the 'Beetle and Wedge' h Moulsford timber wharf. Lots of inte goes went to and from Reading and I that will follow in due sequence. another important centre for waterb Downstream of the main wharf bridge) there was, as in many 1 towns, a ropewalk, which is a lo covered way in which strands of fibr and twisted into rope. Ropes were a tant, albeit expendable, item in th towing; a set of tow ropes lasted thre most, journeys upriver and back short-lived, these ropes were infin than ones of the pre-Roman era sometimes made of plaited withies.

To list all the wharves along the 1 cargoes carried, would make this ch catalogue; however, mention must the very important Hedsor Whar situated in the Hedsor Water, a Wharf; in the last quarter of the 1 both wharves were combined tenancy. Thomas Saunders took where around 1750 and the lovely m ing still on the New Wharf site is c ders Wharf'. This wharf saw the timber – splendid beech from the wo inghamshire. Paper was brought ov the mills at High Wycombe, to be ta London by barge. Coal was unl hauled by horse and cart along d roads, besides which there were the modities required by a busy and h community. At the tail of Hedsor

The oldest lock cottage still in existence, a single room carved out of the chalk at Hedsor.

lock, of which under water are scant remains. The original lock house was hewn out of the vertical face of the chalk cliff; it is a capacious single room with a good fireplace, the flue passing up through the chalk to emerge in the woody growth above. The front of the opening is built up with brick and provided with a door and two attractive windows.

When Cookham Lock cut was driven and the lock opened on November 1st, 1830, the owner of the Hedsor Estate, Lord Boston, who was landlord of the wharf and took all the towpath tolls, was badly affected financially; within weeks of the lock opening the tenant of his wharf sold his horses; due to navigational improvements and building of Cookham lock, all barge traffic by-passed Hedsor and went merrily on its way to Boulter's. The tenant requested, and received, remission of that year's rent; so ended over five centuries of trading at Hedsor Wharf.

Lord Boston commenced proceedings; at the quarter sessions he obtained a little more than half the sum that he claimed. But more important to future generations, he managed, by certain interpretations of The Thames Preservation Act of 1884, and The Thames Conservator's Bill of 1894, to enjoy the Hedsor Water as a private channel and prevent any person from entering upon it. That right once obtained has endowed all subsequent owners of the property with the delightful privilege of owning part of the Thames.

As we go on downriver there were wharves by the score – Maidenhead, Windsor, Staines and so on – some public, others belonging to local merchants. When Hampton Church was re-built in 1830, all the materials were delivered by barges. The former Thames Conservancy once had in their archives a very fine hand-coloured engineer's drawing of the temporary extension to the existing 'hard', which was required to cope with the extra barges whilst church building was in progress. This hard at Hampton is one of the few left that can still be used for its intended purpose; so many are silted up, built upon, turned into public gardens or just lost in oblivion. When battling for one's rights old newspaper cuttings and contemporary photographs can be excellent ammunition in overcoming bureaucracy.

Whilst most wharves were substantially built, some were just sections of level and consolidated bank, where there was a good depth of water and easy access to a local thoroughfare. Regular cargoes of hay for London's great population of horses has been mentioned, but in return large quantities of manure were brought away for delivery to riverside market gardens upstream of London; it goes without saying that on shorter trips fresh produce would be taken by water to London as well as larger Thames-side towns. Barge traffic has existed on the river from the earliest times and probably reached its peak prior to the middle of the last century when railways were beginning to make their presence felt. Ironically, sometimes the building of railways was helped by barges which delivered construction materials to the nearest possible site. One com-

A sailing barge with the now familiar rounded bow. The starboard 'leeboard' is in the up position between the covers and the tumbril (tip cart) on left. This picture was taken at the turn of the century and shows a cargo o— unloaded at the hard, Hampton.

modity that sometimes floated on its own was timber; logs would be lashed together to form a raft and steered downstream to a sawmill. About the last mention of this practice is in the minutes of the Commissioners' meeting of August 1777 when it was 'ordered that for every float of timber be taken at the several pound locks on the river a toll of 2d. at Boulters and a toll of 1½d. at other pound locks'.

The Thames and the canal era

The River Wey was made navigable from Weybridge to Guildford under an Act of 1651, by digging about 10 miles of artificial channel and building 12 locks at a cost of £15,000. The River Kennet became likewise navigable from Reading to Newbury some years later. But it was not until the second half of the 18th century that canal construction got under way in earnest. This

resulted in increased traffic and comr the Thames. The constructior Thames–Severn Canal, which was traffic from Stroud to Lechlade in heralded as a great innovation. In ant the increase in barge traffic, a new c made at Radcot in the north bank, by a narrow stream that was about a metres wide; this watercourse lef upstream of Radcot Bridge and swur the side of the 'Swan' public house, wharf stream, which originally gave a wharves, and was wide enough for t the stone trade. The bridge over the course was a low affair of timber, commissioners replaced with the pre span stone bridge in 1787. It shou that the arches of old Radcot Bridg low to take large barges at times of This re-alignment of the navigati necessitated alterations to, and re-positioning of some of the wharfs.

One of the main cargoes to the Thames was South Staffordshire coal, whilst another important commodity was salt from the Droitwich area. Due to a difference in the size of locks on the Severn end of the canal, the large Thames barges had to trans-ship their cargoes on to smaller craft; Brimscombe became a port for this reason.

The Wilts and Berks Canal joined the Thames at Abingdon in 1810, so linking that town with Semington on the Kennet and Avon. Later, in 1819, the North Wilts Canal was built to connect with the Thames–Severn Canal at Latton. Traffic for the lower Thames could now by-pass the upper reaches and join the main river at Abingdon. With the Somersetshire Coal Canal, authorized in 1794, flowing into the Kennet and Avon Canal further supplies of coal were reaching Thames-side towns, whilst corn and agricultural produce was being shipped in the other direction. The uniting of the Thames and Severn had a small influence on the latter-day West Country barges, which took on a few ideas from Severn trows, which were the traditional carrying craft of the river Severn. They were clinker (clincher) built and of varying sizes, the largest being about 70 feet long with a beam of 18 feet and a draught of 3 feet to 4 feet; they could carry about 120 tons, when they would require a 9 to 10 foot depth of water. Severn trows bore no relationship to trows of the Tyne which were a completely different style of craft used for salmon fishing and netting.

The former Thames Conservancy had until the late 1940s a contract with the Samuel Barlow Coal Company of Tamworth to make an annual delivery of coal for the lock keeper's houses as well as the conservators' steam dredgers. One of

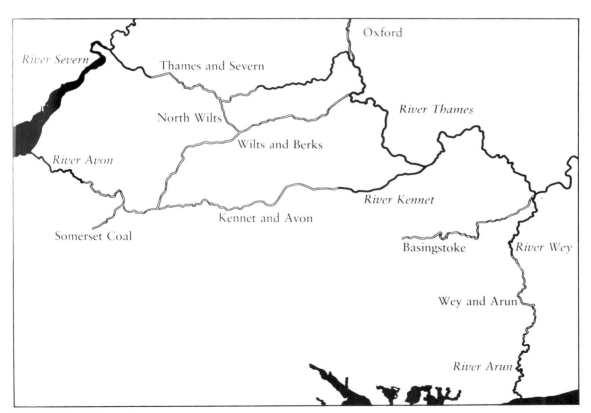

The Thames and the canal system.

the last places to receive coal in this way was Sandford Mill, which had about 200 narrow-boat loads a year until shortly after the last war.

With all this traffic from the Midlands on the Thames, traditional narrow boats became an everyday sight. The completion of the Kennet and Avon canal in 1810 made another great through route, and many trading firms set up at Newbury, Honeystreet, Hungerford, Reading, Bristol and Bath. One Samuel Slocock, of the Newbury family of brewers, had a large fleet of barges carrying malt, timber and commodities of all kinds, including 'Newbury peat ashes' for the market gardens of Middlesex. Newbury barges were capacious craft with a length of 109 feet and a beam of 17 feet; the earliest known New-bury barges were in fact slightly larger, being 128 tonners as against the later ones which car-ried 110 tons. They became popular on the Thames and influenced barge design in the early 19th century, with their rounded bows, fuller lines and attractive sterns. Other well known carriers were: Parsons, who had a fleet of 11 barges in the early 19th century; Horner, who had 3 barges; Townsends, Harwood and Ashley, and of course Robbins, Lane and Pinniger Ltd of Honeystreet, who were also barge builders, their products being known as 'Kennet' barges. They were provided with a cabin aft, for the crew; the helmsman stood on the platform forward of the cabin and steered with a long tiller which passed over the cabin roof. Like the Newbury barges, they saw much life upon the Thames, as well as trading on the Wey Navigation and Basingstoke Canal.

The last commercial carriers on the Kennet and Avon were John Gould Ltd, with the narrow boats *Colin* and *Iris*; these craft were named after the children of their previous owner, Har-vey Taylor, who operated from Aylesbury with a fleet of boats, most being in the coal trade. In 1950 John was honouring a formal contract, carrying for T. Harrison Chaplin Ltd, when the Docks and Inland Waterways Executive (fore-runners of the British Waterways Board) closed the canal, locking his boats in at Newbury. This contract enabled John Gould to enter into litiga-tion: obviously a commercial carrier being

forced out of business had a better c
local protestors, canoe clubs and the
outcome was the inability of the D. &
abandon the canal at that stage. By the
1962 Transport Act came into being
opinion had changed enough for the ca
saved. At the time of writing much of
has been opened and full success is now
John Gould is a wonderful character an
of information on his truly great love, th
and Avon Canal. Apart from a lot of v
work, he still hires out pleasure boats
bury. Just prior to the Chaplin-Gould sa
Knill with his narrow boats *Uranus* a
umba had been delivering salt to Newb
the Cerebos works at Middlewich.

As canal enthusiasts know only to
owner-boatmen were referred to as
ones'. A great number one on the Tha
George Beauchamp Senior. He traded w
from the Warwickshire coalfields for the
part of the year, delivering it direct to to
villages on the Upper Thames, but at
Regatta time he would unload his
Oxford, collect a load of punts and ski
Bossom's of Medley and take them d
Henley where he would hire them out to
enthusiasts. His narrow boat was horse
and his son once told the writer that he co
this trade until shortly before World W

The Oxford Canal was opened in 17
brought a steady flow of traffic to the
for many a long year: coal from the Co
pits, road stone from the Nuneaton ar
cement from Stockton near Rugby.
boatmen were shrewd businessmen, and
their big contacts for trade was the wa
pub, where rest and refreshment could be
as well as stabling and fodder for the f
horses. At Oxford there was a boatman
who, for ten shillings (50p) would arr
cargo. Then some timber wharves or
would display a sign if they wanted a boat

Another well known number one wi
quented the Thames was the late and much
Jack James, who in his later years becam
well known to those visiting the Wate
Museum at Stoke Bruerne; at one period

A pair of Stevens's barges loaded with grain, being towed up the Walton reach on a November morning in 1960, en route for Cox's Lock Mill on the River Wey. The leading craft is a Basingstoke barge built by Harmsworth, the other is a Wey barge built by Stevens.

career he joined forces with Bill Chivers and Jack Garner to form Thames Traders who contracted to tow away barges of spoil for the Thames. Conservancy dredging programme; they supplied boats for constructional projects and also acted as general carriers and towing contractors. Regrettably this concern came to an end with the Depression of the 'thirties, when Jack James returned to the Grand Union Canal. The other two remained at Reading, Bill Chivers later trading on his own account; he was a great character,

well known on both the Thames and the Kennet and Avon Canal.

The Wey Navigation was busy until recent times with loads of timber for Guildford, and grain to Cox's Lock Mill, which trade, using genuine 'Wey barges' (73 feet × 13 feet 10 inches, with carrying capacity of 80 tons) ceased in 1969. However it is good to know that this trade was re-commenced, using modern powered craft, in 1980. The last regular consignment of linseed for crushing at Whittet's Oil Mills,

A William Stevens 'Wey' barge, showing folding rudder which enables the craft to fit into a tight lock.

Weybridge, was unloaded in 1963.

The Wey-Arun Canal, linking the Thames with the South Coast, was a great concept but a lost cause; from the start it had problems in obtaining enough water, whilst the canal itself was not large enough to accommodate boats that would appreciate a short cut to the South Coast. In 1867, the last person to make the through trip was J.B. Dashwood in his Una-rigged sailing boat *The Caprice* (see Chapter 11). An Arun barge (58 feet × 10 feet 10 inches) has been preserved for posterity. She is now moored at Ford near the old wartime fighter aerodrome.

Of individual boats and cargoes on the Thames it is surely worth recording that the great narrow-boat builders and canal carriers, Fellows, Morton and Clayton, designed and built some narrow boats especially for river use; they had washboards (wide boards set into, and rising above the gunwale, so that when the boat was loaded it did not ship water) and also winches so that anchor and chain could be used. Two of these craft, the *Mapledurwell* and *Greywell*, were, amongst others, regular visitors to the Thames and also the Wey and Basingstoke Canal. Of cargoes, the longest haul known to me was bricks from Ruabon on the Llangollen Canal to Harleyford, where they were used in the construction of stables and outbuildings at the manor in about 1816.

The Basingstoke Canal, which joins the Wey near the former Brooklands motor racing track,

was opened in 1796. It was a source of able traffic including timber to Wo' bricks from Natley, at the upper en canal; Basingstoke barges were slightl than their Wey counterparts, being of tons capacity; they were built by Harm of Ash Vale. The Basingstoke Canal is n restored, mainly by voluntary workers ardent enthusiasts.

The Grand Union Canal, formed by t

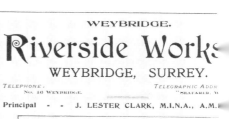

An advertisement of 1896, which includes the bu
tugs and barges.

The great fire at Gridley, Miskins timber yard, Kingston (1928).

of several canal companies in 1929, gave rise to very regular trade in its heyday; however, a great percentage of that trade was for the London Docks and the tidal Thames, via the Regent's Canal or Brentford.

One of the last regular upstream cargoes of any consequence was timber from the Surrey Commercial Docks (London) for timber merchants at Reading in the early days of the last war; this trade gradually faded after the cessation of hostilities. During World War II and for a short time afterwards, motor tank barges (of the type used on both the Severn and the Trent) were transporting petrol from the Walton terminal (which was built early on in the last war to receive oil products sent from Bristol through a cross-country pipeline) to the Pool of London. These no doubt were the largest craft to have traded upon the river. To some octogenarians the sight of these craft must have brought back nostalgic memories of steam barges, such as the *Ambition*, which plied the upper Thames. They had a typical barge-type hull with fairly bulbous bows; the boiler and machinery were set aft,

A rare sight on the Thames: a steam barge of about 80 tons capacity, she is the *Ambition* on her way up the Maidenhead reach in about 1906. Her boiler and machinery are situated right aft and the tall funnel had to be lowered before passing under a bridge. Skindles Hotel is on the far left. The steam launch heading for the centre arch is towing a dismasted rater, possibly from the Upper Thames Sailing Club at Bourne End. The flat on the right is one of Edwards, once well known piling contractors.

Some of Clement Knowling's steam tugs, including *Pamelalice*, together with lighters at Gridley, Miskins Whar Turk's boatyard is just beyond the white flagpole (early 1930s).

beyond the capacious hold. The smoke stack was, of necessity, tall to give adequate draught for efficient combustion. These funnels were hinged and braced in such a way that they could be easily lowered and raised when passing under bridges. It is unfortunate that very little information is available about these noble craft.

Various gas works such as those at Oxford and Staines had called a halt by the 1950s to the waterborne delivery of coal. As the '40s were drawing to a close, Edward Jones of E.C. Jones

and Son, a Brentford firm well know barge- and tug-building, tried to revital transport with the introduction of his pusher tug. This 30 foot tug with a 12 f could push a 250-ton lighter; 'knees' or of the tug pressed against the stern of th whilst wire bonds (cables) attached fro lighter were tensioned with ratchet wi that the two craft became a single mano unit. In addition to pushing a 250-to could also tow another astern. This into service on the Thames in October 1948; however the Thames Conservancy were not enamoured with the new idea, and as a result of a test case held at Feltham Court in January 1950, the tug was withdrawn from service on the river. The Conservancy claimed that the *Bantam* contravened bye law 30, which states that all vessels under way should be navigated singly or separately, except vessels towed alongside or astern of any mechanically propelled vessels. Mr Edward Jones said that he regarded the tug and barge as one unit. His method of control was 50 per cent safer in normal times, 80 per cent safer in floods than the normal method of towing, due

cial traffic faded from the scene. The hustle and bustle at Palmer's Wharf, Kingston, where coasting vessels had regularly discharged their cargoes, came to an untimely end in the mid 1960s. No more were schoolboys able to spot majestic steam tugs such as *Pamelaalice* and *Scorcher* (the latter built in 1888), whose owners, Clements Knowling of Brentford, were to become Clements Tough. These tugs, like others, were not economic to run with the great decline in regular upriver trade.

The beautiful tugs *Ham* and *Sheen*, built in 1925, which towed William Cory's lighters loaded with coal for the waterworks at Hamp-

The Thames Conservancy steam tug *Bourne*, leaving Molesey Lock with a standard type steel barge in tow (late 1930s).

to the fact that barge and tug could be worked adroitly, as a single unit, under difficult and/or flood conditions. With a normal tow there is always the possibility of the barge overriding the tug, especially upon going downstream when there is a strong flow. The *Bantam* became very popular on large gravel pits for towing ballast barges whilst the River Wey Navigation Authority still use a small *Bantam* for moving their maintenance boats.

During the next couple of decades, commer-

ton and Walton, were the pride and joy of Tough and Henderson, who have been in the towing business since the 1820s; however, Tough's are now probably better known amongst river users for their boatbuilding activities, including luxury yachts, which seem a far cry from mundane tugs and barges, at their extensive yard situated close to Teddington Lock.

By the '70s Beckett's timber wharf at Hampton Wick was undergoing changes which brought the cessation of waterborne timber

Meadhurst V. Believed to be the last Thames-based working narrow boat in regular use. She was built as a ho
ice-breaker cum workboat by Bushell Bros. She was converted to diesel power, which necessitated re-building the st
1930s. She is now powered by a 4 cylinder Ford diesel with closed circuit cooling.

transport, including the disposal of their superb
little motor tugs, such as *Pep, Andy, Vim* and
Puffin. Fortunately for those with a nostalgic
turn of mind, some of these tugs are still about

on the river, having been acquired by
Watson Ltd for towing barges during d
operations and on maintenance work.

8 TRADITIONAL THAMES CRAFT

Those accustomed to modern motor boats, with glass reinforced plastic hulls and cabins fitted out in a manner to vie with luxury apartments may be bewildered by the number of different craft discussed in this chapter; but all our contemporary pleasure boats derive from that ubiquitous craft, the Thames wherry. Such craft, like their successors, such as skiffs and gigs, were created by great characters who built a boat by eye that would be a joy to scull and a pleasure to behold.

There was hardly a navigable river, or boating lake, in the United Kingdom, prior to the plastic era that did not have a traditional Thames-built boat, or at least a Thames-designed boat upon it. Thames boatbuilders of the 19th and early 20th centuries were craftsmen of no mean ability, whose products were unique on the inland

A delightful scene in the 1890s with the famous Mrs Lindsay's lawn in the background; the downstream section of the lawn now forms a public open space with mooring facilities under the auspices of Spelthorne Borough Council.

waters of the world; at their zenith, they were receiving export orders from the far corners of the earth. But they were the end of a long line of boatbuilders.

Thames wherries

To begin the story we must go back to the time, long, long before the advent of steamers, when people used the river as a highway. The earliest known type of craft used for carrying passengers was known as a 'wherry'. It should be noted, however, that the 'Thames wherries' bore no resemblance to the cargo-carrying sailing wherries of the Norfolk Broads which, historically, are relatively modern. The Thames craft were lightly built of clinker, or clincher, construction: that is, all of her timbers, or 'strakes', were so attached to each other that the lower edge of each timber overlapped the upper edge of the timber below it, the timbers being 'clenched' or 'clinked' with copper nails and 'roves' (small saucer-shaped copper washers). The action of clenching, or riveting the end of the nail into the rove pulled the timbers tightly together. Wherries were designed to glide over, rather than through, the water. They had little freeboard and long, pointed bows raking well forward; the stern was pointed and cut vertically. Dimensions varied, but a typical wherry would have a length of 26 feet with a beam of 5 feet 8 inches. During the 17th and 18th centuries, people relied to a large extent on using a wherry as a quick and easy means of transport; wherries, depending on size, could carry up to eight passengers, also luggage, subject to the following condition: 'That in all cases when luggage is carried by any of the persons or passengers in the boats licensed under the provisions of the bye-laws, the number of persons or passengers such boats are permitted to carry shall be reduced one respectively from the number of persons or passengers contained in such respective licenses, for every complete hundredweight of luggage so carried as aforesaid.' A passenger wishing to be taken across the river, or on a short journey, was said to be 'taking a pair of sculls' – a wherry sculled by a single waterman (using a pair of sculls). For

a longer journey one would take 'a pair ʘ that is, a wherry rowed by two watern pulling a single oar. On very long joun travelling fully loaded, large wherr rigged 'randan' – that is, handled by thre men, the midships man pulling a pair whilst bow and stroke would have a si Occasionally the crew of three would a a pair of sculls. Wherries, in experience were pretty fast craft. The beam at the g where the rowlocks were placed, was fa than the beam on the waterline, wh reduced to a minimum; this gave the e flared gunwale, and gave the sculler man) the leverage, and elevation c required for speedy propulsion. This design pre-dated the outrigger by so years, the latter being developed in Harry Clasper, a Tyneside waterman, ν set up a well known boat building conc the Thames.

Where river crossings consisted of a was not unusual for the craft to be a wherries were also used for carrying I goes and, in the heyday of houseboa Victorian and Edwardian era, pr groceries, wines and spirits, as well as were delivered by wherry.

In 1514 Henry VIII had passed a stat lating watermen and their fares, recorc it had been a laudable custome and us out of mind to use the river in Barge ʘ Bote'. The watermen carried on acting dently. However, an Act of 1555 a rulers of all watermen and wherrymen between Gravesend and Windsor an Watermen's Company was born. The ι introduced apprenticeship for a perioʘ year for all boys wishing to learn the wa trade. A further Act, in 1603, exter training to seven years. This was a looking provision which was of inc value to both watermen and their ind 1700 the lightermen, who until that been members of the Woodmonger's C succeeded in their petitions to Parliame under an Act of that year they were bro the Watermen's Company, making

Company of Watermen and Lightermen of the River Thames'. The arms of the company were granted to the watermen by Queen Elizabeth I and by the end of the 16th century the company became the proud possessor of its own hall.

Watermen were the first public servants to wear a uniform; in fact before the navy or army had any distinct outfit of clothing, the Thames watermen were known by their uniform and badge. The livery consisted of a pleated coat, knee breeches with hose and a cap with a stiff peak. Upon the arm was a plate or badge, either of the Waterman's Hall (denoting they had the freedom of the river and were licensed) or the badge of his employer. Any person rowing or working a wherry, boat or other vessel for hire who had not served his apprenticeship incurred a penalty of £10.

Watermen used their wherries for racing at the local annual regattas (see Chapter 11); they were standard craft, but made lighter by removing the 'burden' (floor) boards and all surplus gear. Wherries were so representative of life upon the river that in 1845 a race called the 'Silver Wherries' was instituted at Henley Regatta; the race was for pair oars and presentation prizes given to the winners consisted of model wherries in silver. In 1850 the prizes were altered to silver gilt cups with the subsequent re-naming of the event to the 'Silver Goblets'.

Punts

Punts have always been associated with fishing, 'ballasting' (that is, dredging gravel from the river bed for building purposes), ferrying and numerous other river duties. The old time working punts, which were on the wane by the 19th century, were clumsy craft, heavily built and often towed from the bank by a man if they were to travel a considerable distance. Occasionally they were fitted with metal rowlocks, these being termed 'swivels' by some watermen, so that the punt could be propelled with a pair of sculls which proved an excellent method of propulsion. The standard, and accepted, way of handling a punt is with a pole; the pole shows off the efficiency of a punt when negotiating crowded waters or where much manoeuvring is required. A further advantage under congested conditions is that the punter, unlike the oarsman, faces the direction in which the craft is travelling. Fishing punts were fitted with a 'wet well' which is virtually a box running the full width of the punt, the bottom and sides of which form the ends and floor of the well. Gratings are let into the sides of the punt at each end of this box. When fishing, the punt is usually moored athwart the stream, and as the water flows through the well, it supplies the live bait with plenty of fresh water. Dimensions of such a punt are 26 to 27 feet long with a beam of 3 feet 6 inches at the widest point; the craft are somewhat narrower at the ends. Pine was a popular timber for their construction and they were finished with a copious quantity of paint, whilst their bottoms, especially if old or tender, were well dressed with tar.

By the early 1800s punts used purely for exercise and recreation were being built in

Albert Mitchell with his fiancée and chaperone out punting at the turn of the century. Albert's brother Charles founded the Thames Camping and Boating Association mentioned in Chapter 12.

mahogany, were of lighter construction than the everyday 'work punts' and had more elegant proportions. Typical measurements were: length 26 to 27 feet with a beam of 2 feet 9 inches increasing to 3 feet 6 inches at the widest point. By the 1830s punting was becoming more and more popular with a surfeit of elegant craft being produced by the well known boatbuilders of the period. The sides of the punts were built from a single piece of selected mahogany; one end of the craft had a 'till', that is, it was decked. Rigidity was provided by transverse bearers, each of which was braced to the respective sides with 'knees'. Between the bearers and to the height of same were gratings (like duckboards) so as to provide a level surface and a 'bilge' to collect any ingress of water. These gratings were usually of mahogany and made with the finesse and decorative skills associated with the craftsmanship of Thames boatbuilders. The 'saloon' is the area in the centre of the punt arranged to take four sitters on lounge cushions, supported by shaped wooden backs, which face each other. Varnish was the customary finish, although

sometimes the bottom would be painte green was the colour invariably used. small decorative groove, sometimes a groove, would be formed with a routin along the full length of the craft a litt gunwale level. This was invariably rep the inside of the craft. The single groov be gold-leafed, whilst if there was 'moulding' this would be painted black the gold stand out against the varnishe Tills were planked 'fore and aft', and on ity punts alternate planks would be of ing timbers to give a striking effect. Wh a punt it was usual to carry a spare p often than not it was carried in a pair strops slung on the outside of the punt the punter). On some craft the spare p be carried inboard, for which purpose der would shape the backrests accord the cushions would then be tailored t mooring, punts never had a painter line), but were equipped with a chain invariably one forward and the other a as poles, the punt usually also carrie

From the Chaplin family album. This is reproduced from a 'daguerreotype', which was an early photographic p Harrison Chaplin and family in the late 19th century.

A camping punt with awning up and kitted out. A Thames Conservancy bucket dredger is in the background with attendant barge and steam tug (about 1929).

paddles; with two people sitting on the edge of the till, with a paddle apiece, progress, although possibly slow, was peaceful and relaxing. Due to their length and flat bottoms, punts were until the 1930s favourite craft for camping, for which purpose they had canvas covers which were supported by folding iron hoops, the bottom ends of which dropped into small brass sockets secured to the upper inside edge of the punt's sides, so that you could sleep aboard. Alas, the wash from the ever-increasing number of power craft upon the river caused a decline in their popularity; in the 1930s 'wash boards' were very much in vogue as a means of keeping passengers and camping gear dry. As the name implies, these were single boards running from the head of the punt to the till, or sometimes just abaft the rear cushion support. These boards were several inches high, so in proportion with the punt. Naturally they were shaped to fit and showed the builders' attention to detail. They were retained in place by steel straps which slotted into small brackets on the inside of the punt. However, although wash boards increased the useful life of punting, the demise of the punt, other than for racing or pure exercise was imminent.

Shortly after World War I Walter Hammerton of Twickenham developed and introduced a clinker-built punt. It was somewhat shorter than a standard punt, lighter too, and very versatile; although not ideal for camping it was useful for local recreation; it was a handy size for mooring and storage.

A few words on the principal means of propulsion – the punt pole! Poles for working and fishing punts were very often a selected branch from a suitable tree, with the bark removed and the minimum of shaping or rubbing down; the iron 'shoe', or prong, at the bottom would have been formed by the local blacksmith. For this type of pole the straight stem of a young larch tree was ideal. Larch was also used for better poles, although generally this class of pole would be 'made', i.e. shaped from selected deal. A good pole must be straight, free from knots, stiff and well balanced. A pole can soon give trouble if the grain is not straight and/or if the wood is not of equally good quality throughout. Even the best of poles may, after a 'breaking in' period, fail to retain its straightness or stiffness. General pole length is 14 feet with a diameter (excluding taper at the upper end) of between one and three eighths and one and five eighths inches. Poles are

Picnic table erected in the saloon of a punt. Note pole slung in leather strops on the starboard side and the velour cu... till for two people to sit and paddle the craft. Felix hanging from the camping cover dates the picture.

shod with an iron shoe which consists of a socket to take the pole and a fork which makes contact with the river bed in the action of the punting stroke. The shoe itself is of galvanized malleable iron; the fork part of it is available in two styles, either rounded and 'U' shaped, or in a 45° 'V' shaped prong. The rounded style is supposedly less liable to collect stones from the bed, but on the other hand when stones do get in they are far more difficult to dislodge. With the 'V' shape, stones are easy to get out and can often be cleared by giving the pole a sharp jar on to the river bed. Punt poles, when new, are in most cases given a coat of diluted varnish and then rubbed down with very fine sandpaper – a fully varnished pole being too slippery for the hands, especially when wet. Aluminium punt poles were popular between the wars but their use is mostly confined to racing; together with racing punts, they will be dealt with in the chapter on Sport on the Thames.

Gigs, skiffs and dinghies

It was not until the early part of the 19th century that boating for pleasure purposes began to make inroads into life upon the Th... interest in such a leisure activity g... mendous momentum with the adver... ways, which provided easy access ... Thames-side towns. Hence it is easy t... the humble and hard-working ... developed into a sleek and delightfu... this time wherries were very muc... decline, and furthermore they would ... rather large and clumsy for persona... was that the 'gig' came into vogue f... purposes in the later part of the first ... the 19th century. Originally the gig d... the wherry, but was also influence... design. A pair-oared gig was about 2... with a beam of 3 feet 9 inches, and co... people. Like the wherry, it was clinke... had flush gunwale with rowlock ... swivels) placed on the top of it. 'Carv... were developed for racing purposes. ... 'caravel' hull has the planking laid e... on a sturdy framework; planking ... fashion gives a completely smooth su... hull, but on craft built for hard ... section sheathing makes the fin... heavier than its clinker-built counter...

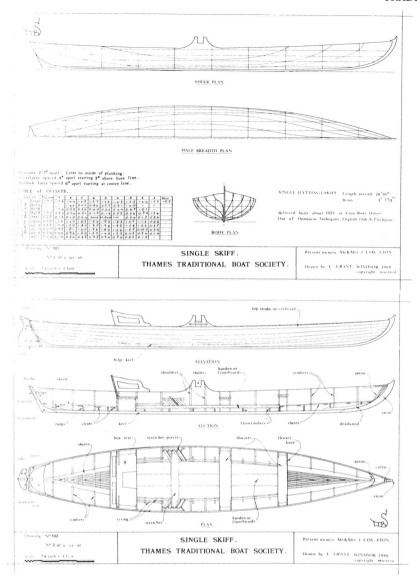

A constructional drawing of a traditional Thames skiff.

dan version of the gig was at one time quite popular and whilst it had the same beam as its pair-oared, or double-sculling contemporary, it was some 3 feet longer. The gig could be pair-oared, or double-sculled; the randan version would have a pair of sculls amidships whilst bow and stroke would have a single oar.

From all accounts the gig was the ancestor of the ubiquitous skiff, which from the 1870s onwards outclassed the gig. Skiffs are clinker-built and of relatively light construction, the bows reminiscent of a wherry compared with the nigh on perpendicular stem of the gig. The stern finished in a very narrow transom whilst the gunwales swept in elegant curves between the rowlocks which were built into the top strake; the sides of the rowlocks were made of replaceable cheeks of hardwood, the name for these cheeks being 'tholes'. There are exceptions, where skiffs have been fitted with swivel rowlocks for special purposes or to suit the whim of an individual owner. Skiffs were generally for

A Thames skiff being built in 1970 by th[e] method, working upwards from the keel with held in position with struts from the floor an[d] plank above.

(*right*) A page from the post World War I catalo[gue] by Messrs Hobbs of Henley.

souble sculling although singles have their adherents: lengths are in the 20 to 26 foot bracket
whilst randan skiffs are about 27 feet; beam can
be up to 5 feet. A few boatbuilders, notably
Salter's of Oxford, built smaller single sculling
skiffs purely for the hire trade; the design being
perpetuated in Salter's little G.R.P. (glass reinforced plastic) skiffs that are now made in
considerable numbers for local authorities and
others to let on hire by the hour.

A feature of the skiff that recalls the profile
of the wherry is the built-in rowlocks with
hardwood tholes. Gigs and skiffs, like punts,
were grand roomy craft for camping; for this
purpose they were equipped with gunwale fittings to accommodate folding steel hoops, over
which a canvas camping cover could be rigged.

The dinghy was adopted for pleasure purposes at about the same time as gigs were coming
into vogue. They range in size from 10 to 16 feet
in length with a beam of up to 4 feet or so. They
were usually built for double sculling, although
the odd shorter dinghy was sometimes arranged
for single sculling only. Dinghies, due to their
beaminess in relation to length, are not as fast as
skiffs, but are extremely handy, easy to lift
ashore and highly manoeuvrable. In the distant
past they must have been the waterman's coun-

terpart of today's mini-van. No do[ubt]
Thames dinghy was developed from th[e]
boat', which is the oldest known Thames
was designed for fishing and hence rece[ived its]
name from the patron saint of fisherme[n]

Peterboats were used for net fishin[g]
attained a length of some 23 feet, but
upriver a smaller type with a length of ab[out]
feet was used. They were double ended c[arvel or]
clinker construction, with a wide beam,
well for the catch and rowlocks flush wi[th the]
gunwale to prevent fouling of nets. The
downriver Peterboats set a simple spritsa[il and]
foresail to make the most of the wind. Th[e last]
surviving example of this noble type of cra[ft was]
seen rotting away at Putney in about 19[..] [A]
Peterboat is depicted in the arms of The [Com-]
pany of Watermen and Lightermen of the [River]
Thames; it also features in the fine oil painti[ng]
'Keen Edge Ferry, Shillingford', by J. T. Se[rres.]

Dinghies were usually of clinker construc[tion,]
the few carvel-built versions being very [fine]
birds which were influenced by the P[eter-]
borough Company of Ontario, whose nam[e is]
synonymous with Canadian canoes. Ding[hies]
have straight gunwales and swivel rowlock[s of]
bronze or gunmetal. On the longer dinghies, [and]
even sometimes on the short ones, a rud[der]

PUNT AND DINGHY.

With one exception the two most popular craft in use on the Thames, for those who do not aspire to a power-driven Boat.

would be hung on the transom in the same way as on a skiff, and operated by white cotton tiller lines. The larger dinghies, like skiffs, gigs and punts, had gunwale fittings to accommodate camping cover hoops. Another feature for camping was that the stroke thwart (seat) was fitted in such a way that it could be removed, although when in position it provided maximum rigidity for the boat.

No 'classic' Thames dinghies have been built since the 1930s. They are superb little craft and there are still a number about but about 90 per cent must have fallen into disrepair, for the average newcomer to boating, unless he is a sailing man or racing enthusiast, now seems to consider the use of a motor obligatory.

Another historic craft popular in the 18th century was the shallop, which was built on similar lines, and in the same way as a skiff, but was much larger and propelled by four oarsmen; the cox sat right aft and between him and stroke were the thwarts and side benches for the passengers, this area being protected with a canvas canopy rigged over a light iron frame, although in some instances the shelter would be a more permanent structure of wood.

A customary feature of gigs, skiffs and dinghies was the drilling of the bow thwart, and the burden board below it, so that a short mast could be stepped. The mast would carry a small lug sail to help one along with a following wind. Although an excellent performance was possible, due to the shallow draught of the craft and the fact that no centreboards were fitted, sailing close to the wind was out of the question.

More often than not, the mast would be used as a securing point for a tow rope, the boat being towed by men from the bargewalk (old Thames term for towpath). This was at one time common practice, as devotees of *Three Men in a Boat* will recall. By having the tow rope coming from the top of the mast, entanglement with reeds could be avoided, while if the mast was stepped sufficiently aft of the bow, the craft would run on course without difficulty.

Boat fittings

The craft in the main categories described were invariably built of mahogany, with oak, spruce and certain other timbers being used as and where required. Fastenings were of copper throughout, with keel bands of iron. Where keel bands were brought up the transom and also over the stem on to the apron, the blacksmith would hammer out the iron to form a fleur de lys or other attractive motif. The boatbuilder would finish off his craft by forming one, or sometimes a pair of grooves in an arc across the transom (both inside and out) then a straight groove along the outside of the top strake with another on the inside of the gunwale. This very precise work would be carried out with a very narrow convex routing plane. The grooves were finished with gold leaf highlighted with a narrow black band, prior to the craft being finished with a rubbing down and building up of numerous coats of the best boat varnish. The standard of finish could be compared only with that of a coach-builder. Rowlocks, if of the swivel type, were of bronze or gunmetal, and fenders were made from leather, in either cylindrical or round disc form, and stuffed with coir. On lower priced craft the fenders would be of painted canvas. Painters (mooring ropes) were of white cotton rope which was also used, as previously mentioned, for rudder lines, due to cotton being very kind to the hands. An item of great comfort, for which even in this modern age there is no equal, were the lambswool pads for attaching to the thwarts; whilst in the stern, for the comfort of the passengers, were horsehair-filled cushions, made individually for each and every boat to ensure perfect fit and maximum comfort. Besides cushions, a shaped and bound carpet of Axminster or Wilton, would be fitted. The back rail of a skiff or gig was generally of woven rush, although hire boats, not surprisingly, often had the latter in wrought iron to stand hard use. The earlier wherries had their wooden back and side rails supported with elegantly turned spindles.

A boathook and paddle were always included as standard equipment; paddles were shaped from a single piece of wood with a widened grip at the upper end, to fit the palm of the hand; they were very useful for handling a boat in a lock or confined space. At one period the combined boathook and paddle became quite popular; they are now regarded as collectors' items.

Sculls and oars were fashioned from a single piece of timber; sculls or 'blades' as they are commonly termed, were paired and balanced for the boat in which they were to be used and were numbered for their appropriate position,

Towing. This is reproduced from a postcard in t[...] river boating' series published by Misch and Co. i[...] 20th century. The artist of this series went under t[...] 'Bob'.

i.e. bow, stroke, etc. Leathers were c[...] and accurately fitted to form a colla[...] the shaft where it rotated in the row[...] 'button' of leather at the upper end [...] collar ensured correct balance and preve[...] shaft slipping through the rowlock. The s[...] the button is such that one can recogniz[...] and left-hand blades quite easily. If you [...] tunate enough to own one of these fin[...] remember that leathers should always be [...] good condition by the regular applica[...] tallow, or, in the vernacular of pre-wa[...] men, 'best two and eight'! It was nor[...] protect the tips of the blades with a ve[...] capping of copper. Nowadays, thanks [...] availability of modern glues, oar and scul[...] ers are able to tip their blades with a narro[...] of hardwood, which is very effective and a[...] ically pleasing. Blades were either square-[...] or rounded; the design of the latter bein[...] buted to a fine old character, William Ben[...]

established his boatyard at Hampton sometime prior to 1704.

This wonderful old yard, with its fascinating boatbuilding loft and fitted rooms for ladies and gentlemen to change into 'boating dress' was very badly damaged during an air raid in the last war and was fully demolished in 1946–7. The last owner and descendant of the original William Benn was the late Louis 'Jube' Waldock. He was a wonderful character, a waterman par excellence and a born naturalist. Provided he was not watching herons nesting, checking the Hampton Deeps prior to the fishing season, or teaching a youngster to use a punt pole correctly, he could, and did, carry out a certain amount of boat building; he executed superb repair work, so good that when finished, including the toning down of new wood, the repair was very hard indeed to detect. The recipe for darkening new mahogany is the skilful use of permanganate of potash, but careful judgement is needed to make the solution to the right strength for the wood in question.

Extras which could be supplied were mast and lug sail, camping cover, detachable centre thwart, and folding picnic table; this fitted athwartships from gunwale to gunwale a little for'd of the stern seat. Other optional extras would be a 'bow box' for the storage of picnic and other gear and a pair of small drawers under, and to each side of, the stroke thwart for stowing lock tickets, tallow and sundry oddments. Sometimes one drawer would be lined with zinc for the housing of a wash leather, that very essential item for keeping varnish work in pristine condition. It was very fashionable with many people to have the family monogram emblazoned in gold leaf upon the bows of their boat as well as on the blades of their sculls. On a nostalgic note here is an extract from the account book of Charles Constable, boatbuilder of Hampton, for 1904: 'To 6 monograms in gold leaf and to numbering sculls: £1.3 shillings. To 6 new leather fenders with brass eyes: Twelve shillings and sixpence. Varnishing and painting punt: £2. 10 shillings. Painting colours on punt pole [a common form of identity]: Three shillings and sixpence.'

Sculling boats

A boat for one person, with no room for crew or passengers, is a sculling boat, fast little craft that were outrigged, that is, the rowlocks projected beyond the gunwales on a light steel framework, so as to provide sufficient leverage for the sculls, which is very necessary in view of the narrowness of the craft. A 'funny' was an open outrigged sculling boat, having stem and stern alike with the keel curving from either end. A 'whiff' was very similar but the stern was vertical. In the latter part of last century outrigged craft, other than racing boats, were looked upon with some disfavour as rowlocks were liable, when present in some numbers, to get entangled when in locks, at regattas and other events where there was a crush of boats.

The number of boatbuilders till World War I was tremendous, mainly small yards; however, there were large concerns, such as Searle and Sons with yards at Lambeth, Eton, Henley and Oxford. Their products were of the very best and their name a household word; to have served an apprenticeship at Searle's was considered the ultimate. Short Brothers, of flying boat fame, built many a fine Thames boat for the sculling enthusiast. Of the famous names, Burgoine, Biffen, Constable, Horsham, Percy Turner, Cawston, Rough, Thomas, Shaw and Beesley are just a few that come to mind, whilst Salter's, Turk's, Tims, Hobbs, Freebody, Bates and others are old-established firms who are still very much in business.

Canoes have always been popular on the Thames, although they do not come into the traditional class of Thames boat. It is interesting to recall that Searle's, mentioned above, claimed to be the originators of the kyak canoe in the mid-18th century: a very light-decked craft, built of cedar and propelled with a now well known double-ended paddle. One of these craft, in perfect condition and over 110 years old, was completely destroyed in a disastrous fire a few years ago at Kenton's boathouse, Hampton. This must have been the precursor of our modern canvas, plastic or glass fibre canoes of the kyak type. The other form of canoe is the Can-

A typical boatyard of the Victorian-Edwardian era, punts and skiffs on the hard for repair and two houseboa
completion; Harris of Laleham is still a famous name (photographed early 20th century).

adian; large numbers, built by the Peterborough Company of Ontario, were brought over to the Thames in the latter part of the 19th century. One of the principal importers was Saunders of Goring on Thames, a boatbuilder of high repute who later founded the firm of Saunders-Roe, who, like Short's, became famous for their flying boats. A number of Thames yards started making canoes on typical Canadian lines, but naturally variations crept in, such as clinker-built canoes. The Canadian canoe, traditionally built of cedar or basswood, with gunwales of ash, varied from 11 to 19 feet in length with a beam of around 31 inches; its design was evolved from the Indian birch-bark canoe but the Canadian is planked with boards one quarter of an inch thick on light ribs generally set about 6 inches apart. Canadian builders were awarded medals at the Colonial Exhibition in London in 1883 and 1886 at which time a 16 footer cost about £8 sterling! These canoes are, in the main 'paddled' – the propulsion of a canoe with a punt pole is, regrettably, a dying art. A few canoes were built with outriggers, which made them into first-class sculling craft. One such canoe has recently

been fully restored by an up and comin
Thames boatbuilder.

Having described an import to the Tha
it be said that Thames boatbuilders wer
main, forward-looking and built up a ve
export trade, often winning medals and
cates at foreign exhibitions. Turk's for e
won a gold medal in Paris in 1885 and an
New Orleans with a mere silver aw
Philadelphia. Claspers exported boats
many, Holland, Australia and seemingly
corners of the globe; Tagg's had a prett
record, including exporting craft to Rus

A hundred years ago (1881) Tom Ta
affected by a strike in the London Docks
extent that several Thames skiffs, all ca
crated for despatch to Burma, remained
dockside for an excessive period due
absence of stevedores.

There was a hardcore of Thames boatb
who pioneered the exhibiting of their war
specialities at overseas exhibitions, a
example being the World's Fair, held in
during the spring of 1889, when Shephe
Dee of Henley (later taken over by Sear

Traditional wherry built by Mark Edwards (winter '81–'82).

A typical Turk advertisement. This one appeared in 1896.

Sons) displayed two beautiful double sculling boats and a model of a punt. Forrest and Son showed a range of sailing dinghies, whilst Aylings had a well arranged display of oars, sculls and paddles. T.G. Tagg and Son exhibited a double sculling skiff backed up with photographs of other craft, whilst R.J. Turk had one of his sailing canoes on view with a model of a skiff, which the present Michael Turk still displays at special events.

Rosewells of Walton, now Walton Marine Sales Ltd, once carried out a thriving export trade, which included building boats for the Emperor and Empress of Russia, as well as for Prince Louis of Battenberg.

Even taking into account that before World War I the cost of living was low, it is hard to see how a highly skilled craftsman, using the very finest materials available, could produce a skiff with sculls, completely fitted out, including impeccable varnishing with mouldings finished in genuine 22 carat gold leaf for as little as £25.

With the inevitable decline in the use of traditional boats, due to the popularity of power boating, a band of stalwarts foregathered in March 1980 to form the Thames Traditional Boat Society; there are a number of aims, but first and foremost is the desire to encourage the better maintenance, preservation and restoration of traditional craft; furthermore, to keep them afloat and in use. A good, well found boat will last much longer in its natural environment – water – than in a museum. The first event held by our society was a sculling/camping trip down river from Lechlade. In all nine superb craft participated, being handled by their owners with the skill and dexterity as of yore. The oldest boat on the trip was a gig built by Hammerton's of Thames Ditton over 100 years ago, whilst one of the youngest was Tom Chaplin's camping dinghy, built by Burgoine of Hampton Wick, which became an octogenarian during the event. This waterborne tour of May 1980 aroused great interest which is being reflected in the ever-growing desire to own and handle a 'real' boat.

9
STEAM POWERED CRAFT

The very thought of steam power evokes an aura of nostalgia; little thought of the danger occasioned by the exploding of boilers, when in an experimental stage; the filthy black smoke that begrimed everything within its range and the very dirty job of 'coaling ship', together with the wretched job of stoking, particularly on a long run such as made by the Oxford–Kingston steamers. Charles Dickens writing in 1891 states that: 'Steam launches are often the curse of the river. Driving along at an excessive rate of speed, with an utter disregard to the comfort or necessities of anglers, oarsmen and boating parties, the average steam-launch engineer is an unmitigated nuisance . . .' Unfortunately much the same can be said today with regard to a percentage of the motor boats upon the river, whose skippers endeavour to bring motorway techniques to the water.

The advent of steam wrought dramatic changes upon the Thames scene; not only were steam tugs introduced for towing barges and large steam vessels built for carrying passengers, but small steam launches became available for private use. Unlike the traditional boats mentioned in the last chapter, powered craft were not unique to the Thames; but they owed much to the river and the very versatile Thames boatbuilders in their design, development and construction.

Passenger boats

The first steamer to ply for hire upon th was the *Richmond* in 1814, so name she ran between London and Richm was built at Great Yarmouth by Leping fitted with a steam engine designed ar that once famous Thames-side engine Maudslay's of Lambeth. The *Richmo* about 50 tons and her engine was of 1 horse power. It is recorded that in boiler burst – a hazard with early st world over. However, she was repair back into service. The first steame regular passenger service between Court and London was the *Locomoti* built in 1840 and equipped with a machinery as found on a high-press engine; consequently she gave the san a locomotive – hence her unusual nar the City of London limited her speed when she caused £300 worth of da banks between Teddington and Court.

One of the noblest and most fam tions of the Thames, now sadly end ter's regular steamer service runni Oxford and Kingston with schedul points en route. Salter's predecess Thames and Isis Steamboat Cor which was formed in 1878 to run a vice between Oxford and Kingston

The *Isis* at Folly Bridge, headquarters of the Thames and Isis Steamboat Company Ltd, formed in 1878, predecessors of Salter Brothers. It ran 2 paddle steamers, *Isis*, built in 1878, and *Thames*, built in 1879, for the Oxford-Kingston service.

summer months with the paddle steamer *Isis*. A second paddle craft, the *Thames*, was built in 1879 and these two launches remained in service until the company ceased operating at the end of the 1882 season. Exactly what happened in the next six years is a little uncertain; however, in 1888, John Salter of Folly Bridge, Oxford, was running his steamer *Alaska*. She was a screw-driven craft built by Horsham and Co. of Bourne End, who were well known for their steam launches, houseboats and the like. *Alaska* left Oxford at 9.30 every Monday morning, reaching Kingston late afternoon on the Tuesday. The overnight stop was at a hotel in Henley. The return trip took three days with overnight stops at hotels in Windsor and Reading. The arrangements were such that each morning the *Alaska* awaited the arrival of a specified train from London so enabling tourists to make the complete five-day trip or any part of it. This Salter steamer service ran from May to September. About a decade ago the hull of the *Alaska* was 're-discovered' on the Oxford canal; she is now

being completely restored by that celebrated boatbuilder, Peter Freebody of Hurley.

Salter's second boat was the *Oxford*, which went into service in the summer of 1889, replacing the *Alaska* on the weekly service. *Oxford* was built by Edwin Clark and Co. of Brimscombe near Stroud, which is on the Thames–Severn Canal. Clarke's and their successors, Abdela and Mitchell Ltd, built passenger vessels, tugs and commercial craft for river use until the 1930s. Clarke's, until handing over to their successors in about 1899, built further boats for Salter's: the *Kingston* (1890), *Swan* (1891), *Windsor* (1892), *Cliveden* (1892), *Henley* (1896) and *Nuneham* (1898). All these boats were fitted with engines built by W. Sisson and Co. Ltd of Gloucester, well known engineers and naval architects, whose compound and triple expansion steam engines were available from 3 to 300 horse power. In the very early days some craft were delivered by going through the Thames–Severn canal, others went down the Stroudwater Canal to the Severn and in most

Delightful Steamer Trips on the Thames.

SEASON 1896.

SALOON STEAMERS run daily between OXFORD, HENLEY, and KINGSTON, from May 18th to end of September.

Down Trip.—OXFORD TO HENLEY, HENLEY TO KINGSTON—Daily (Sundays excepted).

Up Trip.—KINGSTON TO HENLEY, HENLEY TO OXFORD—Daily (Sundays excepted).

FARES :—

Oxford and Henley, 12/6 ; Kingston and Henley, 12/6 (available for 7 days). Oxford and Kingston, 25/- (available for one month).

Intermediate Fares, 3d. per mile ; Minimum, 1/-. Children under 12 half-price.

Passengers' Bicycles at owner's risk, not exceeding 12 miles, 6d. ; 25 miles, 9d. ; 50 miles, 1/-.

The through journey occupies two days each way, but passengers can join or leave the boat at any of the locks or regular stopping places. Circular Tickets for Combined Railway and Steamer Trips are issued at most of the principal G.W.R. Stations. Time Table, giving full particulars of arrangements, fares, &c., post free, 1d.

ROWING BOATS of all kinds for Excursions down the River at Charges which include Cartage back to Oxford.

FULL PARTICULARS ON APPLICATION.

STEAM LAUNCHES for Hire by the Day or Week, and also for the Trip.

Boats of every description, Canoes, Punts, &c., built to order.

A large selection, both new and second-hand, kept in readiness for Sale or Hire. Illustrated Price Lists may be had on application.

House Boats for Sale or Hire, and also built to order.

SALTER BROS., Boat Builders,
FOLLY BRIDGE, OXFORD.

A Salter Brothers advertisement, 1896.

instances to the Thames via the Kennet and Avon Canal. Craft too big for the locks, or for export, were built in sections.

In the 1890 and 1891 seasons respectively, two weekly return trips were instigated by Salter's between Oxford and Kingston. The great step forward came in 1892 with the inauguration of the daily service. With the commissioning of the new boats during the 1890s there was no need for the same steamer to go from Oxford to Kingston; the journey was split into two stages, one boat running each way per day between Oxford and Henley, with morning and afternoon boats each way from Henley to Windsor and Windsor to Kingston. It was then possible to do the whole return trip in four days. The midday stop at Windsor allowed for day trippers to change boats if they wished to return by steamer

the same day. Combined rail/steamer were – and still are – available, and the mooring (just above the 'Donkey Hou conveniently close to the railway station. ing to size, the steamers carried up to 1 engers.

From 1900, Salter's built their own at Oxford, designed by Sissons. In t 1900–31 the following ten craft we *Reading, Sonning, Marlow, Streatley Wargrave, Oxford* (replacement), *Court, Mapledurham* and *Cliveden* ment). With the extra boats the se extended to two boats each way per d entire route; a lunchtime stop at W was added to the itinerary. Salter Br built some nine steamers for the known operators, Mears of Richm were taken over by Thames Launche No new boats were built after 1931, second-hand craft were added to the including Cawston of Reading's M was the last steam-driven vessel v drawn from service in 1966 – all the been converted to diesel. For the rec

The wharf at Folly Bridge, Oxford, in 194 'Head of the River' public house. On the steamer boilers lifted out for winter ov crane is typical of the type that adorned ma or wharf in the 19th century. Earlier crane timber.

The Salter steamer *Cliveden* built at Oxford in 1931. Photograph taken in the 1950s. The original *Cliveden* was built in 1892.

be worth mentioning that steamers consumed upwards of 10 cwt of coal per day.

The last addition to Salter's fleet was the *Mary Stuart* in 1957, which started life as the petrol-engined *Kagerplas* in Holland. She was purchased by Salter's in the Hague in 1956 and brought to Oxford under her own power. She was stripped, completely re-fitted and re-powered with a diesel engine. On the other hand some of Salter's boats were disposed of. In World War I the *Kingston, Windsor* and original *Cliveden* were shipped to Mesopotamia and given names more befitting to their new waters. The original *Oxford* was sold after World War I to Phelps of Putney, and renamed *Gaiety*. In 1929 she sailed through the Kennet and Avon Canal en route for the Severn and up to the Lower Avon at Evesham. In 1933 the *Hurley* went to Evesham, following the same route as *Gaiety*. In 1975 the Oxford–Kingston scheduled service ceased to operate, but Salter's steamer trips are as popular in the season as ever, in a modified form to suit the present need; the vast increase in traffic upon the Thames, which

causes considerable delay at locks, has a serious effect upon scheduled services.

In 1977, Salter's sold off an old favourite, the *Marlow*, which was built in 1902. She now earns her keep taking passengers up and down the $1\frac{1}{2}$ mile long Willen Lake which is near the Grand Union Canal at Milton Keynes.

In concluding these notes about Salter's it is interesting to recall that they built nine steamers for Joseph Mears Motors and Launches Ltd, for use on their downriver Hampton Court to Greenwich service. And a 'special' from Salter's was a stern paddle steamer, specially designed for use on the Congo. She was the *Endeavour*, built in 1892 for the Baptist Missionary Society who required a craft with very shallow draught. Her statistics were: hull 100 feet × 19 feet, with only 8 inches draught. Her boilers were wood burning and after completing her trials on the upper Thames she was dismantled for shipment.

In the '20s and '30s the name 'Mears' became synonymous with steamers. The large fleet of craft was owned and operated by Joseph Mears Launches & Motors Ltd of Richmond; the

La Marguerite, built in the 1880s by Tom Taylor of Chertsey and Staines, shown here circa 1890.

'motor' part of their business title referred, of course, to their fleet of pneumatic tyred charabancs, which they proudly announced on the front cover of an excellent Thames map which they produced in the late 1920s and sold for one old shilling (5 new pence). Although they advertised that they had steam launches for hire 'on any part of the Thames', their main activities were confined to the Richmond–Hampton Court–Windsor area. When Mears came to an end many of the craft were absorbed into the fleet of Thames Launches Ltd, which after the last war and on into the '70s became well known for its downriver service. The company operated from Eel Pie Island, Twickenham, where it had a large dock, slipways and extensive facilities. The firm is now part of the Thames Passenger Services Federation.

After World War II Messrs Odell's of Walton, in the belief that there would be a return to waterbourne traffic, launched their waterbus service in the lower reaches; the boats were of an advanced design and provided all-weather accommodation, with a cabin. The vessels were built at Odell's Walton Yard which was originally the Walton Yacht Works; alas it is now a factory producing decorative building boards. However, the underwater sections of the three

very commodious slipways are still ⁘ firm of R.G. Odell Ltd, which was ⁘ dredging contractor to the former Th⁘ servancy, was founded by Robert G⁘ who was apprenticed in 1897 to lear⁘ of a waterman and lighterman, and ⁘ youngest man ever to win the Dog⁘ and Badge race (see Chapter 11). In 1⁘ awarded the O.B.E. and when he di⁘ later, at the age of 90, he was Presi⁘ Thames Passenger Boat Owner's As⁘ is sad, not only that Odell's waterbus⁘ relatively short lived, but that the ⁘ selves were short lived. Although ⁘ built to a very high standard, th⁘ timber of which they were construct⁘ quality with little or no seasoning⁘ were all diesel-powered and in many ⁘ pattern for the current generation ⁘ craft, which now are of all steel co⁘

It is unusual for operators to desi⁘ their own craft, but David Pickin, he⁘ sor Boats, does just that. The diesel-⁘ welded steel boats are built in h⁘ attractive and efficient yard at Clewe⁘ are in the 50 to 65 foot range and⁘ weather use, having the facility of ⁘ enclosed as well as being equipped ⁘

The King, built in 1902 by Harry Tagg of East Molesey. His works were adjacent to the old Hampton Court Bridge. The compound engine of this vessel was built by Plenty and Son, Newbury. She was run by Harry Tagg until 1915 when she was sold to Mears; thirty years later she passed into the hands of Thames Launches and in 1977 she was acquired by E.B. Smith. Now powered by a diesel engine (photograph circa 1910).

heating. A far cry from the firm's first passenger boat, the *Windsor Belle*, built in 1900. She carried 60 passengers aboard her elegant hull of varnished Burma teak. Although changed to diesel power she remained in the family service until 1977. At the time of her launching, the founder of the firm, Arthur Jacobs (who was David's great-grandfather), had been in the boat hire business for sixteen years. Arthur, one-time landlord of the 'Waterman's Arms', Eton, was a keen part time officer of the R.S.P.C.A. In those days when amphibious craft were not even a wild dream, cavalry on regular exercise from Windsor barracks would trot across the bridge to Eton, gallop over the Brocas as far as its southern boundary to plunge into the Thames and swim to the Windsor shore. After a time it was decided that a guard boat should be on duty during such exercises to help any horse, or soldier, that might get into difficulty. Well, who better to cope with this job than Arthur Jacobs? He jumped at the idea with alacrity. When the cavalry had completed their routine crossing, locals and visitors alike asked for trips in the guard boat and so a new and lucrative business was born!

Arthur Jacobs pictured in 1925, founder of the passenger boat organization now known as Windsor Boats Ltd, and great grandfather of the present managing director David Pickin.

The *Windsor Belle*, built in 1900 and photographed the same year: precursor of Windsor Boats's splendid

In 1925 a new boat was added to the Windsor Boats fleet – the *Windsor Castle*; a commodious and functional craft, but lacking beauty of line, a failing that was perhaps compensated by the fine varnished timber of her hull. She was built on the island at Windsor by an itinerant boatbuilder by the name of Lance Summers.

In the past when many barge owners and, later on, pleasure steamer operators did not have a big enough business to warrant carrying a boat-building staff, they would call in one of the many travelling boatbuilders to carry out their assignment. These craftsmen were fully occupied along the Thames, travelling from yard to yard. Generally the boats or barges would be built by eye after discussion and briefing with the owner; they would be built on his land, mostly in the open and often alongside the bank so that they could be launched beam end on (i.e. side-ways). This practice was of course followed by many builders of canal craft; the late Harry Stevens of River Wey fame was a past master at launching his big barges in this manner.

In addition to regular passenger steamers

already mentioned, in Victorian and days many a Thames boatyard own with which they ran local trips ar business in hiring out for parties ar as illustrated by the following c reports from the *Surrey Comet*:

July 25th, 1896. London City M in *Sunbury Belle* intended to g sor. *Sunbury Belle* had an a Richmond the previous night s did not leave Hampton Ferry t Only made return trip to Staine late start. Arrangements in abl Mr. Bonfield.
August 18th, 1894. One of th cessful river trips from this v place on Monday last. The ste *Her Majesty* was chartered b Langshaw Jnr. and started f head from Hampton Ferry at with over 100 persons on boar nation being reached at 2.30 liven the journey the service

A steamer, possibly *Princess Beatrice*, built by Tom Tagg in 1896, leaving Sunbury Lock in about 1900. *Sunbury Belle* is moored at Clark's Wharf, far left.

Vicary and Kemp had been requisitioned and these gentlemen gave agreeable selections on the violin and piano. A halt was made at Bell Weir for refreshments. Home was reached at 9.45 p.m. Tea was served on board. Mr. Langshaw was roundly cheered for the organisation of a very successful and enjoyable day.

Catering on passenger boats has steadily developed from tea and sandwiches to a wide choice of delightful meals available today.

In 1896 Tom Tagg and Sons of Molesey were running their 'select river parties' from Hampton Court to Windsor in the handsome steamer *Princess Beatrice* every Sunday during the season. The fare, inclusive of first-class rail travel to and from London, lunch and tea was one guinea (£1.05). At the same time Burgoines of Kingston, builders of sailing craft and all types of Thames boats, including steamers, were also running a service similar to Tagg's.

Cawston's of Reading was at one time almost a household name for upriver steamer trips. E.

A typical Tom Tagg advertisement.

Cawston set up his own boatbuilding business after working for Searle's; as the yard progressed he began to hire out craft and in the 1880s owned a shallop capable of carrying thirty people. Like quite a few yards of that era he also hired out ponies for towing. The flagship of the Cawston steamer fleet was the *Majestic*, which was built at their own yard in 1907–8; her wooden hull, complete with bowsprit, was originally varnished. Cawston's was taken over in 1945 by Salter's, after the death of the Cawston brothers.

Another old Reading firm was Maynard's; their fleet included the once very popular *Queen of the Thames*, also the *Grand Duchess*; the former, like a number of other craft, was engined by Plenty's of Newbury who were once famous for their reciprocating steam engines and marine boilers. An Italian, Antonio G. Bona came to Reading in the very late 1870s, bought the Caversham Bridge Hotel, had a boatyard alongside and built up a considerable fleet of steamers which he ran with success until his death in 1905 when the craft were sold, most finding their way into the hands of various Thames operators.

The name Bond, from Maidenhead, means a lot to those interested in the pioneer days of pleasure boating. Jonathan Bond set up his business in the early 1840s with a boathouse and ferry rights after reclaiming a rather poor piece of ground just downstream of Maidenhead Bridge. One of his first craft was a horse-drawn barge for passenger trips but Jonathan moved with the times and soon became celebrated for the steam launches which he built for various customers, and in particular one which he built for himself in 1898 and used for running trips between Maidenhead and Marlow: she was the *Empress of India* which he sold in 1922 to Arthur Jacobs of Windsor. He used her for some 50 years and then sold her to Turk's of Kingston. Another of Bond's celebrated steamers was *Her Majesty's*, which was acquired by Whatford and Sons of the Palace Boat House, Hampton Court, during World War II and then gave over a quarter of a century's service on the ever-popular Hampton Court run.

As steam gave way to diesel power it seemed,

perhaps only by coincidence, that the p of passenger boats, or in plain Tham 'steamers', began to wane. However, ing with tradition and having welded s with modern facilities, all weather p and even heating for cold weather, boats have made a great come-back years from Radcot down to the tidew champion of the cause is Keith French his brothers now runs a regular servi Runnymede and Hampton Court, short trips and booked parties. For wish to view Mapledurham House Tim Deaton is running a scheduled s Reading.

The year 1981 saw the complete circle with the return of the *Sunbu the Thames. She was built in 1894 Clark of Sunbury by H. Tooley o Wick; her teak hull is 75 feet long wi 15 feet. In 1896 she was sold to an Worcester where she started to ear after an adventurous coastal trip. settling herself on the River Sever Sunbury was dropped. In 1980 acquired her, and brought her boatyard at Brentford, where he re her original condition except tha revert to steam propulsion. The v operated by his new company, the Steam Navigation Company Ltd, sailed up to her Maidenhead headq spring of 1981.

Horace Clark had another *Sunbr by Tooley in 1896. Her engine – st – was built by Willans and Rob Thames Ditton. This once well situated at Ferry Works adjacent hotel also built steam yachts and l moved to Rugby in 1898. The la mony was carried out by Mrs (1896, after which the steamer w demand for trips and outings, be carrying 250 passengers. She w craft embellished with a fine pc funnel, which many older remember. She was sold to Whee enham in 1937 and later saw servi

Clark's *Merry Duchess*, advertised as a new launch for the 1890 season. Seen here at Sunbury Lock in the 1890s.

Hastings, another renowned name upon the river. During the last war she was damaged by a flying bomb, and became unserviceable. After this episode, she came into the hands of Fred Robinson, a Sunbury timber merchant; he acquired her from a local businessman, in settlement of a bad debt. Fred patched up the old girl and kept her afloat at her Sunbury mooring in Thames Street, with the idea, when the time was suitable, of taking her apart so as to make full use of her 2 inch thick planking which was of Burma teak. However, at the end of the war he was visited by two gentlemen from Worcester who made him an excellent offer, which was clinched after a little bargaining. *Sunbury Belle* was towed away downstream; Fred believed that she was towed round the coast to the Severn. However, some years later Bradley and Seabourne of Worcester informed the writer that she was taken overland from London to Sharpness and thence by river to Worcester.

The very old established boatyard of Horace Clark at Sunbury was taken over in the late 1970s by an even older Thames firm, R.J. Turk and Sons of Kingston, who in recent years have built up a fine fleet of passenger boats; most of the fleet are of the typical modern type, but Michael Turk has had the courage and enterprise to acquire and run two old timers, the *Empress of India* and the *Windsor Castle*. If fuel prices continue to escalate, Turk's may even take up one of Clark's early diversifications, which was the hiring out of ponies for towing!

Tugs – including the beginning of diesel

Although 'steamers' possessed a certain charm and glamour, and were very much in the public eye, their more humble cousins, the steam tugs, did a yeoman job of work. Until the establishment of the railway, they revolutionized transport; travelling times by water were greatly improved and furthermore a single tug could tow several barges. The earliest tugs built were designed mainly for manoeuvring sailing ships in confined spaces, towing being a secondary consideration and then mainly to get lighters from ship to shore, and vice versa, when a vessel had to load or unload where she lay at anchor. Apparently the first steam tug to appear on the tidal Thames was the *Lady Dundas* in 1832; she was built upon the River Tyne. Within a few months a second tug, the *Wear* from Sunderland, made her presence known upon the

Thames; however, her poor performance hardly inspired enthusiasm for steam tugs amongst Thames watermen. It later transpired that her North Country owners were glad to be rid of her; nonetheless, her new owner, John Rogers Watkins, founder of the great Thames towing firm William Watkins Ltd of London, had great faith in the future of steam tugs and invested in a fleet of tugs that was second to none. John Watkins could be said to be the father of steam tug towing.

Information on upriver tugs is somewhat scant, the first mention is in a report of the Thames Commissioners, dated July 21st, 1780, which stated that:

> A person who signed his name Thomas Hunt having addressed a letter to the commissioners with certain queries relative to a project for towing barges with a steam engine the same is read, his model examined and his ingenious proposal considered but as they apprehended his project would not answer in practice on a river such as the Thames they cannot give him the necessary encouragement to make a trial, but order him a guinea to defray his expenses.

At a meeting held many years later on September 11th, 1818, the commissioners finally were able to take a more enlightened view, the minute reading as follows:

> Application having been made by Messrs Parsons and Co of Newbury to navigate without paying tolls at the Pound Locks a boat with a steam engine on board for the purpose of towing loaded boats – Ordered that they may be permitted to work such a boat by way of experiment without paying toll provided it contains no goods besides those which may be necessary as the apparatus for the engine.

By 1850 steam tugboats were gaining a foothold judging by the following two reports:

At a meeting of the Thames Comm ers held on November 8th, 1850 decreed that steam having been intr as an improved and cheaper m haulage, it is incumbent upon the C sioners to consider so important a in the conduct of their business. general committee therefore be re specially to consider and report to eral body upon it with a view to su lations thereupon as shall pron interests of the body and protect t from injury and damage.

At a meeting of the commissioners ruary 14th, 1851, the committee that the sum of one hundred pound Messrs Allen & Skinner as some r for the trouble and expense incurre the introduction of steam upon t means of haulage, which the Com will greatly improve the trade up gation.' Allen and Skinner must impressed the Thames Commissi March 29th, 1851, 'The Com mended that £150 be given to M Skinner for the trouble of introd

However Charles Dickens, w upon the subject of barges, enamoured of steam:

> Although the extension of rail in the country through whi Upper Thames has very reduced the number of up-; there are still many engaged in trade. That they are useful, r for granted; that they are p mental, may be a matter of they are a decided nuisance v them, under the convoy steam-tug, monopolizes a lo or so, admits of no doubt. A tugs themselves are an abon are driven along with sublin the interest of persons in p boats – in this respect re more distinguished relativ

The steam tug *Ham* with an empty coal lighter in tow, leaving the water works wharf at Hampton in the early 1950s.

launches – and raise a wash which, one would suppose, can be as little beneficial to the banks of the river as it is to the peace of mind of anglers and oarsmen. Nor are the manners and customs of their crews, or of their associates the bargees, such as to conduce to the comfort of Riparian proprietors or of pleasure seekers. Practically, they seem to have things all their own way, and do and say just what they like.

The name Tough Brothers of Teddington is almost synonymous with the Thames. This family firm is now run by Bob Tough, who is the sixth generation, for it was his great great great-grandfather Alexander Tough who founded the business at the beginning of the last century as a barge operator. As mentioned in an earlier chapter on barge traffic, the company at one time traded as Tough and Henderson when a Mr G. Henderson teamed up with Mr Tough. They were one of the early proprietors of upriver tugs, of which they were also excellent builders. The first generation tugs were timber planked on oak frames and were about 50 feet in length; the next generation of their steam tugs had steel frames and then of course followed all-steel

hulls. These hulls had a deep draught and the steam power swung a single screw of very large diameter (between 5 and 6 feet). A great development for upriver work was a shallower draught twin-screw tug which enjoyed the name of *Woodcock*. Before the advent of diesel power and with the low cost of coal, steam power was very well suited to tug propulsion, providing tremendous power at low shaft speeds, which enabled tugs to handle several 75- to 100-ton barges in a single tow.

On the Wendover arm of the Grand Union Canal were Bushell Brothers, boatbuilders of New Mill, Tring. One of their Thames customers was Beckett's, the timber people of Hampton Wick, for whom they once built a large steam tug; she had a wooden hull and to get her through the wide locks of the Grand Union to the Thames at Brentford, her rubbing strake and certain other fixtures had to be removed. The biggest hitch on her journey was at Winkwell, where the swing bridge had to be completely removed to allow a full width passage!

'Tug Spotting' was a popular pastime with past generations of boys, and one very delightful upriver tug that comes to mind was the *Puffin* which was run by Beckett's of Hampton Wick, having been built on the Thames–Severn Canal at Brimscombe Port by Abdela and Mitchell at the beginning of the century.

The late Harry Fennimore, best described as a very skilled artisan who wore many hats, could recount in great detail and with great enthusiasm the construction of all craft built by Bushell's of Tring, but he talked without as much as a pause, so that after an hour or two in his company one had been completely taken back in time, yet was almost too bewildered to make any notes. Harry started work with old man Bushell the day after he left school; he then carried on under two of Bushell's sons, Joseph and Charles, until the business closed down in 1948. Most Bushell boats were built in the open, and due to the narrowness of the canal were inevitably launched sideways. All materials used at the yard were of the highest quality whilst dimensions of timbers well exceeded required standards. Quality of workmanship was exemplary and not even the smallest detail escaped the watchful eyes of the brothers Bushell. It is a testimony of Bushell excellence that the writer's own company is still using two workboats built at New Mill early this century.

An upriver builder of steel-hulled steam tugs was G. Davis of Abingdon; he built boilers, high pressure and compound steam engines as well as boat hulls and carried out general engineering work; that was in the 1800s, but details are scant.

Tom Taylor of Staines built some excellent tugs; the last to come off his slips were a pair of compact diesel-engined craft in the '50s, but of course many of our fine tugs and the few steam-powered barges that traded on the upper Thames were built in the area that strictly speaking does not come within the confines of this book, namely the tidal Thames. However, a firm about which not many records seem to remain was the Riverside Works Co., of Jessamy Road, Weybridge, who built tugs, barges, tenders and workboats, as well as carrying out all forms of marine engineering until the 1930s.

As with rail transport, steam tended to disappear after World War II, and all tugs are now powered by diesel.

Steam launches for private use

Henry Warriner, a 19th century eng
Bloxham, near Banbury, laid claim t
built the first screw-driven private stea
She was launched into a tributary once
from the Thames, the Sor Brook, wh
into the Cherwell. The site of her laun
Adderbury, where she underwent tri
quently she was kept in a thatched
which led off the brook near Bod
Early this century, the craft was bro
her engine given to a London muse
fortunately all records of her were
lost in the last war.

A pioneer and prolific builder of
was John I. Thornycroft. His first lau
Nautilus, a 38 foot craft with a s
knots, no small achievement in 185
launch, the *Ariel*, built in 1863,
longer and attained a speed of 12.
famous *Waterlily* was built in 18
Miranda of 1871 attained the then
of 18.6 knots. These boats, alon
other craft including torpedo boat
boat destroyers for the Royal Na
boats for export, and fast cra
navies, were built at the Chiswick
nycroft not only designed and
hulls, but applied his skills to t
construction of the machinery req
them. At the beginning of the cei
ing of large craft was transferred
to Woolston near Southampton
struction of small craft was trans
Eyot, Hampton; Thornycroft'
Immisch, the boatbuilder situate
This then made it possible for
build their own wooden hulls,
had been contracted out to we
such as Maynard's, Burgoine of
and Immisch. The moves more
with full production of Tho
combustion engines, so there w
this famous firm in the next c

Des Vignes, of Chertsey (for
ton in the yard now owned
was another eminent builde

Waterlily, built by Thornycroft's in 1866, shown here circa 1870, designed and built by Sir John Thornycroft, who is at the helm. *Waterlily* is now in the National Maritime Museum.

steam launches. One of his masterpieces, the lovely *Pierette*, is giving her present owner excellent service, and graces his mooring at Shiplake. *Pierette* was built in 1894 and spent her youth around Bourne End. She sank in 1946 and was salvaged by the Thames Conservancy. She was acquired by Mr J.B. Hickey and her hull was re-plated by Tom Taylor of Staines, prior to fitting new boiler and machinery. She then went away from the Thames to 'foreign waters' until acquired by the present owner. Mr Des Vignes sometimes lent one of his launches for umpiring at regattas. The following is a contemporary report from the *Surrey Comet*:

On Saturday, 24th. July, 1880, Mr. H. Ballard, son of the licensee of the Red Lion, Hampton, set out with his wife, two children and a couple of friends for a trip up river in their two-paired half outrigged gig. On their return journey, the gig was cut down by a steam launch belonging to Mr Des Vignes which had been acting as umpire launch at Kingston regatta. Both the ladies and the two children of the party were drowned. As a result of this tragic accident the Thames Conservancy issued more stringent regulations regarding the navigation of steam launches.

One of the best known steam launches on the Thames to come off the Des Vignes drawing board was surely the *Donola*. She was built as the *Lodona* for Mr A. Palmer, the Reading biscuit maker, by the Kingdon Yacht, Launch and Engineering Co. Ltd of Teddington in 1893. She

(*top left*) Red Cross steamboat built by Tom Taylor.

(*left*) The Thames Conservancy launch *Donola* on lock gardens inspection in 1960. The man in uniform to the left of the pile is Joe Collett, Chief Navigation Officer of the former Thames Conservancy. Alas, *Donola* is now in the National Maritime Museum.

(*above*) Tom Taylor and Son's once extensive boatyard just above Chertsey Bridge (around 1885).

changed hands prior to the first war, when her name was altered to *Donola*. She was acquired by the Thames Conservancy in 1920 and used as an inspection launch; in particular for the annual lock gardens competition. It was in that role that she will be best remembered by many people, for she looked almost regal steaming downriver, with her ensign, bearing the Thames Conservancy coat of arms, billowing from her mizen mast. The conservators with their white covered caps and blue reefer jackets would be seated comfortably in the for'd cockpit, whilst the stewards would be aft preparing an excellent luncheon, the victuals being carried in large

wicker hampers stowed in true seaman-like fashion on the quarter deck. The lock gardens competition was a great annual institution founded in 1898 and carried on until the late '70s; the Sir Reginald Hanson Challenge Cup was for the outstanding excellence of a lock garden; a later award was the City Challenge Cup for the best-kept lock whilst the Association of Thames Yacht Clubs award and the Joe Collett rose bowl were more recent additions to the list of prizes. In 1968 *Donola* made her last lock garden trip before being pensioned off. Sadly, the old lady now resides, like *Waterlily*, in the National Maritime Museum at Greenwich. As mentioned in an earlier chapter it seems wrong for boats to be out of their element; how wonderful it would be if on the Thames we could emulate our friends in the Lake District, who founded the Windermere Steamboat Museum, where craft built in the middle of last century are still afloat and used.

A steam launch often admired when on her moorings at Cleeve, and even more so when her owner, Laurence Weaver, is out cruising is *Thames Esperanza*; she was built by Bond's of Maidenhead as an electric launch although her hull had the classical lines of a steamboat of that period. She was later fitted with a petrol engine and used as a tripping boat at Windsor. It was not until Mr Weaver obtained her that the boat's potential was explored to the full; it was due to his long hours of painstaking work that the hull was re-fitted to make a steam launch of pristine elegance and sparkling performance.

Many builders of traditional Thames boats turned their hand to building steamboats: one was Charles Constable, who built one and only one steamboat. It was a special commission in 1897 for Mr James Restler, engineer of the Southwark and Vauxhall Water Company. She was a lovely craft, carvel-built with teak planking on oak frames, with a length of 35 feet and a beam of 7 feet. According to the late William Chaplin her machinery was built in the engineering shops of the S. & V. Water Company, whose property was adjacent to Constable's. The boat was named *Elfin*, and is currently at Tough's Boatyard, Teddington, where her present owner is refurbishing the little beauty.

The Saunders boatyard has already been mentioned: it was started at Streatley by Moses Saunders, who was followed in turn by his son and grandson, who became almost legendary in the boatbuilding world and renowned for his lightweight 'sewn' mahogany hulls, which were a product of his Springfield Works at Goring. As sewn construction is rather a thing of the past an Admiralty description will surely not be amiss:

Sewn Boats. – These boats consist of two thicknesses of Honduras Mahogany; the inner thickness is of $5/32$ of an inch and is worked at right angles to the keel from gunwale to gunwale; the outer thickness of $\frac{1}{4}$ inch is worked longitudinally with the edges of the planks flush; the three lower strakes, however, gradually increase to $3/8$ of an inch in the rabbet of the keel. These two thicknesses, as well as timbers and floors, are fastened or sewn to-gether with

best annealed copper wire. The plan at the stem and stern and the fasten the keel are the same as for other built boats.

This method of 'sewing' boards toge copper wire, rather than fastening wit tional rivets, enabled very light but i strong hulls to be produced, and not su a number of yards were awarded Adm tracts for small naval craft.

A great tribute to Saunders's sewr tion can be witnessed in the lovely l launch *Victoria*, which glides up anc Thames nearly a century after her la

A prolific builder of steamboats Taylor, of Bridge Wharf, Chertsey, dentally, was the second person to l phone in Chertsey. E. Andrews ar Maidenhead were builders of repute the *Woodland Lily*, built by them once again in beautiful condition, l re-planked by that craftsman Michael Dennett at the Harris and S at Laleham in the '70s. This boat, *Esperanza*, started life as an elec Another builder of steam launches head was Henry Woodhouse. Meakes and Redknap had a very gc steamers, whilst Henley always wa associated with the design and ma steam plant by that grand firm of h Stewart Turner Ltd. The heyda launches was in the Victorian–E and lasted until petrol motors too the first war the number of stean the river dwindled at an alarming the last war, in response to the spr gia, steamboats have been steadily popularity and much has been Steamboat Association of Great B this interest and help newcomers t

10 POWER BOATS

Electricity

Although steam power reigned supreme for a considerable time, inventors dabbled with alternative means of propulsion because boilers took up a lot of space and were labour-intensive. Electricity was the first object of interest; however, the Thames is unable to claim a first here for the pioneering work on electricity was that of a Russian scientist by the name of Jacobi, way back in 1834. Five years later, with financial help from Tsar Nicholas I of Russia, Jacobi built his electric launch; it was propelled by two paddle wheels and, whilst it handled satisfactorily on the River Neva, the crew was overcome by nitrous fumes given off by the motor. It was a couple of decades before another electric paddle boat came on the scene, this being the brainchild of a Frenchman by the name of de Molins. However, the potential of smooth, quiet and odourless propulsion remained unrealized until 1880, when another Frenchman came to the fore. He took out a patent for a detachable electric motor that could be clamped to a boat's transom to drive a propeller by means of a chain. The propeller and rudder were integral so providing very good manoeuvrability. The trials of the boat, and, in particular, the proving of the experimental batteries was successful and from then on electric powered boats really caught on.

The first electric launch on the Thames was the *Electricity* of the Electric Power Storage Company of Millwall. Then in 1883 Yarrow's, the once well known Thames ship and boatbuilders, produced the *Beni*, a 45-seat electric passenger craft that took passengers up and down the Danube during the Viennese Exhibition. At this juncture it is worth recording that Yarrow's, who became famous for their torpedo boats and other fast craft, both at home and abroad, started life as builders of steam ploughing machinery. In the course of progress and expansion they moved from the Thames to the North East.

On the Thames the name Immisch is synonymous with electric launches; Mr Immisch was a designer and builder of electric motors who developed several, with great success, for marine use; he then went ahead with the idea of establishing charging stations for topping up batteries, the first of which was at Platt's Eyot, Hampton. As his factory, the Electric Works, Malden Crescent, Kentish Town, was not sited well, or suitable for boat building, it was not long before he acquired the then small boatyard on the lower end of Platt's Eyot, so that he could construct his own hulls. This yard formerly belonged to one of the Tagg family, who, as we shall observe in a later chapter, built very fine and extremely large houseboats.

On Thursday, December 21st, 1888, a new electric launch was christened at the Platt's Eyot yard of Immisch and Co. The details as reported in a local paper at that time were as follows:

The new launch is similar in mechanism to the well known *Malden*, but more than double as large. It is built of mahogany, and is 65 feet long, and has a beam of 10 ft. It is provided with a comfortable cabin amidships. The vessel has a mean draught of 22 inches, and a displacement of 12 tons. The launch which is christened *Viscountess Bury*, is worked by twin propellers, obtaining their impetus from two 'Immisch' motors of 7½ horse power driven by 200 accumulators placed beneath the floor of the boat. As compared with steam launches, the electric boat has manifest advantages, while it has none of the drawbacks of the evil smelling naphtha launch. The motors were made at the Electric Works, Kentish Town.

The hull was built at Platt's Eyot by Tagg, immediately prior to Immisch taking over his business; the launch could carry 36 passengers.

Immisch's charging stations were very successful and the number increased so that, apart from the island at Hampton, one could stop at Staines, Windsor, Maidenhead, Henley, Reading, Shillingford and Oxford. Some were floating stations, others ashore. Other firms also set up riverside charging plants, including Woodhouse and Rawson at Chiswick and Chertsey. The largest floating plant was a converted barge which carried a semi-portable steam engine driving a large dynamo that was able to generate enough power to re-charge half a dozen launches at the same time; needless to say this portable charging unit earned its keep at great river events such as Henley Regatta; then, as more yards built electric launches, or acquired a hire fleet, so they too had charging stations.

But back to our old friend Immisch. A report in a local paper of September 1889 not only makes interesting reading but shows the excellence of these Hampton-built craft:

The great strides made in the popularity of the electric launch seem fully warranted by the achievement of these 19th century improvements. One of these, the *Eta*,

recently made a trip to Oxford a[n] a steadily maintained speed an[d] delay. It is scarcely necessary to the *Eta* is one of Immisch's vessel[s] is the only firm who are able to t[] electric launch suitable to the Th[ames] *Eta* left Platt's Eyot, Hampton, Maidenhead, a distance of 26 mi[les] hours including all locks. The day the same boat was run to [] miles, and the journey was comp[] morning, when Goring was o'clock, Oxford being reached The *Eta* attracted a good deal o[f] at Oxford, but only remaining a returning to Abingdon for the return journey was made to M[] in two days. The accumula[tors] charged at Maidenhead, G[] Abingdon at night, so that no caused, and the very creditab[le] mance was gone through witho[ut] When it is borne in mind that a 60 miles (Goring to Oxford an[d] accomplished with only one r[] will be seen that the electric grown out of its infancy and has[] adult stage.

Immisch's had a fleet of some 5[] hire; second to them was possibl[y] Valley Launch Company of Wey[] fleet of 40 launches for hire. T[] many of their launches with feat[] lers, which in those days was a gre[at] Full ahead to full astern was effec[] ing propeller pitch, actuated by r[] forward or backward, whilst th[] when moved from side to side, mo[] in the appropriate direction, so whipstaff' steering of ancient ve[]

Andrews and Sons of Maid[e] dozen electric launches, all but which were named after fish c[] Thames (*Pike, Barbel, Dace, Bre[am]* flagship was *The Angler*, which '50s was used as a tripping laun[] although her electric motors had

Electric powered canoe *Gena*, built by Ray Motor Company of Maidenhead, in the early 1920s.

replaced with a petrol engine.

Amongst private owners and, to an extent, hire firms, large electric canoes became very popular; the Ray Motor Company of Maidenhead built a considerable number and had three six-seaters for hire: the *Gena*, *Genetta* and *Genella*.

As mentioned in an earlier chapter, Thornycroft's sub-contracted the building of some of their wooden hulls to Immisch, so it is not surprising, therefore, to find Thornycroft's taking over the Immisch yard, which they re-named Hampton Launch Works. The take-over was at the time of Thornycroft's closing down their Chiswick yard, with the transference of all shipbuilding to Southampton. Furthermore the Immisch yard was ideal for the production of small fast naval craft, the need for which was accelerated by the threat of World War I. The fleet of Immisch electric launches continued for some time under the flag of the General Power and Traction Company.

After World War I the interest in electrically propelled boats began to wane. Efficient petrol engines were more attractive as they obviated the need for charging stations. Few indeed were around after the 1930s, although in 1926 the Ray Motor Company were advertising electric canoes for hire at 3 guineas a day, 4 guineas on a Saturday and 5 guineas for Sundays. As I write this the interest in electric boats is now being re-awakened; Viscount St Davids has not only brought forward the idea of electric propulsion in the House of Lords, but set an example by equipping his own small cruiser *Emys* with suitable batteries and an electric motor, having discarded its outboard motor as noisy and extravagant on petrol. An association of electric boat enthusiasts has now been formed; who knows, if really lightweight batteries can be developed, we may well return to a form of motive power that was popular nigh on a century ago!

Naphtha

Before the development of the petrol engine and the necessity of charging stations for electric boats an engine running on solid fuel had been developed. The fuel in question was naphtha, which is generally derived from coal tar, although it can be formed by the intense distillation of almost any organic substance; to quote from *Motor Boat* (1904): 'The fact that pure white naphthalene is all but insoluble in water disposes to a great extent of the difficulty of storage aboard a boat, for a bunker well lined with felt, or even ordinary boxes would appear ample for its storage.' One Thames firm making naphtha engines was J.E. Hutton Ltd, of Thames Ditton, who laid claim to its clean running. A special mixing valve for melting and spraying the naphtha was, apparently, the key to the success of the whole affair. This mixing valve/spray device was pioneered in the late 1880s by Priestman Brothers of Hull: the name Priestman is still familiar on the river today, for drag-lines and excavators used on river maintenance and dredging are made by that old-established firm. Although great claims were made for naphtha launches, contemporary reports give one the impression that they were very smelly and could be extremely dangerous, causing fires.

Petrol

Whilst the popularity of electric boats was paramount, the petrol engine was conceived, but some time passed before such a power unit was installed in a boat. It was in the hands of Gottlieb Daimler that a maiden trip was made on the River Neckar, way back in 1886. Daimler carried out his trials with great secrecy and even pretended that the boat was powered by electricity and secured wires to ceramic insulators along the gunwales of the craft. But as far as can be ascertained the first British built motor boat was the brainchild of Dr F.W. Lanchester, the motor car pioneer. He designed the boat with the help of his brothers George and Fred in 1893; the brothers built the boat at their home in Warwickshire. It had the appearance of a rather rakish looking punt with paddle wheel propulsion; the wheels were made by Frank Lanchester in his experimental laboratory, the engine was a single cylinder unit of 2 h.p. of his design, built for him at the Forward Gas Engine Works in Birmingham, under the strict supervision of George Lanchester. In 1894 the boat was loaded on to a horse-drawn vehicle and taken to Oxford, where

it was launched into the Thames fro yard. Later in life the Lanchester fami in Weybridge, where they had a fir sweeping down to the river, with, of attendant boathouse.

By the turn of the century petr engines were well developed; initially would be started on petrol and when t warm switched over to paraffin su reason for these engines becoming p best be explained by quoting from a copy of *The Motor Boat*: 'Paraffi obtained in remote places; it is a dom which can be found in at least one h every village in Great Britain, petr article which is required solely for work is, however, only obtainable i tively large centres.' Thornycroft experimental suction gas motor, wh anthracite as fuel; although econom this, along with other ideas, came to to the sophistication of the petrol en rapid evolution of the diesel.

The development of motor boats quickly that by 1909 Temple Pre lished the third edition of their 396 *Boat Manual*: a veritable bible o covering every development and p period.

As already mentioned, Maudsl beth were pioneers of marine stea by no means lagged behind with ment of petrol engines, for the which they had established a facto by the beginning of the century.

Another pioneer in this field croft's; a since deceased, long servi that firm once told the writer h John Thornycroft removed the the 1890s from *Waterlily*, the b he built in 1866, so that her hull c a test-bed for his newly develope bustion engine. Thornycroft er popularity to the extent that a s was set up at Caversham – w throw of the river – for their engines produced at this works 'R' before their name, to indicat

'Reading built'. Several marine engineers and launch builders produced petrol engines in limited numbers; for example the Riverside Works Company, run by J. Lester Clark at Weybridge, was the sole maker of the 'Reliable' marine motor from 3½ to 75 b.h.p. Hutton's of Thames Ditton, Blake's of Kew, Stirling's of Twickenham are names that come to mind as producers of marine petrol engines.

Walter D. Fair of Hampton Wick built excellent small petrol engines, some of which, resplendent with their copper 'pots' and pipework, are still in the few remaining motor canoes; his products bore the trade name 'Watermota' which later became the title of the company which is still in business, although the works has moved from the Thames to Devon. Walter D. Fair produced one of the best known early English outboards, the 'Watermota'. This was available in the 1920s as a service model of ¾ h.p. whilst an 11 h.p. speed model was marketed with great success. The former could be obtained with a rudder and reversing propeller. In 1927 a certain Richard Cole apprenticed himself to the Watermota concern; one of his many duties was testing these outboards upon the Thames at Kingston, a job which from all accounts he enjoyed. After a while, the quiet waters of the Thames failed to offer the challenge that young Dick Cole needed to test his faith in outboard motors, so it was not long before he clamped a 4 h.p. 'Watermota' to the transom of a 13 foot dinghy and sped across the Channel. This was only the beginning of his adventures; later he went to South Africa and then to Canada, and became a prominent designer of outboard powered craft in the U.S.A.

Another once popular outboard, the 'Anzani', was a Thames product. The managing director of Anzani's, Charles Harrison of Hampton, was well known not only for his engineering skills but his watermanship.

With the development of petrol engines, Thames boatbuilders were to the fore in designing and building hulls to accommodate them. Salter's could almost be described as prolific builders of such craft. A few of their early cruisers are still around, and one that comes to mind is the *Flying Spray*, which is currently moored at Moulsford: she is 31 feet long with a beam of 6 feet 9 inches, has a commodious aft cabin, complete with coach roof so as to give good headroom, and has a delightful for'd cockpit, with not only ample space for the helmsman, but room for the crew to relax and enjoy the scenery in comfort, predating the current design of many holiday boats by over seventy years, for *Flying Spray* was built in 1904. By 1907 Salter's were building a wide range of very delightful launches both for day use and extended cruising.

It is not surprising to find that Saunders of Goring lost no time in making the transition from steam to petrol propulsion; one of their early launches, the *Consuta*, must be familiar to all who use the river and certainly to spectators at Henley Regatta. Sometime about 1896 there was a public outcry against the great amount of wash at the Henley Regatta set up by the

A sleek launch by **Saunders of Goring**, who were renowned for their sewn construction (circa 1890).

umpires' launch. The Regatta Committee then investigated the possibility of a launch capable of a speed of 25 m.p.h. with little or no wash; Mr Saunders came forward with his proposals for a craft constructed on his sewn hull system and so the *Consuta* was built and is still used today. On her trials, early in 1904, she attained a speed of $27\frac{1}{2}$ m.p.h. over the measured mile, whilst the absence of wash was a complete revelation, in which respect, to quote from a periodical at that time, 'she almost equalled the racing eights'. Critics at that time asserted that in due course the boat would shake to pieces and that it would be impossible for her to stand the tideway (thinking of the Oxford–Cambridge boat race); however it is good to know that she has outlived those critics!

Although sewn construction was given a mention in the steam boat chapter, it seems fitting at this juncture to give details of Saunders's own method:

Hulls built on the Saunders's principle consist of a number of skins of thin wood solutioned and sewn together with waterproof canvas separating the layers. The hulls are constructed bottom upwards on a mould. The keelson and stringers are first fixed on temporarily, and then the first skin is lightly tacked on diagonally. A layer of waterproof canvas is followed by another layer of wood, this time with the grain running at an angle to that of the first layer. Two more layers of canvas and two of wood follow, the first of the latter going completely round the boat and the second longitudinally. The waterproof solution takes about six weeks to set, and by the end of that time the sewing is complete. This is done by means of a flexible drill, akin to those used by dentists, which carries a tiny cutter for making a little groove on the outside skin for the copper stitching wire to lay snugly in. Boats built on this principle have no ribs, longitudinal stringers being employed instead. The advantages claimed for this system by Mr. Saunders are firstly a saving of nearly 40% in weight;

secondly greater stiffness of hu thirdly more graceful lines wi labour.

Saunders moved to Cowes and f Saunders–Roe concern for building fl and the Goring yard was sold in 1911 old and highly respected Thames firm Henley, which was founded by H. Hobbs in 1870 for the purpose of skiffs and punts, the latter being mair ing. Six of his brothers became invo (Bill), A.J. (Arthur), Fred, Frank, Ernest, and as the business grew new were erected, not only for housing building new ones. A new era of exp begun in 1902 when they acquire Meadows site which now forms the and head office. They acquired ne Saunders yard, but also East's boaty lake and Ellis of Goring. In 1927 the the business of the very old and high boatbuilding firm of Searle and Sons engine brought changes which A.H son of Harry, and father of the prese director, Tony Hobbs, was quick to open launch with a canvas canopy w first craft to receive a marine petro 1917 Hobbs excelled themselves wi ing of the *Enchantress*, a specialist speed of about 20 knots for umpiri and boat races. This launch, like Co on active service and admired by all upon her, particularly when she is special role at Henley Royal Rega fine Hobbs umpire launch is th which they built in 1921.

Nowadays Hobbs build a var including cruisers for their own hire ing launches – they built the Oxfo launch *Bosporus* – besides boats fo tomers, which include narrow bea canals, all of which is quite a far superb skiffs, dinghies and othe craft, as well as electric canoes, wh in the distant past. Hobbs and So the guidance of the present Tony certainly moved with the times w

A very elegant motor canoe built by Hobbs and Sons Ltd and featured in their 1925 catalogue.

way losing personal service and old-fashioned courtesies.

W. Bates and Son of Chertsey have always been great producers of motor boats. The firm started as Taylor and Bates in the latter part of the last century; the Taylors had a small coal and timber wharf immediately downstream of Chertsey Bridge. William B. Bates married into the Taylor family and took charge of the timber side of the business. It was not long after this that James C. Taylor and William B. Bates started boat building, having received encouragement from G.F. Des Vignes who, as mentioned earlier, was a steamboat builder of very high standing.

Taylor and Bates built some houseboats, then embarked on steamboats both for sale and hire, and as soon as the internal combustion engine was on the market they commenced building motor launches. Their fame soon spread and within a short time they were exporting boats to various parts of the British Empire, South America and the Far East. During World War I, in common with other Thames yards, they built motor craft for the Admiralty; however some of these special and interesting assignments will be covered later (see p. 129).

After the war Taylor and Bates became very well known and highly respected for their

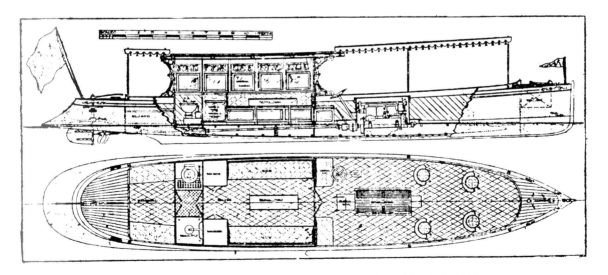

A beaver stern petrol launch built by James Taylor and Bates Ltd for the Sultan of Perak, in 1926.

A James Taylor and Bates launch of 1920. Some of this firm's craft had so-called 'flat bottoms', which were cov patent of 1905: the bottom was concave towards the centre to prevent lifting of the bow and planing.

beaver-stern shallow draught launches which were available in three lengths: 27 feet, 30 feet and 35 feet, the first two having 4 cylinder 10 h.p. engines and the latter a 4 cylinder 20 h.p. unit. A 30-footer of this class, named *Brown Trout*, was once well known to the author. She was built in 1922; her hull was carvel-built of mahogany, the keel and framing were of oak, all being finished with yacht varnish, giving a superb gloss and highlighting the beauty of the wood. Fairleads, cleats and all fittings were of polished gunmetal, whilst her equipment included a canopy and side curtains, carpets, table, ensign staff, helmsman's seat and other etceteras, including of course ropes and the ubiquitous boathook. At the time of her launching she cost a little under £500. By the mid 1930s the firm was offering a range of motor craft, ten in all. Top of this range was a 55 foot vessel powered by twin Parsons engines, the total cost being a trifle in excess of £3,500. The smallest boat in the range was the flat-bottomed 17 foot 6 inch 'Gondacruza' which sold for £48 complete with a 1½ h.p. Stuart Turner engine.

In the late 1930s the Bates/Taylor partnership ended, and the yard was divided in two. Bates carried on under the title W. Bates and Son and

the lower yard was run by Taylor u of James Taylor (Chertsey) Ltd, w date moved lock, stock and barrel In the formative years after the w who was well aware of possible from modern American cruisers designed an entirely new range of powerful boats that went under 'Star' craft, which proved to be m

Bates launches of the 1920s a tors' items, and great is the pit Thames Conservancy inspection *rush*, when pensioned off in 197 Kent School, Connecticut, U.S.A princely sum of £3,500.

Slipper stern (sloping stern) always had a following, particu those who require an open boat be seated comfortably in close p water. They were built in various longer boats accentuated the s graceful lines. Andrews of Bour pioneers of 'slipper' stern craft; been synonymous with them s their trade name 'Greyhound' is A typical Andrews Greyhound have a length of 25 feet with a l

A conventional motor cruiser of the 1930s. This one was designed and built by Taylor and Bates.

inches, and overall height (with hood up) of 4 feet 6 inches the draught being 1 foot 9 inches. The construction was hard chine with mahogany planking on oak or mahogany frames; the decks were laid in $2\frac{3}{4}''$ planks, all beautifully varnished which, in naval slang, gave a very 'tiddly' effect. With a Morris Vedette engine such a launch could attain a speed of 12 m.p.h. Generally a folding hood was fitted for use in inclement weather and the boats were delivered complete with cushions, lines and all customary fittings.

'Greyhound' launches are now treasured collectors' items; one of the early devotees of restoration was the Garrard family of Wraysbury who in 1964 raised a sunken Andrews Greyhound launch, completely restored her and put the original engine (a 1921 model T Ford) into working order so that once again they could enjoy the pleasure of travelling in an open boat. In the past eighteen years such efforts have been repeated again and again by devoted enthusiasts throughout the length of the Thames.

The development of the conventional type of cabin cruiser, with 2 to 6 berths, was perhaps a trifle slow; one of the firms to realize its potential was Bushnell's of Wargrave who produced fine well equipped craft for private owners as well as

for hire purposes between the wars. Bushnell's were established in 1860 and the present Paul Bushnell's late father, Len, was also a naval architect; one of the products of his drawing board, the current chief inspection launch of the T.W.A., named like her predecessor *Windrush*, is seen by all who use the Thames to any extent. Len was a great river man, he loved his sculling and enjoyed the Thames in every way, so it was extremely fitting that he was a Queen's Waterman, following in the steps of his father John, who in his day was a King's Waterman.

The boats already described were specifically designed as power craft; however, a traditional Thames vessel to receive a petrol engine was the ubiquitous punt, and it was not long before purpose-built motor punts were being produced. By 1904 that great punt builder, Harry Mileham of Strawberry Vale, Twickenham, was building and marketing such craft with a $2\frac{3}{4}$ h.p. Smith and Dowse (of Isleworth) petrol engine. These punts were 27 feet long with a beam of 3 feet 2 inches and a draught of only 9 inches in running order, so, to quote from a contemporary report: 'With such a small draught it would be quite possible to explore all the backwaters and reach out of the way spots which the ordinary type of

Motor punt of 1904 built by James Taylor of Chertsey. Some of the last motor punts, powered with Stuart Turne run as hire craft by Hobbs of Henley.

small motor boat cannot hope to get near.'

The punt described, built of selected mahogany and finished to a very high standard, complete with cushions and requisite fittings, cost £75. A number of other yards, including Taylor and Bates and Hart Harden of Hampton Wick, built motor punts. Cuss of Oxford built an interesting variation in 1901, which was propelled by a small paddle wheel so that it could navigate the very shallow and extremely weedy sections of the river in the vicinity of Cricklade, which was its home base. Hobbs of Henley had motor punts for hire until well after the last war; however, the excessive wash from the ever increasing number of power boats upon the Thames made punting for relaxation almost impossible.

The once very popular Canadian canoe set the pattern and general style for power-driven versions, the first being electric, followed of course by the petrol engine. Size of these canoes varied according to the builder's ideas and/or customer's requirements; however, most popular models were about 21 feet long with a beam of 4 feet. The general construction was almost the same as on a 'Peterborough' canoe as already described in an earlier chapter (see p. 100). A number of Thames yards, such as Bond's, Cawston, Ray Motors and Burgoine, built beautiful examples of these delightful, swift, yet clean

Thomas Sopwith's 1914 Schneider Troph off in the Kingston reach for trials after re-designed floats made by boatbuilder S

C.M.B. no. 4. The Coastal Forces torpedo boat, built at Thornycroft's Hampton Launch works; this famous boat sunk the cruiser *Oleg* in 1918, under the command of Lt Augustus Agar. It is now on view amidst old aircraft at Duxford, Cambridge. The craft on which C.M.B. 4 is sitting is one of several floating docks that were built for seaplanes in World War I.

running, canoes. Just off the Thames, on the Medway, Short Bros, of flying-boat fame, excelled themselves with their production of motor canoes.

No Thames book would be complete without a modest mention of a few of the special and famous power craft built upon the banks of our river. Burgoine's of Hampton Wick had an interesting assignment back in 1914, when Tom Sopwith commissioned the then young Syd Burgoine to produce a pair of floats for his Schneider Trophy seaplane; after tests on the Hamble the plane came back to Burgoine's yard for modifications, then, due to shortage of time, it was tested on the Thames; take off and landing were in the early hours; altercations with the Thames Conservancy ensued, but it seems all was forgiven when Sopwith set up a new record with the seaplane!

In World War I many yards built launches and pinnaces for the navy, whilst some of the bigger ones built fast craft for coastal forces such as C.M.B.s (coastal motor boats, which carried torpedoes) and M.L.s (motor launches), which were general purpose craft. Possibly the most famous coastal forces boat of all time was C.M.B. No. 4, built by Thornycroft's at their Hampton Launch Works. Until Thornycroft's

were taken over by Vospers and the Hampton yard disposed of, this vessel was on view for all to see, complete with the Victoria Cross painted on her side. Under the command of Lt A.S. Agar, No. 4 torpedoed and sank the cruiser *Oleg* at Kronstadt in the Baltic; for his courage and devotion to duty in carrying out this epic raid, Lt Agar was awarded the V.C. After Thornycroft's were taken over, the boat was moved to Southampton, before taking up residence at Duxford aerodrome, amidst veteran wartime aircraft, like a fish out of water. Perhaps one day the Coastal Forces Veterans Association and the Thames Heritage Trust will get together with a view to her being returned to her birthplace.

In World War I Hampton Launch Works turned out some 120 odd C.M.B.s, most of which were powered by Thornycroft V 12 or the larger Y 12 engines. Another famous Thornycroft boat from Platt's Eyot was *Miss England III*, in which Kaye Don set up a new world speed record of 119.75 m.p.h. in 1932. At the turn of the century a hull (of unknown make) had been designed to perform at 36 knots; she had a concave bottom and was powered by twin petrol engines. On her trials she succeeded in travelling at 3 m.p.h., whereupon further development was abandoned; she lay moored at Tagg's boatyard for a time and then was converted into a 'flat' for ferrying horses from Hampton to Hurst Park Racecourse.

With the outbreak of World War II, Thames yards were soon producing craft for the services and in particular a variety of torpedo and gunboat for coastal forces. The only was to build up large fleets of these craft was to organize a mass-production scheme on a vast scale. It was the Fairmile Company of Cobham, Surrey, who proposed the building of pre-fabricated craft for anti-submarine and escort duties. This prefabrication system enabled woodworking firms to shape timbers, fabricate sundry assemblies and so on for delivery to yards where the vessels would be completed and launched. One of the first yards to become closely involved was Tough Brothers of Teddington; at this point it is surely fitting to recall that it was the late Douglas Tough who was very much involved in 'Operation Dynamo' – the evacuation of Dunkirk Beaches in 1940 – the spirit of which is kept alive by the Association of Dunkirk Little Ships, many of which are either Thames built and/or based. The scheme started off with the Fairmile 'A', but, in spite of being powered with three 600 h.p. engines, its topmost speed was only 25 knots;

'B's and 'C's were built, followed by the boat, which was a complicated packag fabricating. Within its 115 foot hull we away four 1,250 h.p. Packard engin could be up to 30 knots depending ment; they were considered to be the r ily armed boats of their kind in the the last ones commissioned as M.T equipped with four tinfish (torpedo Taylor (Chertsey) Ltd were also proli of M.T.B.s and M.G.B.s.

A spin-off from torpedo boat de came from the Italian Navy in the f now almost universal 'Z' drive.

Von Muller Thomamuhl of th Hungarian Navy deserves the credi the first person to propose the air-cu ciple of hovercraft; his prototype ac knots way back in 1916.

Since 1945 many fine craft for bo and those of foreign countries have various Thames yards, along wit firefighting, missionary service, e luxury cruising and record breakin out and basic trials of the very early powered boat also took place on t

Thames sailing barge discharging cargo at West Molesey Wharf about 1890, from watercolour by W.E. Ch right is Platt's Eyot before it was built up with spoil from excavations for nearby reservoirs. The term 'eyot Anglo-Saxon 'Ey' indicating an island.

Rowing

The oldest form of professional oarsmanship is attributed to the Thames waterman, whose prime concern in life was providing locomotion, largely for carrying passengers, who would have hailed him from the nearest 'stairs' (landing stage) in the same way as one hails a taxi today. As stated in the chapter on Traditional Craft, all watermen had to be licensed, and for this they had to undergo a period of apprenticeship. They had then plenty of opportunity, and even encouragement, to take part in competitive rowing. Races or wagers would have been rowed in ordinary working wherries, with the exception that they may have been made slightly lighter by the removal of any unwanted gear, burden boards and the like. Once watermen were licensed they still enjoyed a certain amount of competitive rowing in their very limited leisure time.

The most famous race is The Doggett Coat and Badge; not only is this the oldest regular aquatic contest, but the most ancient *regular* sporting event in the world, having been held every year since 1716 to date. Thomas Doggett was an actor, but he is remembered as founder of the race, which began on August 1st, 1716. The announcement of it read as follows: 'This being the day of His Majesty's happy accession to the throne there will be given by Mr. Doggett an orange livery with a badge representing liberty to be rowed for by six watermen that are out of their time within the year past. They are to row from London Bridge to Chelsea. It will be contested annually on the same day for ever.' It is still held by the watermen on August 1st, except

The Doggett coat and badge won by Charles Constable in 1852.

when the 1st falls on a Sunday, in which case it is held on the Monday. In the course of time the livery was changed from orange to red and the design of the silver badge was slightly modified. Originally the men rowed their standard wherries; gradually they lightened their craft until 1796, when new rules were drawn up. The original course was five miles against the tide, nowadays it is with the tide: from the Old Swan at London Bridge to the Old Swan at Chelsea – a distance of about $4\frac{1}{2}$ miles – and light craft are used. The six contestants were drawn by lot from the list of entrants; in consequence, it often happened that the best man never rowed. In 1873 a system of heats was instituted, thus giving an equal chance to all competitors, who often numbered several hundred. Although today the number of competitors is small, the enthusiasm is as great as ever and rightly proud is the young man who wins his Doggett Coat and Badge. It was not until early last century that amateurs began to take up rowing as a sport and contests appear to have encouraged the idea of competitive events among watermen.

'Champion of the Thames' was a title bestowed on R. Campbell, who beat fellow waterman C. Williams in a match held on September 9th, 1831. In the race of 1846 Campbell lost to another waterman, Coombes, and within a few years racing between watermen became fashionable. Instead of using their working wherries, lighter craft were made specially for matches and contests, and were known as 'wager' boats. In 1855, Messenger, a name well known on the Thames, became champion, whilst in 1857 the honour went to Harry Kelley, who according to some contemporary reports was the best waterman the Thames yielded, both as oarsman and judge of rowing.

The year 1829 made history in the calendar of rowing. In February of that year Mr Snow of St John's College, Cambridge, was asked to write to Mr Staniforth, of Christ Church, Oxford, suggesting a match during the Easter Vacation, to be rowed near London. As rowing at Oxford at that time did not begin until after Easter, the date had to be postponed till the summer; the race was finally rowed on June 10th over a $2\frac{1}{4}$

mile course from Hambleden Lock Bridge; Oxford won by several len eight that was typical of the perioc clinker construction and just over length, built at Oxford by Davies ar spite of various challenges, no furthe held until 1836 when it was rowed a the flood tide from Westminster Bridge on the $5\frac{3}{4}$ mile championship c used at that time by professionals. crew wore white jerseys with dark b just before the race a piece of pale ribbon was attached to the bow o bridge boat for luck. Cambridge w easily and from that time adopted l their colour. Oxford first used a boat for the race of 1841 and th outriggers were used for the first tim details are given in the chapter on Craft); the keelless boat, which was in 1856, was lighter and faster. The with its increased leverage was, in revolutionary as the outrigger; it Thames invention, but the brainc Babcock of the Nassau Boat Club, N was used in the University Boat Ra With sliding seats and outriggers, t boats steadily became narrower and overall length of 66 feet. From 18 exception of the two world wars, th Boat Race has been an annual ever

Sculling

An amateur event comparable wi for the professionals is the Wing originated by Henry C. Wingfield, trophy in 1830.

Over the years racing 'eights' matter 'fours', single scullers and craft have become lighter and m cated, as too, have the design and of both oars and sculls. The slidir tioned with regard to the Universit was apparently first used on the T London Rowing Club in 1871. Th of very high esteem, was founded

Regattas

As rowing grew in popularity, so clubs increased and regattas became annual events. 'Regatta' is a Venetian word meaning a 'rowing match of gondolas'. The first use of this word on the Thames, or for that matter in England, was in 1775 at an event off the Ranelagh Gardens (near Chelsea Bridge) in the presence of the barges of the Lord Mayor and City Companies. Such an event must not be confused with water pageants, or processions, with elaborate barges, beflagged and gay with musicians and colourful costumes which date back to Tudor times at least. The second regatta to be held on the Thames was on the Walton reach; thereafter the idea grew with rapidity.

The greatest of all regattas is of course Henley, which dates back to 1839 and became Henley Royal Regatta in 1851 when the Prince Consort became patron of the then two-day event. The original course was from above the island to the upstream side of the bridge; the new course – from the bottom of the island on the Buckinghamshire side to Poplar Point – was inaugurated in 1886. The original racing three abreast came to an end in 1885 in which year a third day was added to the event and both sides of the course marked with piles. 1906 saw the first four-day regatta, whilst the new straight course, which entailed cutting away and re-campshedding of banks, was ready for the 1924 regatta. The length of the course is 1 mile 550 yards plus the average length of an eight (20 yards).

Rowing and sculling races became popular with schools, who established their own rowing clubs, the most famous being the Eton College Club which dates back to 1793. Westminster School had a rowing club by 1813, whilst Radley College did not follow suit until 1847, after which there seems to have been a marked increase in school rowing. Eton started racing Westminster in the year of the first Oxford–Cambridge boat race, and soon it became a traditional event. It would appear that Eton scholars have always regarded the Thames as nature's gift for exercise and relaxation; once a boy can swim he takes to the boats, or, in other

A racing eight shares Iffley Lock with a Bert Bushnell hire cruiser in the 1950s.

words becomes a 'wet bob'. By the 1930s Eton had a remarkable fleet, including the superb ten-oared *Monarch*, and eights, fours, pairs, 'perfects' (these were open clinker-built coxed pairs, with short outriggers), whiffs, of which there were 140, and no less than 336 'riggers' which was the Eton name for craft otherwise known as 'funnies', 'wager boats' or 'best boats', to which reference has already been made (see Chapter 8).

Apart from regattas, other forms of competitive rowing have developed, especially 'heads', which are held in the early part of the year; these derived from the Head of the River race, which originated in 1926. Today, regattas are thought of as club events, with highly trained crews in superb racing craft, and competitors coming not only from the other end of the country but from other nations. However there was a time when watermen's regattas were commonplace; sometimes they were combined and watermen, fishermen and sometimes members of the local constabulary, who had their own rowing clubs, would take part; a favourite name for a police boat was *True Blue*. With the decline in the number of watermen, these local events dwindled, although a few lingered on until this century.

Watermen's, or local, regattas were largely

aquatic sports. Two very popular events were always water jousting and walking the greasy pole. The former is a contest between two people, armed with mops, standing on the tills (ends) of separate punts. Each man thrusts the mop at his opponent, endeavouring to push him into the water; but not infrequently the attacker misses his mark, loses his balance and ends up in the water; in either case plenty of unexpected dunkings and splashings result, to the immense delight of the spectators. The amusement in walking the greasy pole is in the same category; rarely can the competitor reach the end without losing his balance and having a ducking or two before reaching his goal. The original form of this entertainment involved a pig in a box on the end of the pole; the pig was released by the man who first managed to reach it, then a pig hunt in the water ensued, the pig trying hard to escape whilst the determined hunters struggled to grab hold of the slippery porky boy and so lay claim to its possession. An alternative to walking the greasy pole was climbing one that was driven in a vertical position; the target was to remove the leg of mutton hung at the top. A development of water jousting was the water tournament, where the players are ranged on two sides, each man being provided with a canoe and a mop. The two sides endeavour to push their opponents into the river, or to overturn their canoes with the mops. If coracles could be obtained for a race, fun was guaranteed when these seemingly frail craft from Wales got into the hands of a Thames man! Punting Canadian canoes was a popular event, and furthermore it was one of great elegance, especially when a woman was competing. Some of Molesey Boat Club's members were considered to be the finest exponents of the art; possibly the last Molesey member of repute was Fenwick Atkinson, who, on succumbing to a power boat after the last war, at least chose a classical motor canoe.

Dongola racing has always drawn the crowds; it is a popular event at the present Sunbury Regatta. The skill is in the ability of the crew to keep their punt from running into the bank, their rival crew, or nose diving so that the punt becomes submerged. If a well trained crew of six

Walking the greasy pole: a very popular local and watermen's regattas. Note sna~ 1890).

— mixed sexes — paddled their p٤ line without mishap the specta very disappointed indeed; they of the crew miss a stroke and ، next fellow with ensuing chaos. bow heavy and cross the path then turn right round; with ١ water slopping aboard, one of ally becomes immersed as it str finishing line. The fun is gene٢ to the fact that crews are mos٢ volunteers with little or no pr٤ Another competition involvin of-war. A circus-type event w؛ ing through a paper screen anc canoe without upsetting it.

Dongola racing about 1890: still a popular event at some regattas.

Women have always shown a keen interest in rowing and sculling, and history was made in 1930 with the holding of the first ever women's inter-varsity boat race, which was between Reading University Women's Rowing Club and Newnham College, Cambridge. In the succeeding 50 years great developments have been witnessed in female participation.

Punting

Punting, as a leisurely pastime, has virtually been killed by motor boats, or rather the wash therefrom. However there are still a number of punting clubs in existence, who, thank goodness, are keeping alive the graceful art of propelling a punt with the dextrous use of a pole. Competitive punting takes place at a lot of our smaller, but highly successful local regattas, where one can also witness some really good skiff racing. Early punt racing was of a spontaneous nature enjoyed between watermen, with little or no organization until the formation of the Thames Punting Club in 1886. This club was started in Sunbury by a few men interested in the sport; they instituted the Amateur Punting Championship which was decided at Sunbury Regatta from 1887 to 1890. The club did not flourish due to lack of funds, but in 1890 it was reorganized

with W.H. Grenfell – who later became Lord Desborough – as chairman of the committee. The first Thames Punting Club Regatta took place in 1891 on a new course a little below Sunbury Lock. In 1893 this event moved to Staines, in 1894 to Maidenhead and thence to Shepperton; it has now ceased. As eights in the rowing world became longer, narrower and sleeker, so did racing punts; the celebrated champion, B. Rixon of Staines, used in the events of 1895 and 1896 a punt 34 feet 4 inches long with a beam of $14\frac{1}{4}$ inches in the middle and $7\frac{1}{2}$ inches at the ends with a depth of 7 inches in the centre. Punts of this calibre were termed 'the finest' or 'best and best'.

It is interesting to recall that the late William Henry Grenfell, Baron Desborough of Taplow, was a great punter, oarsman and sportsman and a most observant and knowledgeable lover of the Thames. It was fitting that he was the longest serving Chairman of the Thames Conservancy, being in office from 1904 to 1937. His boating activities were widespread; for three consecutive years from 1888 he was the winner of the Amateur Punting Championship; as an Oxford undergraduate he rowed in two boat races, whilst a little later in life he became the only man to compete at Henley for the Grand Challenge Cup whilst a Member of Parliament. On another

W.H. Grenfell, the punting champion. He later became Lord Desborough. He is seen here in a 'best and best' racing punt.

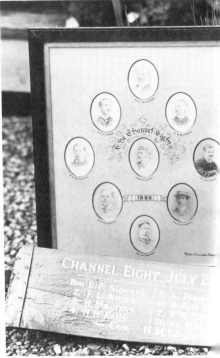

No. 6 blade of the Channel Eight with phot crew.

dangerous and thoroughly worth v
brothers in the crew, Arthur and Ed
who were relatives of the author's
keen Thames men and also connec
Newbury barge proprietors menti
Arthur Slocock was a personal fr
great Thames historian and wri
Thacker and in fact, helped fina
work.

Skiffing is still very popular wit
the skiffs themselves are clinker-bui
itional design, and with fixed seats
has a good following, but one woul
greater interest considering that t
arduous and possibly more relaxed
boat' racing.

Sailing

Sailing has been a popular sp
Thames for many years; some
craft dating from the 1830s wer

occasion he sculled in a crew of three from Oxford to London in 22 consecutive hours, including locking times. One of his daring adventures, in 1885, was rowing a conventional eight across the English Channel; he was stroke of the crew and described the episode as 'A typically British Feat, quite useless, exceedingly built, but simply standard gigs, skiffs and dinghies equipped with a mast, which was usually stepped in a hole cut in the bow thwart. Hoisted from this mast would be a small lugsail, but due to absence of a centre board, or leeboards, it was not possible to tack, which made the craft difficult to handle in a narrow reach. However progress could be quite good in an open reach and a skiff running before the wind can give an exhilarating performance. As time went on standard craft were modified by fitting centre boards, and, in the early 1800s, Clark and Sons of Sunbury were building a special line of Thames gigs with centre boards and full sailing rig. Their hulls appeared to be the same as any other gig and provided a dual purpose craft for sculling and sailing.

The great 'home' of the superb 'A' class raters (see p. 139) was the Thames Sailing Club at Surbiton, which was founded in 1870. Another early organization was the Thames Valley Sailing Club, founded at Hampton in 1876. This club had its headquarters at Benn's Boathouse until 1880, when it acquired a fine club houseboat, which was moored on the mainstream side of Benn's Ait, where the clubhouse of the present, and third, Hampton Sailing Club now stands. The old T.V.S.C. houseboat was burnt down to waterline in about 1902 when boatbuilder John Constable, whilst working upon her, had an accident with a blowlamp. An old and much respected organization is the Upper Thames Sailing Club, Bourne End; a report covering one of this club's activities, dated March 1889, reads as follows: 'The first match for prizes presented by the club was sailed on Saturday. Wind W.S.W. varying considerably in force, necessitating a beat against the strong stream. Only four rounds of the short course were sailed, being four miles. Mr. Chas. T. Ricardos' "Tigress" was left to complete the course alone. She is a new craft of the turn-about design.' It was at this time that Burgoines announced the launching of their new 'turn-about' centre board sailing boats of 17 feet 6 inches and 16 feet 6 inches waterline measurement. In April of 1889 they supplied two of these craft for members of the then popular Thames

A skiff rigged for sailing (1907).

United Sailing Club at Egham, which is now the Laleham Sailing Club. Other sailing clubs of similar vintage were Tamesis and the Oxford University Sailing Club both of which still exist. 1896 saw the birth of Henley Sailing Club – again, still flourishing – once renowned for its sailing punts and recognized for pioneering one-design boats.

After the first war, dinghy sailing became more popular and the 14 foot boats came to the fore with the establishment of the National Class 14 foot dinghy, which later received international status.

The Royal Canoe Club was founded in 1866, and as well as encouraging paddling both in 'Canadian' and 'kyak' styles, it took a great interest in sailing. With the advent of the centre board, sailing activities began to exceed paddling. Immediately prior to the R.C.C. having their own headquarters, in 1897, upon Trowlock Island, Teddington, they were based at Kingston at the yard of R.J. Turk; very fitting too, when one considers that Turks were pioneers in the building of sailing canoes which they later fitted with the 'Radix' patent folding centre board; one of their 'Nautilis' sailing canoes, so equipped, was awarded a silver medal at the International Inventions Exhibition in 1885. Sailing canoes were elegant craft, generally of ribbon carvel construction and often planked with cedar: the mainmast was stepped well for'd whilst the mizen mast was a little abaft the cock-pit; sometimes a foresail, or, more correctly, a forestay sail was hoisted. A fairly broad rudder was hung from the stern post and controlled with a tiller. The stem of these canoes was purposeful in shape, and needless to say pleasing to the eye.

Another craft that fell to the fancy of the sailing man was the humble Thames punt. First, the basic punt was fitted with a mast, which was stepped in a thwartships member at the beginning of the 'huff' (i.e. the point where the bottom of the punt begins to slope upwards); the mast would be about 19 feet long and supported by a forestay and shrouds. They were rigged with a mainsail and foresail, totalling about 150 square feet of canvas; a rudder was hung beneath the till (the aft deck) and iron leeboards were pivoted on either side of the hull. The mast and boom, like many contemporary sailing craft, were usually of bamboo. That doyen of punt builders, Harry Mileham, of Strawberry Vale, Twickenham, produced some superb sailing punts and with his perfectionism, the leeboards, instead of sticking out like crude appendages, neatly retracted into cases built into the inboard sides of the hull.

A great exponent in the art of sailing punt racing was the aircraft pioneer, Thomas Sopwith; punt sailing seems to have reached its zenith around 1901 and the great 'playground' for these craft was the Kingston Reach, with Henley a close second.

One of the earliest purpose built, centre board craft was the 'Una' rigged boat. Most of them were around 16 feet long with a beam of about 6 feet and a draught, with 'sliding keel' – the early form of centre plate – in the down position about 18 inches; with the keel up, about 8 inches. These boats were partly decked, had a freeboard of about 9 inches and were extremely stable; the Una rigged boats had their mast stepped well for'd, the single sail was large with a gaff (the spar to which the head of a fore and aft mainsail is bent) and overhanging boom (a spar on the foot of the sail which also extends the same). For river work Una boats were ideal as they sailed closer to the wind than most other boats of the

A sailing punt in a becalmed situation i? reach in the 1890s.

period; they would 'come about deft movement of the tiller and, ? tant point, the unsophisticated ? owner to enjoy single-handed sai? was very strong, reefing, in sp? boom with about 4 foot overhan? simple. W. Bossom, of Medley? celebrated builder of Una boats; was E.A. Burgoine of Staines.

C. and A. Burgoine of King? 1870s building centre board sai? ous types, their most famous, s? still being sailed, being the 'rat? built about seven between ? Other builders of this class Brothers of Bourne End and

It was not until around 1925 that the remaining Thames raters were converted to Bermudan rig and mast height was limited to a maximum of 50 feet, for taller masts had been used, although 45 feet proved a popular average. A great designer of Thames raters was Linton Hope, who, in World War I, put his talents to the development of seaplane floats and flying-boat hulls.

Although rallies of all kinds have been increasing in range and popularity for the past twenty years, it was not until 1978 that the River Thames Society inaugurated the now annual Traditional Thames Boat Rally, which has become a most popular event, where a wide range of craft participate, from traditional Thames boats, such as gigs, skiffs and punts to veteran and vintage motor boats, together with early Canadian canoes, a smattering of smaller sailing craft, and those much beloved steamboats from Victorian and Edwardian days of which most are genuine, although nowadays the odd replica, or old hull converted to steam power may mingle with the gay and elegant flotillas.

The 'Year of the Disabled', 1981, saw further interest in Thames Sport with the first 'Challenger' regatta for the disabled; organizers and hosts for the event were the Oxford Sailing Club. For the non-sailing man the 'Challenger' is a trimaran specifically designed for the disabled sailor. Another milestone in the same year was work at Fairmile Hospital, Moulsford, enabling patients to get afloat.

Sailing enthusiasts now have an annual event at Bourne End in early June: the Vintage 'International 14' Regatta, where owners of that superb class of sailing dinghy, dating from 1921, can foregather and enjoy competitive sailing. The craft of 1921 is number four, and is still owned and sailed by the same family, namely, the author's!

Canoeing

Canoeing exploits have always provided an aura of exploration and romance to boys of all ages; one of the earliest recorded canoe excursions on the Thames was that of two Oxford under-

Beecher Moore's rater *Vagabond*, which was built in 1907 by Townsend's of Bourne End.

Hampton Wick, as well as that great builder and designer of sailing boats, Theo Smith, of the *Phoenix Barge*, Medley Weir, Oxford, who in the 1880s and 1890s built a very wide range of centre board sailing boats, sailing canoes and canoe yawls. Raters have beamy, but scow-shaped hulls of considerable overall length, although at waterline they are about 15 feet 7 inches long, giving the impression of a skimming dish. Masts were tall, and like the spars, of bamboo; by the turn of the century hollow spars were coming into use, which were light in relation to their strength and rigidity and were not prone to splitting which was a common fault with bamboo. Rigs varied in the early days but steadied up on sliding gunter early this century.

graduates making a trip from Oxford to Hampton Court in a birch bark canoe at the beginning of the 19th century. This craft was very light, weighing barely sixty pounds, for its covering was from some handsome great birch growing in an Arcadian forest; before coming to the Thames the canoe was used by a Micmac Indian, and was apparently a very fine specimen of the craft used by his tribe: on either side of the stern a representation of the moose and the fish of Nova Scotia was neatly etched into the bark. From time to time a few leaks were encountered, but these were overcome by daubing the weak places with a mixture of resin and soap boiled to form a 'goo' the consistency of thick molasses.

Canadian canoes have been described in some detail in an earlier chapter, when mention was also made of the kyak, often referred to as a 'Rob-Roy' canoe, due no doubt to its being popularized by a 19th century schoolmaster, John (Rob-Roy) MacGregor who in the 1870s wrote entertaining accounts of his canoe-touring trips of the late 1850s. The design of the 'Rob-Roy' was inspired by the sealskin clad, reindeer bone framed 'kyaks' of the Eskimo. Here is a contemporary description of a Rob-Roy:

> The canoe is fourteen feet in length and two feet nine inches wide, with a good sheer [or rise] at the ends, so she may be dry and comfortable in rough water. She is built of thin cedar planks, with good frames of English Oak within, and decked with still thinner cedar, leaving only some four feet of a 'well' within which one sits in order to propel the craft with a double-ended paddle, jointed in the centre so as to be taken into two parts for stowage.

These canoes, like Canadians, could be rigged for non-competitive sailing, usually with lugsails of Chinese style on bamboo spars. Wooden lee-boards were made up in such a way that they could be clamped to the canoe, to prevent drifting sideways from the wind. In 1887 an attempt was made at building a collapsible canoe, whilst around 1876 an American took out a patent for a folding boat. The first commercially viable

folding canoe was produced by Johan K 1907; its arrival greatly advanced in canoeing. The folding canoe becam developed between the wars, and v extensively for both touring and sportir At the same time the canvas-cove framed canoe had its adherents; for th close to the river it was ideal and could can, be made by any person capable simple tools. Many a youngster has be duced to the Thames by building a ca youngsters have been helped by buyin full-scale easy to follow working which were produced by a well kr schoolmaster/Scout Leader Percy B and most of the designs are still avail

Canadian canoes featured in regatt example in 1880, it was reported in th Magazine of the Goring and Streatley '. . . the increasing popularity of the Canoe has probably never been so shown as was the case on Saturday. tively swarmed . . .' The kyak type of generally used at canoe club meeting tures, rarely if ever participating in regattas.

One of the most popular competitiv events is the 'slalom'; for this a course in a weir stream, with a series of ma contestants have to paddle their cours in and out of the 'gates' formed by th or poles. The first slalom event he Thames was at Hambleden in 1954; sor and Shepperton weirs are popular slalom events, for which fast water is

Marathon races are held from tin the hardy 'annual' being the Devize minster race every Easter. It was sta event to publicize the Kennet and Avo 1948, planned by Frank Luzmore. over a long course – from Devizes Kennet and Avon to Reading and Thames to Westminster, a total of 12, 77 locks – and lasts the whole weeke within 8 years of its founding, the be been reduced to 24 hours.

Eton boys swimming, whilst others have lessons (circa 1870). Note sculler in 'whiff', right background.

Swimming

How long man has been interested in swimming as a recreation and sport is anybody's guess but we know, from the baths they built, that the Romans were fond of it. Nowadays one often notices youngsters holding on to a small polystyrene float, so as to practice their leg strokes. These floats are supposedly a new idea, but believe it or not, Roman boys and girls learnt to swim in the same way, the only difference being that their little rafts were made of short lengths of bamboo lashed tightly together.

River swimming was extremely popular until the '40s and most riparian towns or boroughs had a 'bathing place' with springboards, a swimming instructor and changing facilities; in some places there would be a boom or booms to keep the area completely free of boats.

Such a site is the one still run by Henley Council, on the Berkshire bank opposite the tail of Rod Ait; most other authority bathing places have disappeared leaving only slight evidence of their former function. At Runnymede the well-built and fully shuttered changing rooms stand like a monument to the past. Bath Ait at Windsor formed the outboard boundary of the old swimming place, which is now a mooring area for visiting boats. Wallingford once had very good facilities on the northern bank, whilst all traces of the Chertsey site vanished as the bank was steadily eroded by the combined action of floods and wash from passing craft.

Unfortunately now the preponderance of powered craft upon the river, and the fact that many are handled as if they were cars on the motorway, makes long-distance swimming on the Thames without an escort almost a non-starter. Whilst swimming in the public baths may be useful for training, or in the depths of winter, there is nothing comparable with the joy of being in communion with the Thames. When on a camping trip what is more delightful, or invigorating, than to slide out of one's sleeping bag and take a header into the pure soft waters of the Thames?

There was a time when swimmers were pretty free from regulations and could swim as nature intended; however the Thames Conservancy tightened up on the matter and in due course regulated hours for bathing; their Acts and Bye Laws, 1857 to 1885, state under the 'Thames Preservation Act, 1885': 'that no person shall bathe or prepare to bathe at any place where or between any hours when bathing is for the time being prohibited by the Conservators'. This was followed by: 'No person shall bathe without proper bathing dress or drawers, unless properly screened from view', which in many reaches gave the bather plenty of scope, and for that matter still does, to the joy of modern naturists.

Long distance swimming races were at one time quite commonplace, but are now somewhat limited in both distance and regularity and more often than not, in the 1980s confined to charity and fund raising events. The races for the amateur swimming championship of Great Britain took place on different reaches of the Thames until 1874, after which it was decided to hold them on the Grand Junction Canal Reservoir at Hendon (now the Welsh Harp). Although no Thames waterman or swimmer seems to have swum the Channel, at least Henry Bran, a great swimmer, waterman and ferryman at Hampton, escorted David Dalton on his successful cross Channel swim of August 23rd, 1890; Henry's escort boat was his time-honoured and locally built Thames dinghy. Henry's son, Bill, followed in his father's footsteps and was a swimmer and life saver; in fact he was one of the few who could swim through a bed of reeds when on a rescue mission.

The cleanliness and purity of the Thames is of the highest standard, and in fact sets an example in river management to the rest of the world. Except in cases of extreme drought, such as in the long hot summer of 1976 (when at Molesey weir large pumps were installed to fill the reach above), the number of weirs throughout the length of the river ensure that adequate oxygen-

ation takes place, so enabling the natu purification process to be maintain Water Authority is constantly testing sa water taken from points not only a Thames itself but throughout the enti ment area of some 3,800 square mile undesirable matter is being dischar; quickly found and matters rectified ver Solid matter, that is erosion from bank washed off fields, amounts under nor conditions to a little over $1\frac{1}{2}$ cwt p gallons of water. No apologies are ma digression on water purity; the m recently tended to give the impression liness of the Thames as a whole was b dard and possibly not ideal for s whereas in fact it ought to be clearly st was the tidal Thames, otherwise ref 'London's River' that required clean the keen observer of nature, the qu river is more than apparent by the quantity of various species that can readily, be they birds, mammals, fish

Another of 'Bob's' postcards, this time in bathing' series.

HOLIDAYS AND RECREATION

Jerome K. Jerome may not have been far from the truth when he remarked in his *Three Men in a Boat* that Julius Caesar was a regular upriver man! But, joking apart, it would appear that spending leisure time on the Thames goes back into a distant past of which there are no records; the first references seem to have been made in the *Universal Gazetteer* of 1801 which devoted a substantial section to Thames holidays.

Pleasure boating

Pleasure boating became really popular in the early part of the last century, when people began to take boats out not just for the day but also overnight – sleeping on board or camping by the river. Boatyards lost no time in having iron hoops and canvas covers made for their sculling craft and punts, so that people could sleep aboard and have the advantage of making extended journeys with complete freedom, without the worry and bother of arriving at a suitable inn or hotel before nightfall; furthermore, sleeping on the boat obviated the need to find a camping site with the attendant work of pitching a tent, which can be rather a chore if it happens to be a wet and windy evening! Canadian canoes were also quite popular for camping

'Brewing up'. The occupant of this camping skiff is keeping an eye on his primus stove (1972).

trips; in wet weather they could be used Canadian-Indian style, that is, set on the bank upside down, with the upswept heads of the respective stems pushed lightly into the ground, so providing a dry and well ventilated sleeping area.

As railways developed, forward-looking yards were not slow to arrange a one-way system for the hire of boats with an inclusive fee covering the cost of returning the skiff or gig by rail to base. It was Salter's of Oxford who really pioneered these 'one-way' trips with camping skiffs, gigs, punts and dinghies, provided the craft was left at one of the approved yards and the additional fee of two shillings and sixpence (12½p.) was paid.

A fashionable type of Thames holiday in the latter part of the 1800s was the hiring of houseboats for attending some major event, or just to enjoy the tranquil beauty of the river. The following contemporary advertisements sum up the situation rather well:

> Houseboat to let for Ascot, Jubilee Show Windsor and Henley Regatta. Roomy and convenient; 35ft × 8ft making up four beds ...

> Houseboat wanted for month from middle of August next − full particulars to Bartletts, Solicitors, Abingdon.

> Houseboat to let, sleeps four; 30ft × 9ft; saloon, bedroom, dressing room, kitchen, sailing dinghy: competent man in charge. £20 for Henley week, or £20 from August 2nd to 26th − write, Coxen c/o Moore, Hampton-on-Thames.

Salter's really were pioneers in the holiday afloat game; apart from their regular Oxford–Kingston steamer service, which has already been described in detail, they hired out steam launches with crew for excursions as desired. For example, a launch with a for'd awning, a cabin with accommodation for six to ten people, lavatory, a crew (including a captain and engineer), fuel and lock fees, cost for six days £15 15s. with the provision that the hirer was

expected to provide the crew with thei[r] meal. That was in 1910 and by 1928 th[e] risen to £31 10s.

In the early 1900s, Salter's were h[...] motor launches which they advertise[...] powerful than steam launches; forty [...] recommended as being sufficient fo[r] excursion. A launch with a saloon a[...] cost £4 4s. for a two-day journey. [...] trip from Lechlade to Oxford, whic[h] sending the launch to Lechlade, [...] £3 3s., or a four-day trip from L[...] Kingston, inclusive of the time occup[...]ing the launch to Lechlade and retur[n] Oxford to Kingston, cost the gra[nd] £11 11s.! By the 1920s Salter's we[re] some very handsome 28 foot 6 inch [...] cabin cruisers at a cost of £12 per w[eek] built a number of very attractive aft [...] with a very comfortable forward co[...] one could relax and enjoy the splen[...] They still had a few of these boats fo[...] '50s; the layout was interesting for [...] pre-empted the 'Caribbean' and sim[...] cruiser that have become so popu[lar] times.

However it was not until the b[...] period that motor cruisers becam[e] available for hire. In the 1930s [...] Bourne End were advertising their [...] as the 'most up to date cruiser on [...] and went on to say that 'the cost [...] boats ranges from £7 7s. to £14 [...] according to size. They are insured [...] lock passage for the whole of the [...] are so arranged that it does not req[...] to navigate them, or Messrs Andre[...] a competent man to give full inst[...] the hirer is confident.'

In the same era Meakes Ltd of [...] advertising two- and four-berth [...] for hire, whilst at that time ma[...] now so well known to us for the[...] cruisers, were still advertising '[...] and boats at moderate prices', 'C[...] speciality' or 'Skiffs, punts and c[...] the hour, day, week, month or [...]

It was not until after Worl[d...]

Thames holidays afloat really went ahead with modern motor cruisers and, to give an idea of post-war progress, at the first ever National Boat Show, held from December 30th, 1954, to January 8th, 1955, the only Thames yards exhibiting were Bond's of Maidenhead, Bossom's of Medley, Arthur Jacobs Ltd (now Windsor Boats), Maidenhead Court Boathouse and Maid Line Cruisers Ltd (now Maidboats Ltd). In 1950 the only firms advertising hire cruisers in *Thames*, a monthly periodical of the period, were Maid Line, who were then based at Shepperton and Lincoln Arms Boatyard at Weybridge, along with Horace Clark and Son of Sunbury.

In the late 1940s the late Eric Vereker was building up his 'Swallow Cruiser' fleet based at Lincoln Arms Boatyard, Weybridge; some of his early craft in those difficult days were converted wartime hospital boats which were hard chine, had an aft cockpit and were of shallow draught, which made them excellent hire cruisers. Some were re-engined, whilst others had their original Chrysler or Ford V8 motors governed down, else their speed would cause excessive wash.

Many old-established Thames boatyards did much to encourage holidays afloat; amongst them were Bates of Chertsey, Bushnell's of Wargrave and Maidenhead, Tims of Staines, Dunton's of Shepperton, Townsend's of Bourne End (now Bourne End Marina), Hobbs of Henley, Parr's of Surbiton and Allen's of East Molesey besides the firms already mentioned. In 1955 the Thames Hire Cruiser Association was formed with a view to co-ordinating activities between various Thames fleets and providing mutual service facilities. Founding firms of the organization were: Allen's, Andrews, Bates, Bushnell's, Horace Clark, Dunton's, Maidenhead Court Boathouse, Maidboats, Parr's, Salter's, Swallow Cruisers (Weybridge Marine) and Townsend's.

Narrow boats for cruising are now really commonplace upon the river, but it was Lionel Munk of Maid Line Cruisers who in the early 1950s did so much to create an interchange of boats between the Thames and our inland waterways.

Sailing craft for holidaymakers, whilst popular on the Norfolk Broads, never became common on the Thames. It has produced superb sailing craft and has many fine reaches for competitive sailing, but the nature of the river, with in places wooded banks, and in others steeply rising hills, not only gives rise to fluky winds, but in a narrow reach leads to much tacking, which is hardly conducive to long-distance cruising under sail.

A trio of post World War II cabin cruisers so popular with holiday-makers (1960s).

Houseboats

A delightful feature of the Thames was, and still is to a limited extent, the handsome custom-built houseboats (as opposed to residential boats which have become more commonplace). Most of these elegant and commodious houseboats were products of the Victorian and Edwardian era. Houseboats varied in size considerably, from a 30 foot × 9 foot craft to an 85 footer with 13 rooms and every convenience. A few of the elite craft had varnished upperworks, but the majority were painted and very fine they looked, often with window shutters in a contrasting colour and canvas blinds in multi-colour stripes to match the awning of the main deck. The final touch was the mass of colour provided by beautifully planted troughs and hanging baskets which, quite often, were augmented with a splendid collection of indoor plants within the main saloon. Sometimes at a weekend, when a special party was being held, houseboats would be enhanced at night with a myriad of coloured lanterns; the light came from tallow night lights, which gave a soft but twinkling light. Houseboats were furnished to the highest Victorian standards; quite often London firm Maples were commissioned, not only the furniture and furnishings, but to a layout and prepare the colour schen houseboats required a cook and serva designer of the boat had to fit in sui accommodation. The kitchen, althoug by to-day's standards, was well fitted c ing was by an elegant coal range, polis with all bright parts of metal burni mirror-like finish with emery cloth (a c for some poor young Daisy). The larde was a small room, for often the cook, as housekeeper, would buy whole chee a larger variety were required it mig cheeses – no buying by the pound! W would be delivered, bottled fruits by the finest butter, pure lard, prodigious of eggs and goodies galore. They did n modern convenience of a fridge for th craft were provided with an ice bin feature was the wine cellar which accounts was as well stocked as the lar rooms had running water, but if they connect direct to the mains, some stro member of the crew had to pump wate

Houseboats at Shiplake: a scene from the late 19th century.

storage tank in the bilges, to the header tank on the roof. There were elegant bedrooms whilst the main room would be the lounge, with big windows opening out on to the verandah or mooring platform.

Some of the biggest concentrations of houseboat moorings were at Hampton Court/Hampton, Shiplake, Reading and Oxford; an important factor in their siting was the proximity of a railway station, for the majority of these boats were for holiday and seasonal use, enjoyed by city dwellers, some of whom during the summer months would commute to their place of business in London.

The houseboats were built by yards such as Horsham of Bourne End, Meakes and Redknap of Marlow, Stevens of Abingdon, Tims of Staines, Bates of Chertsey and Tagg's of Hampton. Tagg was a master of houseboat building; he established his yard on Platt's Eyot, Hampton, in 1866, and started by building skiffs and canoes which he exported to places as far away as Ceylon and Rangoon together with a special order for a randan to San Sebastian. By the time he had sold his yard to Immisch (as mentioned earlier), he had built some of the largest and finest houseboats ever seen afloat.

Tom Tagg, who started a boatyard on Walnut Tree Island, trading as T.G. Tagg and Son, just upstream of Molesey Lock, was a relative. His fame as a boatbuilder soon spread. Adjacent to the boatyard he built a successful hotel and the name of the ait was soon changed to Tagg's Island, which name it still enjoys. Of the many craft he built, one was a barge for Jesus College, Oxford. Jack Tagg, a relative, was a great sportsman and rowed in many races, not only on the Thames but in France and Holland; in his time he was considered to be one of the best river pilots between Oxford and London.

Tagg of houseboat fame had the backing of a Mr Hewett, for whom he built several splendid vessels. One of them, the *Kingfisher*, moored at Hampton, was in its day the largest houseboat afloat, in fact it was so beamy that it could not pass through any locks above Molesey. Her owner, being determined to make excursions upriver without denying himself the comforts and luxuries to which he was accustomed, commissioned Tagg to build him a new, and even larger and more sumptuous craft – with a difference, for she was built in two sections, running fore and aft, so that she could be taken apart from end to end, and towed in two reasonable width sections. This leviathan houseboat, built in the late 1880s, was named *Satsuma*, no doubt from the glazed Japanese pottery with which she was decorated and which appeared to form the theme of her interior decor. The furnishings were of the finest Victorian elegance, or fussy trappings – according to one's views. The *Satsuma* had her attendant steam tug to tow her around; mind you this was no ordinary tug, it was a real mongrel combining the virtues of tug, launch and houseboat. As well as towing the *Satsuma*, it provided accommodation for the crew, numerous servants and maids who staffed *Satsuma*. The name of this peculiar vessel was *Tom Tug*. Realizing the fire risk on *Satsuma*, the owner forbade smoking; sadly, soon after he sold the craft she was burnt out. She was replaced with a smaller but very elegant *Satsuma*, complete with vases.

The vast majority of houseboats in those Victorian and Edwardian times were used as delightful 'retreats' by their owners for holidays, weekend parties and other jollifications; they would be towed up or downriver for Henley Regatta and other events, where the owners would entertain friends and have a grandstand view of the racing from the top deck. Other than two-storey houseboats such as *Kingfisher* and *Satsuma*, most houseboats could use their upper decks for sitting out; not surprisingly they were, in the main, rigged to receive awnings of a gay but practical nature to give protection from scorching sun and squalls of rain alike. Some craft boasted a small but comfortable room upon the upper deck, which could be described as a miniature version of the 'Texas', a small, superior cabin, found upon the great Mississippi steamboats.

A few houseboats were used as permanent living quarters for the whole year; most were used only for the summer season, particularly if moored close to a railway station so that businessmen could commute to London. Houseboats were quite often let for Henley week and not a few were let for the whole season. An advertisement for such in the 1880s reads thus: 'To let for entire season pitch pine houseboat with verandah and bow windows, furnished, piano, good saloon, upper deck, fine kitchen'; another advertisement reads: 'Handy man wanted, to live on houseboat; must be able to prepare breakfast, do simple cooking and make himself useful, good character for honesty, civility and sobriety indispensable.' Having mentioned the seasonal use of houseboats, a quotation from an article of 1889 will not be amiss: 'Mr Hudson's houseboat *Little Billie*, does not, like the majority of houseboats, lie up for the winter, but in season and out remains snugly ensconced under the trees opposite the Roebuck at Tilehurst. I wonder how it is that no other houseboater has discovered the delights of an all-the-year round floating residence on the Thames.'

Towing of houseboats was throughout the season quite commonplace prior to the first war. Towing was by steam tug or by hauling from the bank with a horse or mule. Horses were pretty easy to hire from many sources, whilst the hiring out of the latter was a speciality of quite a few boatyards. Some owners, like Mr Hewett, had their own private tugs, or shared them with other owners. A 19th century report on towing makes interesting reading: 'The *Heron* house-

boat was unfortunate in her choice of a week. Moving down from Cookham to quarters, she procured a horse rather th for wear to drag her along, but under th Lacey's Boathouse [now Turk's] he slip then toppled into a boat drawn up u towpath, which he damaged not a litt

When a houseboat with a 25 foot 5 in had to be towed from Tagg's yard to C the Thames Conservancy said it was no because of the width, but they had not a for the builder's ingenuity in desig walkways on either side to hinge into position, so enabling the boat to pass locks.

Most of the houseboats on permane ings had a landing stage for attendant craft; sometimes this would be cantilev the main structure, such as on the *Riv* but often a separate pontoon was buil ured alongside the main hull. The *Velma* was unusual, inasmuch as afte war her leaky pontoon was replaced crete unit, which in fact was one of th experimental narrow boats moulde crete, at Cubitts Basin, Chiswick.

Possibly the most expensive hous built was the *Astoria*, which was con by Fred Karno, who felt that his exis boat *Highland Lassie* was too cramped. The hull of the new boat Brentford; the superstructure was bu

Astoria, the luxury houseboat built for Fred Karno in 1912.

craftsmen, the last of whom, a woodcarver, died only a few years ago. Besides local craftsmen, some of Fred's own carpenters – from his 'Fun Factory', where he built stage scenery and effects – worked under supervision. The gunmetal window frames were fitted by Crittalls, whilst other specialists carried out such duties as cladding the bathroom throughout with marble. The upper deck was a dance floor, complete with glazed canopy, and as can be seen to this day at Hampton, there is a bandstand at the after end of this deck. When the *Astoria* was completed in 1912, she had cost Fred Karno £20,000! Like his previous houseboat, the new one was moored at Tagg's Island, and the story goes that it was from standing on the deck of *Astoria* viewing the island in its entirety that Fred conceived the idea of building the *Karsino* and making Tagg's Island the most dazzling entertainment centre in the country. But that is another story which brought the great entertainer into the bankruptcy courts.

In the year that Tagg established his Platt's Eyot Works (1866), the writer's grandfather, Thomas W. Chaplin was establishing a waterborne service for victualling houseboats; apparently the quantity of provisions, wines, spirits and beer, besides groceries, supplied during the height of the season was prodigious.

Purpose-built houseboats are steadily coming back into their own, and would be more popular if sufficient moorings were available. The present-day Residential Boatowner's Association is a strong organization; it has problems with the authorities, but that is nothing new; in the 1890s it was stated that 'Houseboats have become increasingly popular in late years' and that 'Riparian owners are tending to look upon them, not without cause, as unmitigated nuisances'. At the beginning of the last century, when houseboats were just about beginning to make their presence felt, there was certain ill feeling that they were 'undesirable residences' – but that no doubt stemmed from the very late 1700s when the odd redundant working barge was converted to a floating home, to which, according to some reports, could be added the words 'of sorts'.

To some, houseboats gave a sense of insecurity, problems in times of flood if left unattended, and high maintenance costs, particularly with regard to slipping fees when the boat had to be pulled out for cleaning down, scraping and re-coating with pitch. When some of the houseboats began to show weakness under water, it was not uncommon for them to be encased in steel. A craft to be so treated was the *Astoria*; the whole operation of fitting her with a prefabricated 'over' hull was completed in one working day under the skilful supervision and expertise of the late Commander Frank Hucks, whose well equipped boatyard in Hampton complete with slipway and dry dock, graced by a genuine Swiss chalet is now run by his son Dick, ably assisted by his wife Jean. In 1977, Dick Hucks carried out a major re-fit on a veteran houseboat from Datchet, the *Ateraxia*, a handsome old girl with painted diagonal cladding to her upperworks and some six pairs of really large sash windows, besides French doors leading out on to the deck; she was built in the 1880s, reputedly by Salter's.

To overcome the problems associated with a floating holiday retreat, people began at the end of the last century to acquire riverside plots and set up small chalets; such developments grew to alarming proportions. Planning regulations have always been with us to a lesser or greater degree; however, many of the early chalet owners overcame the regulations by claiming squatters' rights, inasmuch as they took over huts that had been erected by 'withy cutters'. When the growing of willows was a big industry on the Thames, itinerant folk would come down for the harvest season to cut the wands, peel them on site and tie them into 'bolts'. The fact that the season was fairly long, combined with the habit of one family returning to the same site year after year, naturally encouraged permanent camps that could be re-used and thereby established a use right. As chalets became more and more popular as leisure spots, so building manufacturers started producing standard units; one of the oldest family firms to do so, who are still in business, are Walton's of Newark-on-Trent. They did a good trade on the Thames and some of their octogenarian units are still around.

A type of building for summer and occasional use that evaded most bye laws was the timber-framed and floored chalet, which was clad with very heavy quality canvas, so enabling it to be classified as a form of tent. As time went by the canvas was replaced with more durable material, such as asbestos; extensions were made and surreptitiously over a long period of time the 'tent' pupated into quite a sophisticated dwelling.

The early chalets were comfortably furnished, but of course lacked domestic equipment to which so many people are now accustomed. Cooking was by oil stove, or that truly excellent appliance the 'Primus' pressure stove. Water supply would be from a small bore hole, drawn up by means of a hand pump, of either the jigger or semi-rotary type; in some cases water was taken by bucket straight from the river. Sanitation was of the good old 'earth closet' variety. But all worked well and happy days were enjoyed by many; in fact some old timers talk nostalgically of the glow of hurricane lamps or the bright light of a pressure-petrol lantern, after an energetic day, out in God's good air.

For those addicted to fresh air and close contact with nature, together with absence of crowds, camping is ideal. However some folk prefer slightly more sophistication coupl a touch of community spirit, which gav the setting up of permanent camp sites p with a modicum of facilities. This m was really pioneered by the Thames (and Boating Association, whose camp si Walton Reach, at Sunbury, is much t today as it was shortly after the soc formed in 1889. The T.C.B.A.'s aims provide suitable camping grounds Thames and its tributaries, to protect t ests of camping and boating men, and reduced railway fares and certain othe sions.

Boathouses

In the early part of the last century, a boating began to make inroads into lif Thames, the construction of boatho riverside private properties incre reached its peak around the turn of th In spite of the considerable age of mo structures, and the fact that many received the minimum of maintenanc still a great number of elegant boatho ing lawns beside the Thames. Unf with the decline of the skiff and the boathouses are no longer in use beca

The Thames Camping and Boating Association site, as depicted in this souvenir of 1906, still looks much the s for the preponderance of skiffs.

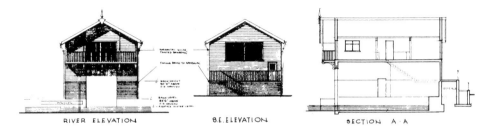

RIVER ELEVATION   B.E. ELEVATION   SECTION A·A

A typical 'wet' boathouse, that is, a boathouse built over a dock, of the great Victorian-Edwardian period.

too small for powered craft; but those built to accommodate a pair of such craft are sometimes used in this present age to take a shallow-draught launch. Some boathouses can accommodate larger craft, due to their being built to house a steam launch; an occasional indication of such structures is the louvered 'pigeon-box' in the roof, built there to allow smoke and steam to escape.

A few boathouses were built out in the river parallel to the bank, with the roof and side cladding being supported on substantial timber piles. Very few of these structures remain, having suffered badly — not only from age, but the ravages of floods. Repair, too, is usually very costly and is difficult because new piles, if a good and pleasing job is to be carried out, have to be driven inside the building.

Most boathouses were built at right angles to the bank, some with a concrete floor ramped at an easy angle from the normal water level to provide a slipway for craft; these are known as 'dry' boathouses compared with the more popular 'wet' boathouse which was built over a dock of suitable proportions. In general the sides of the docks were campshedded in the conventional way, with timber. In a few cases, the dock sides revetted with concrete, but upon close inspection it will be observed that, in general, concrete work has been built up on a timber sub-frame. In many cases where the timber is now showing its age, the task of underpinning and carrying out restoration work is, to put it mildly, a tricky job requiring skill, patience and experience.

All praise must be given to the men who built these docks, where excavation had to be carried out by hand. In the construction of some, where there is a concrete bottom and solid sides, a coffer dam would have to have been driven across the river face of the excavation, in order to minimize the amount of water entering the excavated area — no easy task without the aids of today such as watertight interlocking steel sheets, lightweight petrol and diesel pumps and easy-to-handle hydraulic excavators. A great problem with these docks, irrespective of the structure over them, is that they are 'catch-pits' for silt in time of flood, and veritable trash bins for all the rubbish that people will fling into the drink; judging by relics found during dredging operations, man has not altered in this direction during the past 2,000 years or more! Possibly Sextus Julius Frontinus, who was Water Commissioner for the City of Rome in A.D. 97, had the right idea: he imposed a heavy fine on any citizen found throwing rubbish into a watercourse. May John Coleman O.B.E., Founder and Chairman of the Thames Heritage Trust, have great success with his organization's anti-rubbish campaign, a problem that other river organizations have failed to treat seriously.

When cruising on the river it will be observed that many of the boathouses are of timber construction and invariably have tiled roofs; often the ridge is finished off with a gargoyle or some other embellishment in terra-cotta, which the firm of Henry Doulton produced in great numbers and infinite variety. Some local firms also produced such finials; around the Marlow area many came from the Binfield Brick and Tile Works. A lot of boathouses were virtually two storeyed, the upper room invariably having glazed doors which opened out on to a balcony.

In some instances, several rooms are incorporated over the boathouse; in a very few there is an actual flat upstairs, whilst in one particular instance at Wargrave a lovely and spacious boathouse is integral with a very fine house! Generally, though, the upstairs room, or rooms, were used as 'summerhouses' for convivial parties in the season, and for changing into swimming gear. In winter they provided good storage — away from floods — for boating gear and paraphernalia.

Some rooms are veritable rivermen's 'dens' with trophies for rowing, sculling and sailing hanging upon the walls; photographs in fading sepia cover club, regatta and family events of the past which add to the collection of old enamel Thames Conservancy registration plates, dating possibly from the commencement of registration. (Registration of all pleasure boats came into being under the Thames Preservation Act of 1885, although two years prior to this the Thames Act of 1883 required the registration of steam launches.)

Some dry boathouses, if in an area liable to heavy flooding, had no cladding between the supports for the room above; in winter the boats would be hoisted and slung from the beams. Invariably the sides of these boathouses would be 'slatted' so that flood water would not be impeded; these slats were referred to as 'modesty screens' so enabling menfolk to change into their swimming costumes downstairs without embarrassment to the fair sex. An excellent example of such a boathouse is at Keen Edge, Shillingford. There are several jolly boathouses at Cookham Dean, a couple of which have had their walls underpinned recently in conjunction with re-campshedding. Wargrave has some excellent boathouses to its credit, including what is possibly one of the very few built in recent years. It does not look new, as it was built to an old design and the dock was excavated on the site of the original. Cleeve boasts some good examples. At Marlow there is a very old, and very lovely, boathouse built out into the river; considering that it is in the weir stream it is in remarkably good condition. There are a couple of lovely old boathouses at Sunbury and a fine brick-built

Victorian one at Broom Park, Teddingt

On some large estates it was not unc for the dock and boathouse to be approa a small 'cut' from the river; this usually c when the towpath fronted the property tion. The remains of such a cut can be Dockett Eddy, Shepperton. A cut at complete with small footbridge, is used by the tenant of the boathouse which More interest is being taken in these boathouses and many owners would l them to good use if only they could cle silt; in many cases this can be done wit barge mounted equipment, but som narrow, or have too little headroom working room, whilst the scraping of s river, which at one time was permis contravenes T.W.A. regulations.

This advertisement, published shortly b gives an idea of prices and facilities at

13 ROYALTY AND THE THAMES

In the past, the Thames was regularly used by royalty both as a means of transport and for pleasure. Even King John of Magna Carta fame had his victuals delivered to Windsor by water! Elizabeth I loved the river and it was her custom to be informally rowed in a small boat, quite apart from her official trips and essential journeys. Henry VIII was another ardent riverman and used to enjoy commuting between Windsor and the capital by water.

The Thames was possibly seen in its greatest splendour in Stuart and Tudor times; in that period the Court seized every opportunity to use the river for every sort of triumphal event, procession or water pageant. However, these splendid events seem to have been confined to the London area, there being no records of upriver pageantry. Before, or since, people have possibly never been so river-conscious. Windsor Castle, the royal palaces at Hampton Court, Richmond, Westminster and Greenwich, together with a large number of noblemen's palaces along the Strand, added a great touch of magnificence to the humdrum everyday traffic upon the river. Then the City Livery Companies had their own magnificent barges, a few of which are still in existence, mainly being used by Oxford University Rowing Clubs, as river users may have noticed. The Lord Mayor of London had his own ceremonial barge, but more about these craft anon. It is said that the coronation of Anne Boleyn, second Queen of Henry VIII, was probably one of the finest river spectacles ever produced; she was at Greenwich and the Lord Mayor was ordered to attend her to Westminster. On the journey upstream she was accompanied by some fifty barges which were highly decorated: 'Their decks, sail-yards, and top-castles were hanged with rich cloth of gold and silk; all the barges were newly painted and gilded for the occasion and the Lord Mayor's barge was outstanding with its draping and fluttering of pennants.' Two riverside houses at Cookham Dean are on the site of the former 'Stonehouse', once allegedly owned by Henry VIII; it is said he incarcerated Anne Boleyn there.

Catherine of Braganza, consort of Charles II, first came to Whitehall from Hampton Court, when it was reported that the number of vessels on the river was such that spectators could not see the water! Ever-beautiful Hampton Court must have provided innumerable waterborne spectacles over the centuries, with the everyday coming and going of royalty and important personages – but what a tough time the poor watermen must have had, rowing heavy, ponderous barges down to, or up from, Westminster, for they did not always have the tide, current, or wind in their favour! Contemporary reports suggest that in Wolsey's time a crew of lusty watermen, under favourable conditions, could row the cardinal from Hampton Court to Westminster in about the same time as it takes today to make the journey by public transport –

a sobering thought. The present Banqueting House, on the river bank at Hampton Court, is on the site of an earlier tower, where, it is said, Charles II entertained his lady friends, who arrived and departed by water – unbeknown to the residents of the palace.

Henry VIII organized a mock fight with political significance in a most spectacular manner upon the river at Westminster: 'Two barges were equipped with ordnance of war, one for the Bishop of Rome and his Cardinals, and the other for the King's Grace.' In due time the 'Pope' was overcome and he and his crew thrown into the Thames.

A great pageant marked Elizabeth I's progress from Westminster to the Tower, whence in those days the Coronation procession set forth. Three days before she was crowned, the Lord Mayor and City Companies met her on the Thames 'With their barges decked with banners of their craft and mysteries'. The mayor's own guild, the Mercer's, had a 'Bachelor's Barge and an attendant float with artillery shooting off as they went, with great and present melody of instruments, which played in sweet and heavenly manner.' The Queen shot London Bridge about two o'clock, at the still of the ebb, the other barges following her, and she landed at the private stairs of Tower Wharf. Three days later she returned to Westminster in the same majestic way.

In the year 1610, when Prince Henry Frederick was created Prince of Wales, the Lord Mayor and Aldermen greeted him with a river show devised 'out of Neptune's spacious water wilderness'. To mark the wedding of the daughter of James I, a great sea fight, in which 38 vessels participated for three hours, took place between Lambeth Bridge and Temple Stairs, the opposing sides being courtiers dressed as Christians and Turks.

Probably the last of the really great river pageants was when Lord Nelson's body was conveyed on its final journey from Greenwich in 1806, in the barge originally built for Charles II. This barge is now preserved in the H.M.S. *Victory* museum at Portsmouth.

Edward VII was a keen river man; his interest stemmed from the days when he was Prince of Wales. Although unfortunately little is recorded of his personal activities at that time, the following report makes interesting reading, from *Lock to Lock Times* dated August 1889:

On Sunday the Prince of Wales together with the King of the Hellenes had a pleasant trip on the river in the electric launch *Viscountess Bury*. The party which accompanied his Royal Highness numbered about a dozen. The afternoon turned most enjoyable and the party went on board at Kew shortly after four o'clock, the launch having been ready sometime previous. Being quite an unexpected visit, very little attention was paid to the boat as it proceeded past Teddington, Kingston and Ditton. The white ensign floating on the flagstaff was the first intimation to the sightseers at Molesey, as the *Viscountess Bury* approached the lock, that some distinguished personage was aboard . . . a few minutes past six Molesey Lock was cleared, and the launch proceeded to Immisch's charging station at Platt's Eyot, where the party went ashore and inspected the charging plant for the new electric boats which have so recently jumped into popularity. The Prince of Wales personally examined the *Alpha*, one of the small boats of the firm, and under the guidance of the manager put the launch in motion (in fact he gave the craft a test trip). The return journey was commenced at seven o'clock; and at Molesey an enormous crowd – close on four thousand people – had congregated, whose enthusiasm was a further indication of the popularity of the Prince of Wales. A slight delay occurred in getting through the lock, the *Viscountess Bury* being 'locked' with a host of small boats . . . a rapid run was made to Chelsea Pier after leaving Teddington, which was reached at 10.30, the party then disembarking.

Strange to say, on that same Sunday, and only a short time before the Prince of Wales, the Prin-

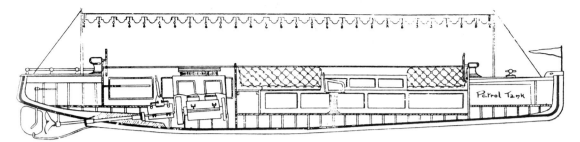

The 33 foot 6 inch long motor boat built by George Tagg in 1904 for His Majesty King Edward VII. She was powered by a Thornycroft petrol engine.

cess Frederica passed through Molesey Lock in a skiff; due to her informality and the normality of the craft, she proceeded on her way unrecognized!

It would appear that the Prince of Wales, like many of his future subjects, greatly enjoyed the pleasure of spending a Sunday on the river: on one sunny Sunday in August 1898, he enjoyed an upriver trip, in company with the Earl and Countess of Lucan, on James Taylor's launch *Favourite*; all arrangements for this cruise were made under the supervision of Mr Bates, who was Mr Taylor's manager at Bridge Wharf, Chertsey.

When the Prince of Wales became King Edward VII in 1901, he still maintained his love for the Thames, often enjoying lively parties at the 'Fisheries', Bray, or sometimes a peaceful spot of fishing in the Staines reach from a site known as 'The Fishing Temple', which is now a residential caravan park.

When he had a motor launch built in 1903, he personally took her out for a test run so as to check details before taking delivery. In 1904 he commissioned George J. Tagg of Hampton Court to build him a new motor launch. She was 33 feet 6 inches long, with a beam of 6 feet and a draught of 18 inches. The hull was of triple skin construction, the two inner skins being laid diagonally across each other, with $\frac{1}{4}''$ cedar planking; the outer skin was $^3/_8''$ mahogany planking running longitudinally; timbers were of American elm. The fore well, or passenger compartment of the boat, was 13 feet long and panelled with American walnut and white ash; cushions were of dark blue morocco leather, whilst the burden boards ('floor' in household terms) were covered with a heavy pile carpet of a colour to match the cushions. The canopy, supported on brass stanchions, was of silk, complete with suitable decorative effects. The power unit was a 4-cylinder Thornycroft petrol engine developing 20 h.p. at 900 r.p.m.

The next Prince of Wales, who became the Duke of Windsor, was another member of the royal family who had close contact with the

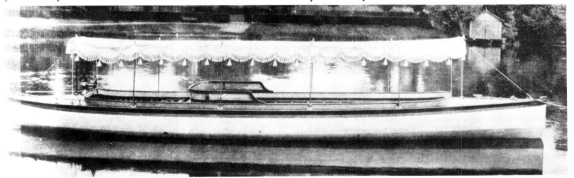

The 33 foot 6 inch launch with 20 h.p. Thornycroft petrol engine built by George Tagg for Edward VII in 1904.

Thames. As a young man he often stayed at that gracious riverside house, 'Monksbridge' at Sunbury, which was then owned by his friends the Dudley Ward family. From Monksbridge he enjoyed river activities, swimming and aquatic sport. When he was courting Mrs Simpson she bought a residence, complete with boathouse, at the lower end of the Datchet reach; this somewhat rambling building was originally constructed as a country club for the Café Royal and would of course, have been ideal for entertaining. It is reputed that the prince, who kept his sculling boat in the Royal Boathouse at the upper end of the reach, used to pull down incognito to Mrs Simpson's, where of course his boat could be tucked away in the boathouse until required for the return journey.

The Queen, as Princess Elizabeth, together with her sister Princess Margaret, when youngsters, enjoyed a cruise upon the Thames in the Conservancy launch *Windrush* – the original and very elegant *Windrush*, so befitting to our

river. In 1946 the then Princess Elizab[eth] her sister Princess Margaret attended post-war Henley Regatta and went a Hobb's elegant launch *Enchantress*. Queen Elizabeth conducted the open emony of the new London Bridge, travelled in the Port of London A launch *Nore*, from Westminster steps monger's steps beside the bridge. Un bridge-top banquet enjoyed by her pred in the 19th century on the opening of vious bridge, the Queen walked am crowds in friendly greeting.

Princess Margaret, on a summer's ev 1972, landed beside the Thames at She in a helicopter of the Queen's Flight, to the opening ceremony of the new launching and mooring facilities prov the Sea Rangers at Dockett Eddy. Then the Princess continued her interest in matters by performing the naming cere the boat *Windsor Sovereign* at the bo[a]

Princess Elizabeth and Princess Margaret attending the 1947 Henley Regatta in *Enchantress*, the umpire launch bu in 1917. Tony Hobbs is in the stern behind the helmsman. The gentleman standing, breast rope in hand, is his

Her Majesty Queen Elizabeth leaving Hurley Lock on her way down to Magna Carta Island, Runnymede, October 18th, 1974.

Clewer village; on another occasion the Princess, accompanied by her children, Lord Linley and Lady Sarah, went out in a motor launch to watch 'swan upping' and to witness the traditional counting of the Queen's swans by Her Majesty's swan keeper, Mr John Turk of Cookham.

Our own Queen, Elizabeth II, made modern history on October 18th, 1974, when she embarked on the launch *Windsor Regent* at Hurley lock and proceeded downstream to Magna Carta Island, where she planted a walnut tree to mark the end of her river tour of the Royal Borough of Windsor and Maidenhead. She made several stops en route and stepped ashore at Bisham Abbey, Cookham, Maidenhead, Bray, Eton Brocas and Datchet. The weather on that momentous day was far from good but that did not seem to deter Her Majesty from taking a very keen and active interest in everything around her. Appropriately, she travelled in a Thames-built boat owned and operated by the local firm of Windsor Boats Ltd.

In July 1981, Prince and Princess Michael of Kent were guests of honour at 'Thames Heritage'; this was a superb son et lumière, held on the water at Windsor reach, off the Brocas, with the castle as a backdrop. The event was organized by the Thames Heritage Trust, under the guidance of Margaret Powell. The theme portraying the River Thames down the ages was written, produced and directed by Avril Lethbridge whose name must be recorded as one of the 'greats' in Thames history. This memorable event far and away surpassed the Runnymede Pageant of 1937. In some inexplicable way a river pageant seems to exercise a spell of magic that is not obtained from the most outstanding spectacle on terra firma!

Although not a royal event, the waterborne ceremonial attending Sir Winston Churchill's funeral from Tower Pier to the Festival Hall site is without equal in modern times. The naval officer involved in the organization of that occasion, Gerald Perry, upon retirement entered the boating trade and became the genius behind a well-known chain of marinas and leisure equipment shops across the country.

In the National Maritime Museum at Greenwich is the most famous of all royal barges, upon the stern of which is the inscription 'Barge built for Queen Mary and King William III 1689'. The last time this vessel was used was in the peace celebrations of 1919 with King George V and Queen Mary aboard. With its long oars, the blades of which were painted scarlet, it took the royal party, including Queen Alexandra, from the Custom House to Chelsea. This superb barge, known as the Queen's Shallop, is 41 feet 6 inches long with a beam of 6 feet 6 inches and was originally rowed by 10 oars; until 1953 she was kept in the former Royal Boathouse at Windsor, in which year she was removed to the National Maritime Museum at Greenwich. (The entrance channel [with attendant towpath bridge] to the old boathouse can still be seen a little upstream of Datchet's public moorings, on the other side of the river.) This royal craft must have looked remarkable with its dazzling white

The Queen's Shallop, built in 1689 by William III for Queen Mary, being removed from Windsor (1954) to its final resting place, the National Maritime Museum.

hull encrusted with gold and scarlet, w̶ after end, a splendid canopy in green which was replaced in 1912 by a finished in red and gold. In the reign o VII the craft was modified by redu number of oars from ten to eight, bec Majesty complained that stroke threatened to butt the royal party! ̶ must have looked resplendent in the tunics and breeches, which were set off stockings, black shoes with silver bu black caps. The bargemaster would ha̶ equally splendid in black and scarlet, c the tiller in a rather crouched position could see under the canopy but o̶ Majesties' heads. This fine craft was Queen Victoria for the opening of Exchange; Edward VII and Queen Vict it to visit the June the Fourth celebr Eton; in 1912 King George V and Qu used it for their visit to Henley Regatta. course, Queen Mary who presented t̶ derful craft to the National Maritime way back in 1931, although it rem Windsor for a further 22 years whe overhauled by that old-established Th̶ of barge building and lighterage fame Cory, before going into a place of hon̶ museum. It is interesting to record that timbers, cut from oak trees grown in Forest, were still sound.

Another important craft in the muse barge built in the 17th century for the Commissioners, and used by their Lor official visits to the Naval Victuall downriver, also by the Brethren o House on their annual visit to Deptfor time Queen Victoria had her own, decorated 33 foot long barge, which in Admiralty, with the permission o Elizabeth, presented to the Maritime M Canada situated in Halifax, Nova Sc

The Queen's Shallop, although buil̶ did not become the state barge until 1 *The Prince Frederick* was pensioned of that date she seems to have been us̶ consorts of sovereigns, or by their re̶ lowing behind the royal or state b̶

King George V in the Queen's Shallop at the Henley Regatta of 1912.

Prince Frederick was built in 1732 for Frederick, Prince of Wales; it was used by him until his death in 1751 when it passed to the Crown and was used by succeeding sovereigns until, as earlier mentioned, 1849. She has superb lines, reminiscent of a Thames wherry, and is decorated in an ornate manner; hardly surprising when it is revealed that the man responsible for her design and decoration was none other than the celebrated architect, William Kent. The craft is 63 feet long with a beam of 7 feet, and now resides, for all to see, in the National Maritime Museum.

Mayor's *barge and livery companies*

Ceremonial events upon the river had become almost *de rigueur* by the 15th century as a result of the prosperity of the city livery companies, the great number of which became established by charter in the 13th century. Prior to having sumptuous craft built to suit their particular needs, livery companies tended to hire barges for special occasions; these were then temporarily furbished as required, and fitted with gay awnings along with tiltcloths, banners, shields and flags. All livery company barges would present themselves in glorious array to accompany the Lord Mayor of London in his own ceremonial barge, which was much used until the Lord Mayor's procession abandoned the water route to Westminster in the mid-1850s; this really brought to a close a very colourful and romantic chapter in the history of State waterborne

events. The last of the mayoral barges was the *Maria Wood* which ended a line of such craft dating back, as far as can be ascertained, to 1454.

The *Maria Wood* was built in 1816, when the Lord Mayor was Sir Matthew Wood, by Field and White; she was 140 feet long by 19 feet wide and drew 2 feet 6 inches of water. The grand saloon, 56 feet long, was capable of seating 140 persons for dinner. This great civic craft was sold in 1859 and then used for pleasure parties; sometimes she was hired by regatta committees for use as a grandstand; she regularly went up river to Moulsey Hurst (original spelling) for the Happy Hampton Races which preceded the Hurst Park Racecourse. The barge was kept at Teddington, although her original home was Strand-on-the-Green. From the former mooring it took 8 horses to tow her upstream, but 4 or 5 less when travelling with the current. A contemporary report (from *Old and New London*) gives an insight to an outing on such a splendid boat:

The fair sex look forward to the *Maria Wood* excursions with great expectation, and more or less rule the roost on these occasions. The prohibition of smoking on board is still adhered to, the elderly members who are anxious for a weed after lunch having to embark on the smoking tender which is hitched on behind. This floating smoke room is like a local Great

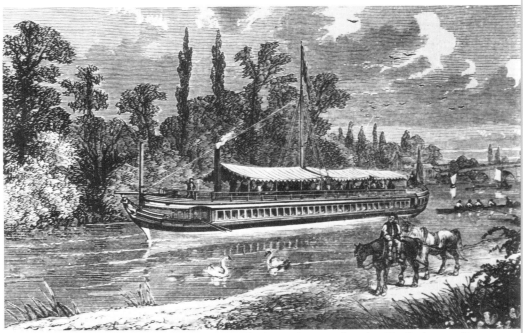

The *Maria Wood*, the last of a long line of barges built for the Lord Mayor of London. Her final mayoral journey was

Eastern third class carriage set down on a lighter. Whilst nicotine is being consumed in the stern, the maternal members indulge in tea and gossip forward, and the younger branches glide down the main deck to the strains of 'Love's Golden Dream'.

Maria Wood ended her days as an excursion boat in 1896 and the writer is grateful that he had a first-hand description of her from his late father.

Even before the Lord Mayor's barge was sold off in the mid-1850s City Livery Companies were beginning to dispose of some of their craft and in 1846 the Oxford University Boat Club started a trend by buying a City barge from the Merchant Taylor's Company. This idea was taken up by various Oxford Colleges so that by 1856 about half a dozen barges had been bought and then towed up to Oxford. All this was inspired by one of the colleges first hiring a Salter built and owned houseboat in 1815, and then one or two other barges from local boat hirers, to be used as places for rowing men to change.

The ex-livery company barges proved so

popular that in 1854 the Oxford Univer[sity] Club had a barge built for its especial [use] 1860 a number of college boat clubs [fol]lowed suit with a resultant 6 or 7 cust[om] barges. Between that time and the e[nd of the] century another 13 were built, and a [few] more in the first quarter of the present [century] Some of these barges were utilitarian [in design] and construction, so as to provide [changing] rooms, and on the roof a railed area wit[h seats to] provide facilities for watching races. O[thers] had the flair of olden times and now e[nhance] river art of the Edwardian period.

In concluding this chapter it seems a[ppropri]ate to mention a few of our famous [Thames] boatbuilders who held a royal warra[nt. Salter] and Sons were foremost – they were no[t only by] appointment to Her Majesty Queen [Victoria] but also to H.R.H. the Prince of Wal[es. Fred] Messenger the boatbuilder from Te[ddington] and Kingston was bargemaster by app[ointment] to Her Majesty. Those ubiquitous boa[tbuilders] C. and A. Burgoine rightly and proudly [displayed] the royal coat of arms, as did R.J. Tu[rk and] R.H. Turk was a waterman to Her

An Edwardian river scene at Oxford, with a college barge in the background.

Queen Victoria. Charles Wheeler, boatbuilder at Richmond Bridge, was waterman in ordinary to Her Majesty. T.G. Tagg and Son held the royal coat of arms; Harry Tagg, with the nearby boatyard at Hampton Court Bridge, modestly displayed the fact that he was a Freeman of the Waterman's Company! Whatford's of Thames Ditton were boatmen by appointment to H.R.H. Princess Frederica. Robert Allen, the houseboat, boat and punt builder of Windsor was by appointment to Her Majesty Queen Victoria; Bond's of Maidenhead were under 'royal patronage'. John Tims and Sons of Staines, who at one time had a second yard at Reading, were by appointment to H.M. King Edward VII. Both Tagg and Son, and Turk's, went on to serve His Majesty King Edward VII. W. Redknap of Marlow was a Queen's (Victoria) waterman and his firm, Meakes and Redknap, the steam launch and boatbuilders, displayed the royal coat of arms.

Somewhere about 1869 Searle's acquired the patent to built 'water velocipedes' which were basically catamarans with two skiff-like hulls, propulsion being by paddle wheels worked in the same way as an old-fashioned tricycle, except that instead of being astride a saddle, the operator sat in an upholstered seat. They became popular abroad, which stepped up export trade, but as far as we are concerned the great interest lay in the fact that Queen Victoria used one of these craft, which was normally kept on Virginia Water and maintained by Tims of Staines.

Tims of Staines kept the flag flying, for they followed on with an appointment to H.M. King George V. Whilst in the late '20s Shillingford Bridge Hotel, like Arthur Jacobs, the boat proprietor of Windsor, was 'patronized by royalty'.

In the previous chapter mention was made of the barge built for Jesus College, Oxford, in the latter part of the 19th century; after the last war she was beginning to show her age in no uncertain way, and due to the munificence of Mr John Smith, High Steward of Maidenhead, she was completely re-built by Tough's over a period of two years from 1967 to 1969. The barge is moored at Maidenhead, but it is understood that it will go back to Oxford at the end of Mr Smith's stewardship. Most contemporary literature states that the barge was built by Salter's in 1910; however the *Surrey Comet* of January 8th, 1887, stated that Tagg's built the barge! Be that as it may, the Trust for the Preservation of Oxford College Barges, is, as its name implies, doing yeoman work in this direction.

14 RIVER MAINTENA AND TRAINING

The majority of holidaymakers, and indeed very many boat owners, take for granted the fact that the Thames has beautifully maintained locks, fine weirs, modern services such as fresh water points and waste disposal facilities, not to mention carefully positioned buoys, well dredged channels and good moorings. Thames Water navigation officers, in their trim blue-and-white inspection launches are a familiar sight, but their brothers in arms go along unrecognized – the engineers, land drainage teams and purification officers whose work in the smooth running of our river, and the well-being of the catchment area spreads over ten counties.

River management has become a business catering for many, often complicated, needs. For instance water must be provided for recreational purposes, effective land drainage for farmers must be carried out, the possibility of flooding reduced by systematic dredging and improvements to weirs, the vast needs of water undertakings must be fulfilled to the tune of some 1,000 million gallons per day, and within reason waste disposal must be allowed after purification, which is carried out with meticulous care. Maintenance and improvement of fisheries is yet another aspect of river management. Much rewarding work has been done in this field and highlights the achievements of our purification officers.

Sewage contains valuable nutrients for crops, so it is not surprising that some of the really early

sewage treatment plants irrigated the su ing land, hence the idea of the 'sewag Prior to 1876 sewage was often channel houses, via the nearest stream, to the that year the Rivers Pollution Preventior a stop to such practices by making it an to discharge raw sewage into a river.

Today the modern sewage works ser water so clean that it is really pure before back into the river. Regular tests are find out how much dissolved oxygen a pended solids are present, as a guide to and whether traces of toxic substanc entered the water.

Clean, pure water is obviously desiral wide variety of reasons, and essential fo ing water supplies, for not only is two t London's water drawn from the Than 24 other water undertakings draw fr catchment area. With the passing of th ropolitan Water Act in 1852, the drav water from below Teddington was pro hence the establishment of the various Water Companies (as they were then) al the river at Surbiton, Hampton, Sunbu Walton. These companies eventually ur 1903 to form the Metropolitan Water which is now a division of the Thames Authority.

Another aspect of management is d and river training; the Thames, like all ri alive and active and requires the same at and care as a colt. A small river such as the Churn, which is the first large tributary of the Thames, rises on high ground and has a short and steep fall to the main river; therefore it flows swiftly and cuts a relatively straight course; with the momentum gained in its downhill drop, the bed is well scoured and silting prevented. However, in a fully developed Thames which flows in a valley that has been somewhat levelled out, through the passage of time, and only affords a gentle drop from source to sea, the amounts of general matter, soil and so on washed down to the river by heavy rain, plus the amount eroded from banks by the action of floods, cause the river bed steadily to silt up. Once a river comes against an obstruction caused by silting, it takes the line of least resistance and makes a course through the easiest ground, and in so doing changes the direction of the channel.

This change of direction gives rise to a winding course, known as a 'meander'. Meanders more or less conform to a rhythm, being bound by the inevitable laws of nature. Once the river has cut a way to miss an obstruction it becomes impossible for it to get back to its original course. The changed, and faster running current hits the opposite bank which it undercuts, causing it to fall away; the undercurrent, which is

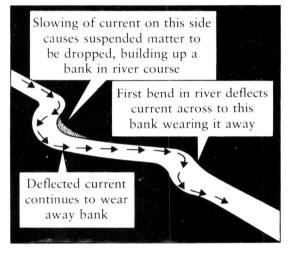

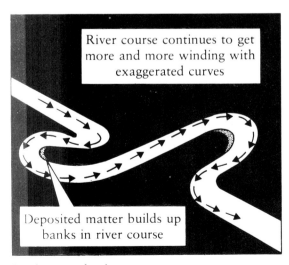

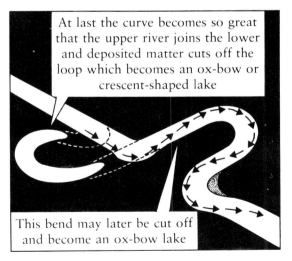

Development of ox bows.

The public gardens, Surbiton, with Kingston Bridge in the far distance. In the foreground two men are operat dredger. Dredged material can be seen piled up in their ballast punt. The paddle steamer proceeding upstream i *Elizabeth*, which was built in 1895. She had three owners, the last being J. Mears Launches and Motors Ltd (cir

slower, carries the sediment on a shorter and fairly direct route. Halted by the obstruction, its suspended matter is dropped on the inner curve, so causing a 'spit' or projection of land to build up. As currents again rebound on the other bank, a further meander is formed; this of course is a repetitive business resulting in a winding river. The word 'meander' is from the Latin name of the river Maeander in Phrygia, whose windings are phenomenal. On an uncontrolled river, meanders can become so exaggerated that in the process of time the loops meet; once united, the river flows through in a direct route, so abandoning the old crescent-shaped course which eventually becomes cut off due to the deposition of silt. These crescents, or crescent shaped pools, are known as 'ox bows'; this name is taken from the curved part of a yoke which fitted over an ox's neck when the beast was put to work. In an endeavour to keep the river 'on course' and ensure adequate depth of water for navigation, besides making due allowance for floods, the Thames Water Authority, like its predecessors the Thames Conservancy, have to carry out a strict dredging programme. When working, the dredger maintains a distance of 30

feet from the bank – or is supposed to! ensure that there is an easy gradient bank to the main channel; if dredging ried out too close to the bank, und collapse of revetments or 'toeing out' shedding could ensue.

Thames dredging used to be called ing', simply because the old fashion dredgers played the double role of ballast, i.e. sand and gravel, from the for building purposes and at the s removing shoals and other hindrances tion. These dredgers were small flat-craft, generally termed 'flats' or 'balla they were equipped with a long pole o of which was a purse-shaped bucket sometimes this was a wrought-iron f lip, covered with hide. The crew consis men: one guided the pole, whilst turned the small winch affixed to the boat; this raised the spoon through wi line attached to it. This operation until the boat was loaded, with gunwa awash, then it was poled ashore to be where the cargo was left to drain, a sifting was carried out to isolate the sharp sand. On site the flat was kept in position by lashing it to 'ryepecks' thrust into the river bed. Ryepecks are long straight poles with the bark removed; they are roughly tapered and fitted with a heavy iron point to facilitate driving into, and withdrawal from, the river bed.

Looking back to the year 1771, we find that the commissioners only paid 7d. per ton for ballasting, including unloading at the wharf. By 1808 a decree was passed that 'no ballast or gravel [was] to be taken from the Thames without leave of the District Committee, under penalty'. Six years later the commissioners' surveyor inspected a 'ballasting machine' on the Oxford Canal; at a cost of £1,800, it was not considered a worthwhile proposition. However a year later moves were made towards using steam power for dredging, which, very, very slowly, almost imperceptibly, took over from hand ballasting on the main course of the river.

The last of the old-fashioned ballasting machines persisted until just before the last war, providing a well known Sussex grower with sharp Thames sand; it was an excellent medium for rooting his cuttings.

Besides dredging, another important facet of river training, was, and still is, the careful and well calculated siting and positioning of weirs and ancillary works, in an endeavour to maintain desired currents and minimize eddies. Such

works are not just the prerogative of highly qualified 20th century engineers; our forebears were pretty canny. For example, at Benson in 1789 the commissioner's Area Engineer ordered 50 feet of campshedding to be driven to prevent the eddy from the lock gull (gull is a swift flowing, shallow area of the river) running into the tail of the lock cut.

The true beauty and tranquillity of a Thames river bank is a world of its own with the fragrant scent of the sweet rush, the bright colour of water forget-me-not and the strong spires of purple loosestrife. Unfortunately the wash from the ever-increasing number of motor boats upon the river is eroding the banks, which is reducing the number of small and shallow rooted plants and in return affecting wildlife. It's not a new state of affairs, as was noted in Chapter 5.

New methods for stabilizing banks that ensure a natural appearance and haven for plants have been developed: like anything new there are snags — particularly the age-old one of conservatism. Towpath banks are at last receiving attention, thanks to various riparian councils with help from the T.W.A. and other organizations. Some local authorities take an enlightened view, but there are others who would, it seems, be quite happy to see a river bank of ugly and costly concrete bags from Teddington to Lechlade. Runnymede is a council which has shown

A Thames Conservancy steam-bucket dredger. Note the long reach steam ram rising up from the bucket. This ram not only pushed the jaws of the open bucket firmly into the river bed, but also actuated the opening and closing of the bucket. Boathouse with white verandah rails is where the late Percy Turner built his beautiful traditional craft. The stern of a Salter's steamer is on right against the local wharf (circa 1890).

A ballast punt, positioned by four ryepecks, to which it is lashed. The man on the left is guiding the spoon dredge affixed to the end of the pole. The fellow on the right is winching the dredger to the surface.

aesthetic sense in using 'gabions' for revetting and reclaiming a considerable amount of their riverside land.

The first recorded use of 'gabions' was in the 16th century, when they took the form of rectangular lidded wicker baskets, which were packed with stone and positioned like building blocks with 'headers' and 'stretchers' to ensure a good bond. Two centuries later the principle was re-established in Italy with the introduction of wire-mesh gabions. Basically, modern gabions are wire-mesh containers in rectangular mattress or sack form; however they are still filled with quarry stone, flints, large gravel rejects or in some instances crushed concrete or hard (emphasis on the hard) secondhand or rejected bricks. A most important factor is to choose gabions that have a woven mesh; this gives flexibility to the structure and allows them to yield, without loss of strength, to changing ground conditions. Properly filled and laid gabions are permeable, therefore no provision has to be made for pressure relief; they weather well and growth soon establishes itself. As well as revetment work they are ideal for building weirs, dams and spillways. For the latter the mattress type gabion can prove indispensable.

The time-honoured Thames-side revetment of hessian bags filled with concrete is very ugly;

costly too: not only are the materials ex but the job is labour intensive. If the wate shallow, the bottom of consolidated gra the bank low, then there is a possibility faction. If a high vertical 'wall' is requirec be suitably 'battered', i.e. angled from bottom, whilst first-class footings must on the river bed, for such a wall, when p laid and bonded, is of enormous weigh

Many riparian owners, whose timbe tages are deteriorating, make the mis levelling up with concrete; this adds trem top weight to old and creaking piles and tates their even earlier demise. Mass co other than for engineering purposes, i medium for *protecting* river banks. Rare river bed suitable, or can correct footings except at enormous cost; the structure is ible and not suited to the changes that tal along the river bank, added to whic extremely ugly.

For centuries, bank protection on the 1 has been carried out by driving boards i river bed. However, with relatively wi narrow section timber it is sometimes diff achieve adequate penetration because in or chalk, the ends of the boards 'cauliflow refuse to move. So for strength and securit piles of square section timber are driven a foot centres. These piles are pointed and often steel shod, so they can be driven right home; in turn the king piles hold in place two horizontal members, a waling at the top and a point cill at the bottom, both of which press tightly against the vertical sheathing boards, so preventing them from moving, or toeing out at the bottom if penetration is only minimal. Finally the king piles are braced back with steel tie bars taken to an anchor pile driven down into the bank below ground level, although sometimes in the past tie rods would be secured to a concrete block referred to as a 'deadman'. This type of bank protection is referred to as 'campshedding' although in the 18th century and earlier the word 'campshot' (see Glossary of River Terms) was used. For example, in September 1778, the commissioners ordered that 'A Campshot be made with oak at Mr M. Mackason's paddock at Medmenham.'

Similar type of work carried out on the Norfolk Broads is termed 'quay heading', whilst in America it is often known as 'bulkheading'. The modern and generally accepted material is steel, in the form of interlocking sheets. Quality is consistent; whilst for extra long life they can be galvanized; when driving, the required penetration can be obtained and the use of king piles and point cill are obviated. Heavy section asbestos was developed for quay heading in America; it has been used on the Thames and the Ouse with considerable success, but its main attraction at the start was low cost. This, however, was soon eclipsed with the introduction of lightweight interlocking steel sheets which provided a far stronger job with less labour.

Sheathing with concrete piles has been carried out. They are heavy and clumsy, but paved the way for the experimental light section glass-reinforced cement sheets. New materials for stabilizing banks, as already mentioned, have been used with very good results whilst some are still being evaluated. One material of woven polypropylene and galvanized stranded wire is ideal for holding graded banks in position; once established it becomes buried in the soil and does not prevent the growth of plants and grass. A steeply angled bank, so treated, in the weir pool at Buscot is now passing the test of time with

Campshedding at Eton, just upstream of the bridge (1979). Beyond the jib of the crane is Firework Ait, which was restored in 1971 and subsequently received a conservation award.

flying colours. In deep water, such as in the Buscot situation, a steel campshedding had to be driven, but with the advantage that the freeboard was only just above normal summer level which enabled the bank to be kept as aesthetically pleasing as possible.

When campshedding was required in shallow water, and cost had to be kept to a minimum, horizontal sheathing without point cill or waling was sometimes used. A more modern variation is the dropping of concrete panels between slotted piles driven into the bed. In both cases tie rods are taken back from king or slotted piles as the case may be. As a river bed is liable to movement, this type of bank protection, being devoid of river bed penetration, is not very satisfactory.

The driving of piles, whether small ones to brace campshedding, or large fellows for mooring purposes, or to support a jetty, is a task that is as old as the commercial use of the river itself. The old-fashioned drop hammer, together with its big brother, the ringing engine, have already been described in a very early chapter, due to their being used by the Romans. The principle of modern units is much the same except that an engine is employed instead of manpower. An old boy who still used a hand-operated drop hammer in modern times was once asked by the writer why he started work so early in the morning. He replied with a twinkle in his eye, 'If I get under way before anyone is out and about I can "drive" the awkward piles with a saw.'

Writing about piles leads one to consider the many and various woods that are found suitable for river work. For the simple ryepeck, barge pole or rough jetty, European Larch is excellent; it stands up to immersion very well, is light in weight and easy to 'work'. At the other end of the scale *the* timber for mooring piles and large scale construction, including lock gates, is greenheart, an extremely hard and very durable wood yielded from the tree whose botanical name is *Ocotea rodiaei*, a native of Guyana. In the heyday of timber campshedding, pitch pine was one of the most popular timbers; not only would it tolerate total immersion, but also the alternate wet and dry conditions along the waterline. Furthermore, fifty or so years ago pitch pine could be obtained in really long lengths. Today there are quite a few Malayan hardwoods from which to choose, but although many are very beautiful in appearance they are not all suitable for riparian duties. Now that there is an excellent British Standard for pressure treating timbers with preservative to a high standard for marine work, it is coming about that softwoods such as Canadian Hemlock, when used for jetties or campshedding is outlasting many of the more exotic – and expensive – hardwoods. English Oak is still used for some structures; however it does not have a really long life, being classified as 'durable' and extremely resistant to the absorption of preservatives. It is a timber that tends to split and shake with climatic changes. Another home-grown timber, English Elm, whilst considered to be non-durable, stands

up very well if never allowed to dry out; that reason that it was often used for she It had another virtue: it was available boards, although length of timbers, greenheart, was limited. The latter car tained in lengths of 90 odd feet and tho: of Guyanian forests have been playing t in the construction of Thames locks fo century.

The Thames holds many hidden sur its river bed. It is common knowledge bed at Clifton Hampden is of rock, but erally appreciated that further dow there are outcrops of ironstone only 1 beneath the clay bed; driving steel sh this requires some very special technic the south bank of the river at Bray, t point where the bed changes from hard a deep bed of clay within a distance of some reaches the ballast can be so har crust takes much force to penetrate; seems that nature has washed, grade and consolidated the material in the sa Macadam built his roads.

In other areas hard ballast can stratum of almost running sand, w versely one can strike a crust of ironst examining the bed for the driving o many reaches of the river chalk pred sometimes in a rather loose muddy others it is packed down in large ma: can make the driving of sheathing or going. 'Hog holes' in the bed are area the river is exceptionally deep, somet 30 feet, when perhaps the adjacent ma is only 12 to 13 feet deep. These holes by punters but sometimes appre fishermen. There are of course othe the bed caused by high explosive bom in the last war.

The training, control, and mainte river, which is a living sinuous entity ending task presenting countless pro fessional expertise apart, it is a job th handled with love and understandi with experience and good common s it is a challenge for all who enjoy we nature.

15   THAMES TREASURES

The Thames being a great and natural highway, as well as an important boundary from both domestic and military viewpoints, it is not surprising that her river bed is rich in treasures. Many of the articles that have fallen into the river have perished in one way or another; however Thames mud has rendered great service in preserving objects in a remarkable way; even wooden items have on occasions survived the passage of time through being well immersed in mud. Of course items of stone and pottery are almost indestructible except under the impact of a barge or punt pole, or the jaws of a dredger. Bone, too, survives quite well on the river bed. Where the river is tidal, 'mudlarking', that is, searching for interesting objects at time of low water, is often practised, whereas on the upper river most objects have been recovered when ballasting or dredging.

An authority and outstanding collector of

The long object at the bottom of the picture is the end of a barge pole; above it on the left is the end of a ryepeck; above that the end of a barge hook used when breasting up (going side by side); above that a boathook end. On the right are two smaller ryepeck prongs and two punt pole shoes.

Thames treasures was the late Charles Roach Smith. He spent much time upon dredgers, keeping an eagle eye on the ever moving buckets. One of his most remarkable finds was a bronze Roman model of a peacock, now in the British Museum. A quote from Ivor Noel Humes's description in *Treasures of the Thames* is a must:

> More remarkable still was the story of a small bronze peacock whose tail was recovered from a dredger by Roach Smith but which could not then be identified. A year later when he was watching the buckets of dredged gravel being tipped into an adjacent barge, he noticed a small bronze object amongst the pebbles, and on picking it up found it to be a model peacock that had lost its tail. The two pieces are now re-united as a result of Roach Smith's phenomenal stroke of luck.

Surely there can be few greater coincidences! On the upper Thames most of the outstanding finds have been due to the quick and observant eyes of workmen engaged on dredging operations. The former Thames Conservancy used to award ten shillings (old money) to any of their staff finding an object of antiquarian interest. It takes considerable skill to spot the tip of a sword, a small piece of pottery or some other treasure whilst working a dredger; however, at least three Thames Conservancy employees really excelled themselves, judging by the number of items in Reading Museum that are credited to them. The men in question were: A. Whitman, W. East and A. Lewendon. When these men were dredging in the Staines reach in 1955 the river bed yielded secrets of varying antiquity. As the steel buckets of the dredger groaned and clanked upwards to discharge their contents into the hold of an adjacent barge a great variety of items were retrieved, including a bronze spear head, numerous pieces of Roman domestic pottery, ancient British skulls (of both sexes), a German machine gun from a raider shot down in the last war, a fine collection of pewter tankards which were the result of regatta celebrations over the years, Stone Age axe heads, pieces of Bronze Age

The remains of a spoon dredger brought to the sur dredging a mooring that once belonged to the Chaplin Snr.

domestic utensils and items of modern equipment.

Some of the swords and weapons r from the river are 'doubled back', bent twisted into some grotesque shape; th freak, or action of a dredger's buckets intentional destruction of the weapon be owner finally flung it into the Thames. I the Stone Age axes that have been found as one would suspect, of local flint but from as far away as Cornwall and W land. Geological factors determined th stone used for axes and other implemen south east of England flint was univ other areas where flint was not availabl men used certain local stone; some of ducts from these rock-bearing areas p good that they were distributed over a very wide area – even to the flint lands of the south, hence the finding of stone axes in the Thames that were 'manufactured' in Great Langdale, Craig Lwyd and Cornwall.

Anyone discovering an item of archaeological interest should either report the matter to the Thames Water Authority, or hand the object in to them for examination and recording. Thames relics are housed and displayed quite widely in various museums; items from the lower Thames are principally in the British and London Museums. On the upper Thames there are exhibits in numerous small museums but the *pièce de résistance* is the Thames Conservancy collection housed in the Reading Museum; much of this collection is on display but stored items can usually be seen by prior arrangement. Some of the finds are so striking that a brief description, rather than a full and detailed list, would seem appropriate.

On display there is a 'gisarme' or bill, which was an infantry weapon of the Middle Ages; it was found in the backwater below Cookham in 1931. A mediaeval carpenter's axe of the 9th – 11th centuries came to light at Wheatley's Ait, Sunbury. A fine Bronze Age hunting spear head (1000–450 B.C.) from Shifford is displayed with a similar item found at Surbiton. Then there is amongst items stored away an interesting Bronze Age sword found just above Platt's Eyot, Hampton. From Benson there is a Roman cooking pot (1st – 2nd century A.D.) on which there is a white encrustation, this being a lime deposit which often forms upon objects lying upon the river bed. Above Bray Lock W. East found a late Bronze Age spear head of very unusual type (1000–450 B.C.). A large axe head made from rock, which occurs at Great Langdale in the Lake District, was found near Bell Weir in proximity to a New Stone Age camp discovered by aerial photography. During the New Stone Age period these axes were made at Great Langdale in large numbers for trading throughout Britain. A truly remarkable single-edged sword of the Saxon–Viking period is from the river at the site of the former Keen Edge Ferry, a little above Shillingford Bridge. The blade is decorated by

the insertion of copper, brass and silver; the tip of the blade is missing, it being quite likely that this sword was broken intentionally upon the death of the owner, or for some other specific reason, before being thrown into the river. A ground flint axe head hailing from Garrick's Ait, Hampton, is the colour of ochre due to the staining by iron oxides in the river gravel. Specimens of bronze and copper Roman coins of the 1st and 2nd centuries A.D. have been recovered from Whitchurch Weir Pool, whilst at Raven's Ait, Surbiton, a flint axe head of the Middle Stone Age came to light. Axe heads such as this were used by the peoples who first came into Southern Britain about 8,000 years ago, when the barren wastes following the end of the Ice Age were giving way to forests of birch and pine. An interesting item of the New Stone Age is a finely made flint sickle found at Monkey Island, Bray. The

A collection of pot lids dredged from the river bed. Ceramic pots were popular for retailing edible pastes, toothpaste and certain cosmetic preparations during the Victorian period. Most lids were under-glaze transferred showing designs that identified and advertised the product. All the ones illustrated are black and white except the centre one with figures which are in colour.

New Stone Age folk would have been in the Thames Valley about 3200 B.C. at a time when farming was progressing with the rearing of domestic animals and cultivation of crops; a flint sickle such as this would have had a wooden handle.

From this gallimaufry attention must now be focused on boats; unfortunately little is left of early craft other than scant remains dredged out of the mud from time to time. However, excitement was stirred in October 1966 when Fred Saunders, whilst working in the Walton Reach, raised an almost complete dugout canoe. It was buried in about 4 feet of mud in shallow water against the Middlesex, or northern, bank. The craft had been hewn out of a solid piece of oak and measured just over 18 feet in length with a beam of about 3 feet 3 inches. This interesting vessel went to the Reading Museum, but, as yet, is not on display. The writer, when on dredging operations, always keeps a sharp eye open for the possibility of discovering a sunken West

Country barge. No living person has eve example of one of these, once famou tional commercial craft of the Thames. must have been discarded and left to de and sink along many an unused moor sort of place where a hull could lie is in silt deposits of many a channel long s carded for navigational purposes, suc backwater of Holm Island, Staines, w years ago was the navigation channel, b barely deep enough to float a canoe; the the old Swift Ditch at Abingdon; Heds is another possibility, although underw veys carried out there, prior to structur only revealed large deposits of coal on bed (a legacy from unloading barges a wharf). Let us only hope that in the f time, a dream may come true, so that th can be proud of its own equivalent to *Rose*.

In addition to all the archaeolo; coveries, many interesting items and b

A selection of ginger beer and boot-blacking stoneware containers dredged from the river.

The bottle on the right is known as a 'Hamilton' due to a W.E. Hamilton patenting a filling machine for this sort of bottle in 1809. A similar type of bottle was used by J. Schweppe in 1790. The shape of the bottle ensured it was kept on its side, so keeping the cork stopper moist. Bottles of this type were used for aerated mineral waters for something like 120 years.

The bottle on the left was dredged up at Staines, not far from the former Ashby Brewery, whence it started life. Note Ashby's trade mark – the City Stone. This type of bottle was known as a 'codd' for it was patented by Hiram Codd in 1870. The stopper consisted of a glass marble pushed against a rubber washer in the neck by gas pressure from the aerated water. The constriction below the neck prevented the marble from falling into the body of the bottle.

are found, or acquired, by people collecting 'Thamesiana'. The enamelled licence plates issued by the Thames Conservancy are firm favourites, then boot blacking, gingerbeer and other stoneware jars have their devotees, some of the open-top ones proving popular with flower arranging enthusiasts. To bottle collectors the Thames yields a, seemingly, never ending store of those early lemonade bottles of which there were three main types: the pointed bottom style which had to be laid on its side, so ensuring the cork was kept moist; then the 'pinched neck' bottle which retained a marble to seal the contents (opening was performed with a special tool that pushed the marble down into

the bottle); the third type was a crude version of a modern bottle. Another favourite find, especially near Victorian construction sites, where there were plenty of navvies working, was clay pipes. Of course collectors have plenty of scope if they are interested in collecting books, maps, prints and paintings of or on the river; the limiting factors are now scarcity with the inevitable appreciation of value. This also applies to guide books, journals such as *Lock to Lock Times* and *Thames Boating News*, and a wide range of excellent picture post cards. The most sought after items for decorative purposes must surely be those fascinating, and very accurate, little models of steam tugs and lighters that were pro-

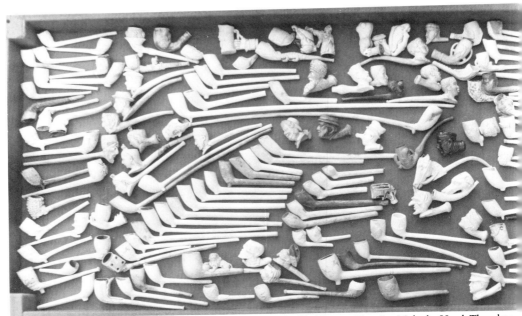

A remarkable collection of clay pipes recovered from the river bed by Thames historian Malcolm Head. They date 1979. Separate heads had wooden stems which have long since rotted.

duced by Doulton's of Lambeth. In the porcelain world there were a limited number of figurines

of past Doggett coat-and-badge winn[...]
still exist they must be worth a smal[...]

We shall take locks and weirs as they fall going downstream:

St John's Lock

There was a weir here in the last quarter of the 18th century. A pound lock was built in 1790. First lock house built 1830. Previously, lock keeper possibly lived in nearby 'Trout' public house. Quite often publicans doubled up as lock keepers. Lock and house re-built in 1905.

Buscot Lock

Original pound lock was built in 1790. At the beginning there was a resident lock keeper, then it became general practice for it to be kept under the eye of the St John's lock keeper, leaving boatmen and/or boatowners to work the lock for themselves. After the war a relief lock keeper was present in the height of the season and resided in the delightful, and adjacent, stone cottage which has belonged to the National Trust for a number of years. A full-time lock keeper was installed when a lock house was built in 1971, due to the popularity of this remoter part of the river with holiday-makers and hire cruisers. 1979 saw the building of a new weir and channel at Buscot.

Downstream of Buscot, and close to the former 'Anchor' Inn, which was burnt down in the winter of 1979, was at one time positioned Eaton Weir, which was one of the few remaining flash locks on the river, and which the author

remembers when in those parts with his late father. There were many flash locks on the Thames above Oxford. The site of some are today remembered by the names of footbridges that span the river, such as: 'Tenfoot Bridge', 'Old Man's' and 'Harts'. Boydell, writing in 1794 of the latter describes it as follows:

> On approaching Hart's-weir, at a distance of somewhat more than a mile from Newbridge, the banks are so thickly planted, that the river appears to be passing through a wood, whose trees, extending their branches from either side, over-arch the water and form a sylvan canopy. Here the Thames divides itself into one large and two lesser streams forming as many islands; one of which is inhabited. The weir stretches across from the meadowbank to these islands . . . A range of floodgates crosses the larger current which pours through it in frothy agitation, while the diminutive streams, that divide the islands, tumble over their sluices in unbroken waterfalls.

Grafton Lock

The pound lock dates from late 19th century, having succeeded earlier flash locks. A new lock and weir were built by the Thames Conservancy in 1898. The lock house at Grafton, like many others upriver, is very remote and had poor access. It was only in the latter days of the former Thames Conservancy that better facilities and good access roads were provided.

Radcot Lock

Not surprisingly, on the site of former flash weirs, which were built and re-built over a period of two centuries until the construction of the pound lock in 1892.

Rushey Lock

This lock in its splendid setting with fine garden and attractive house is always popular with photographers. The earliest lock was recorded in 1790. The Thames Conservancy built a new lock and weir in 1898.

Shifford Lock

This lock, with its attendant weir, was built on a virgin area in 1898, so making it the last modern lock site upon the Thames.

Northmoor Lock

Like Shifford, this lock with its adjacent weir is 'modern', for it dates from 1895.

Pinkhill Lock

Earliest pound lock here was in 1791. Like other upriver locks, Pinkhill was re-built in 1898.

Eynsham Lock

This too dates from 1791; there were numerous flash weirs on this site, the last one being removed in 1927. In the latter part of last century a boatslide with rollers was installed for the benefit of those in skiffs, punts and rowing boats in general.

King's Lock

The original pound lock was proposed at a meeting of the Thames Commissioners held on December 27th, 1817, but proposals dragged on for a mighty long time, so necessitating the regular repair and patching up of the old flash lock. In the 1870s small boats were afforded the facility of a boatslide. The Thames Conservancy built the pound lock in 1927 – only one hundred and ten years after the first proposal!

Godstow Lock

This was opened in 1790. In 1927 the re-constructed and deepened. In the int years there were the usual succession repairs, disagreements and dissatisfact

Medley Weir

Although no longer in existence, it is o to give it a place of honour, inasmuch the last operational flash weir on the Th was not removed until 1937.

Osney Lock

A weir existed at Osney in the 13th cen property was then owned by Osney Ab first pound lock dates from 1790. In 1 Thames Conservancy carried ou improvements to the weir and then in 1 chased land alongside the lock for e> their repairing yard and works.

Iffley Lock

Iffley Weir dates back to the 14th–1 turies. The original pound lock was the built upstream, under an Act of James Oxford-Burcot Commission in the lat The present Iffley Lock was built in 192 Thames Conservancy. At a Thames (sioners' meeting of December 30th, 182 'Ordered that henceforth no barges or permitted to pass through Iffley pound Sunday during the performance of di▼ vice, excepting only when the state of w; require the aid of flashing for the purpo navigation.' (N.B. a 'flash' is a surge of help any boats stranded on shallows.)

Sandford Lock

The first lock here goes back to the 163 the Oxford-Burcot Commission installe their three new fangled locks, so making the first three pound locks upon the r other two being Iffley and Swift Ditch. ¯ followed by subsequent locks of an ir nature over the years. A completely n was built in 1836, alongside the chamber, which was later used by the mill as a leat for a further millwheel; this was the result of a Thames Commissioners' meeting on March 28th, 1880, which 'Resolved and ordered that Mr. Swann be allowed to purchase the site of the old pound at Sandford at the price of fifty pounds, Mr. Swann now undertaking, as a condition of the purchase, not to put in any wheel, other device within such site excepting only such as shall be approved and allowed by the Commissioners or their Surveyor . . .'

Sandford lock was re-built in 1972–3 being opened to traffic on March 31st, 1973. The design incorporated a new feature on Thames locks, entailing the use of an underfloor system to enable rapid filling with reduced turbulence.

Abingdon Lock

There was a weir here in the 14th century. Camden the map-maker notes that a flash lock existed in 1720. Thames Conservancy built a new lock in 1905; a new lock house was built in the late '20s.

Culham Lock

This dates back to 1809. In 1957 the lock house was completely re-built.

Clifton Lock

Quite a junior amongst Thames locks, dating from 1822. It had no predecessors.

Day's Lock

There was a flash lock here in the late 16th century. Pound lock opened in 1789. In 1868 a new weir was built, followed by reconstruction of the lock in 1871. A new lock house was built in 1923 and the present lock was built in 1925.

Benson Lock

Like Day's, there was a weir here in the late 16th century. By the mid 1700s there was a flash lock and towards the end of the century there was a pound lock. A new lock was built in 1870, for the then princely sum of £3,500! In 1913 a new lock house was added to the scene.

Cleeve Lock

Original pound lock of 1787 replaced 16th cen-

tury flash lock. The new lock was built in 1874. In 1793 barge tolls were at the rate of 2½d. per ton.

Goring Lock

There are records of a weir here in 1538. The first pound lock was built in 1787 at a cost of a little over £1,000. Original toll was 4d. per ton but in common with Cleeve was reduced to 2½d. in 1793. In 1921 the Thames Conservancy built a new lock, complete with an intermediate pair of gates.

Whitchurch Lock

This, like numerous other locks, is more or less on the site of a 16th century flash lock. It was in the summer of 1787 that the first pound lock became operational. It was 'turf' sided, that is the lock walls were not built in a vertical manner to the very top with timber or masonry, they were just protected to a reasonable height from whence the grass, or turf, bank sloped back at an easy angle. Along the sides at suitable intervals were timber riding posts to prevent boats hitching up on the land as the water dropped. Such locks can still be seen, and used, on both the River Wey and Kennet and Avon Navigations. Whitchurch lock was completely re-built by the Thames Conservancy in 1875 along with constructing a new weir.

Mapledurham Lock

The weir here had to be maintained by the owner of the Mapledurham estate, and goes back to days before Magna Carta; one of its great functions would have been in the operation of the Mill. The first pound lock went into use in 1777. In 1867 the Thames Conservancy re-built the greater part of the lock: then in 1888 it was thoroughly restored. The lock was again reconstructed in 1907, then 49 years later it made history by being the first automated Thames lock. The system, which was electro-mechanical was an experimental system pre-dating the now universal hydraulic system by five years.

Caversham Lock

Locks here go back to the 15th century. A meeting of the Thames Commissioners (July 12th, 1777) decided that £1,000 must be borrowed to build a pound lock. This was opened to traffic in 1778, when use of old (flash) lock was discontinued. 2d. a ton had to be levied on barges passing through the new lock. Later in the same year the Surveyor reported that 'A Campshott is absolutely necessary to prevent the stream at Caversham (flash) lock from injuring the wing of the new pound lock there.' The Thames Conservancy re-built the lock in 1875. A new lock house was built in the late 1920s.

Sonning Lock

There was a weir here, presumably with flash lock, in the late 1500s. The first pound lock was opened in 1773. It was the highest lock upstream, of the first block of eight constructed under the Act of 1770. Within seven years the lock was in need of major repairs, due mainly to the unsuitability of the timber used. Be it the 1780s or the 1980s the same sort of problems occur! In 1827 the old flash lock was revived and put into sound working order whilst the pound lock underwent major repairs. The Thames Conservancy re-built the lock in 1868 and again 35 years later. 1916 saw the building of a new lock house.

Shiplake Lock

The weir here was, like many others, used in conjunction with the mill. A flash lock operated way back in the 1400s by all accounts. The first pound lock went into use in 1773. 1874 saw the re-building of the lock by the Thames Conservancy, who in 1914 took over land that had been acquired on Shiplake Lock Island by the Corporation of London as a camp site; the conservators carried on by administering it for the same purpose. Shiplake made outstanding history in 1961 by becoming the very first Thames lock to be fully automated by hydraulic power.

Marsh Lock

Originally a flash lock going back to the 15th century. The first pound lock was opened in 1773. Like Sonning, within a span of seven years it was needing major repairs, mainly due to the

poor quality of the timber used. Lock 1787, by Thames Commissioners. Again by Thames Conservancy in 1886, who out a similar operation exactly 28 years provide the lock we use today.

Hambleden Lock

A weir was here in the 14th century, wh for navigation as well as the miller's use; was provided for hauling barges up thro opening in the weir. In 1772 there was plaint against Constructor Mr. Bradsl slowness in completing Marsh and Har Locks. To be discharged if he does not un to finish Marsh Lock in 2 months and F den in six weeks, on penalty of £500 ea Thames Conservancy replaced the lock i

Hurley Lock

Way back in the 1580s the weir here was as 'Newlock'. A pound lock was put int 1773, being the fifth of the series of eigh the 1770 Act. Like other locks alread tioned, troubles began seven years after o This is indicative of the quality of local timber. In these days, if greenheart o super quality timber proves too expens can at least have our wood pressure-treat preservative, to British Standard Specif for marine timbers, so assuring a life of years plus. At a meeting of the Thames Co sioners in 1786 'A complaint having bee by Mr. Morton's Steward that the wa been suffered to rise 5″ above the high mark at Hurley Lock greatly to the dan the meadows above the said lock, [it ordered that the Clerk do give notice Pengree the occupier of the said lock c complaint and that a prosecution will b menced if the said offence be repeated.' It be noted that Mr Pengree was the owner old flash lock, which was an essential sta troubles arose with the pound lock. A many flash locks a winch was strate placed for hauling barges upstream throu opening. In this case it was on the left ba the lower end of the Danesfield Estate, wh remains are still visible. In 1932 the T

Conservancy purchased Hurley Lock Islands and enclosed a section of land to form a bathing enclosure.

Temple Lock

The weir here, serving both the mill and fishery interests, from mid 16th century, incorporated a flash lock. A pound lock was opened to traffic in 1773 (it was the sixth of the series of eight). A small lock cottage was built 4 years later. By 1782 the lock had to be re-built due to deterioration of the timbers coupled with poor workmanship. The River Inspection Committee of the Thames Commissioners reported in July 1780 that: '. . . In the course of our examination we have observed that the Fir Piles, rails and planks liable to be sometimes wet and sometimes dry, or partly buried in the earth, cannot be expected to last above 7 or 8 years. We therefore recommend all such woodwork in future to be of well-seasoned oak.' In 1890 Temple Lock was reconstructed on a new site and was equipped with a boatslide.

Marlow Lock

A flash lock and winch were here at the beginning of the 1300s. The first pound lock (of the series of eight) went into use in 1773; it was on the right bank, so opposite the present lock. In November 1826 a new lock was built on the current site. In September 1847 the old pound lock was sold to a firm by the name of Wright for £39 on condition that they filled it in. The Thames Conservancy reconstructed Marlow Lock in 1927.

Cookham Lock

This lock, a pound one, was ready for traffic in November 1830 after completion of the lock cut, which by-passed Hedsor Water and the old Hedsor Lock and Weir. This lock was lengthened, and a boatslide provided, in 1892. Cookham Lock was completely re-built during 1956–7, it being fitted with three pairs of gates and all machinery powered by electricity, giving the lock keeper push-button control from the comfort of his cabin, which unfortunately precluded him from having a clear view of all the craft in the lock chamber. The new lock was officially opened on June 14th, 1957. The old bottom gates were taken downriver and put to good use in providing entrance gates for Ditton Marina. As stated in an earlier chapter, electric operation had its drawbacks, so after the success of hydraulic power at Shiplake in 1961, it was soon adopted at Cookham.

Boulter's Lock

There was a flash lock here in the 16th century and possibly earlier, for the adjacent Ray Mill would have required a weir when it was operating in the 14th century. The name Boulter's did not appear until the mid-18th century, which coincides with the period when a lot of mills undertook 'bolting', that is the sieving and dressing of flour, rather than leaving it to the bakers, and probably is the origin of the name. This theory is supported by the fact that in a document of 1764 the spelling of the lock is 'Bolter's'. The first pound lock went into use in 1772; being across the river from the present lock, it was on the left bank. When a new lock was being built on the present site in 1827, it was found necessary to purchase a 6 h.p. steam engine at a cost of £350 in order to keep the excavations clear of water. In 1868 the Thames Conservancy re-built

The somewhat elaborate conveyor system that once enjoyed popularity at Boulter's, by enabling small craft to by-pass the locks (pictured in the early 20th century). At most locks 'rollers' consisted of steel rollers running in brackets set at intervals in a concrete ramp so that one could pull a skiff or other craft out of the water and convey it from one level to the other.

a large portion of Boulter's. The boatslide followed in 1888. In 1909 the Conservators purchased Ray Mill Island, including the water rights, so as to improve Boulter's Lock, which was in bad condition and inadequate to cope with the vast amount of summer traffic. Until the building of Romney Lock in 1797 Boulter's was the last lock on the Thames!

Bray Lock

Of the locks built below Maidenhead Bridge, this is the highest upstream, albeit not the first, after the repealing of a clause in the 1770 Act. A 'turf sided' or open type lock with timber riding piles along the sides went into use in 1845. Apparently when the river was well up after heavy rains the lock was left open, only being used in times of low water. The Thames Conservancy built a substantial new lock in 1888. A new lock house was built in 1911.

Boveney Lock

At a meeting of the Thames Commissioners on May 18th, 1836, it was proposed:

> To make a pound lock and Weir near Surley Hall, the former to be placed in a cut to be made through Boveney Point and the latter across the present navigable channel below the entrance to the Clewer Mill Stream, this latter to be made to pen 4ft. 6ins at low water time. To make a weir or dam across one or other of the channels at Parting Eyot and perhaps at Queens Eyot also, to ballast some of the shallows at Gills Bucks and construct the channel there by weir hedges if necessary and to raise the weir at Romney to pen one foot more head water than at present, and to round off Clewer Point. It is estimated that the execution of the whole of these works will not much, if at all, exceed £6,000 and they may for the more part be carried out without interference with the navigation . . . Your Committee feel satisfied that these works when completed will be sufficient to enable the Barges to travel full laden at all times between Boulter's and Romney

without having recourse to the per practice of flashing.

The above plans were rescinded, but a on June 25th of the same year fresh were made and the lock was, in d constructed and put into daily use in 1838. The Thames Conservancy re-c the weir in 1907. Details of earlie Boveney are very scant and possibly the 13th century. Brindley's survey shows 'Gill's Bucks' hereabouts.

Romney Lock

After much debating, study of altern and sites, and a lot of frustration, thi finally built in 1797. (The method barges from the lock to the distant to already been described in the chapte traffic.) Our present, large and fully n lock was built in the winter of 1979

Old Windsor Lock

This lock dates back to September 1 years earlier there had been suggest building a lock at Wraysbury. On 1882:

> The General Committee reported ι several points referred to them f last General Meeting.
> 1. That they were proceeding ι campshedding at Old Windso
> 2. That they had inspected the sta new pound lock and cut at Ol sor, and had great satisfac observing that although the di which the contractors had enc from the flowing of the wate very formidable, yet that th were in progress, and that a rea hope might be entertained that be open for the passage of boa last week of August.

In 1846 the bridge over the lock cι dangerous state; the estimate for the r bridge was £135; the erection of a ne up old materials was £180. The conservators decided in 1889 that the lock should be re-built. A new lock house was built under the 1928–30 scheme, whilst in 1953 the lock was completely re-built again. A new departure was the use of pre-stressed concrete piles to form the walls of the lock chamber.

Bell Weir Lock

At the Commissioners' meeting of June 4th, 1816, authorization was given to forthwith purchase the land required for making the cut and lock at Egham. At a meeting held four months later it was minuted that: 'The Committee specially appointed at the last meeting to view and report on the most eligible mode of remedying the shallows at and above Bell Weir . . .' Then on October 28th, it was reported that 'Expense of proposed Cuts and Works at Bell Weir: £6,940 including £1,800 for a weir which leaves £5,140 for making the cuts and pound lock. Ordered that the said works be proceeded on by contract as soon as can conveniently be done.' The above was confirmed at a meeting on November 29th, 1816. Work on the site commenced in 1817. In August of that year it was reported that: 'The contractors had made the pound lock at Bell Weir too narrow. It is recommended that the Surveyor do see that the Contractors do construct the pound lock according to the plan by making it 18 ft. in width at the ledge between the Upper and Lower staple posts and every other part of the Pound Lock.' The winter of 1817–18 saw the opening of the lock to traffic. Then in April 1918 the surveyor suggested the towing path be repaired, then to deepen and ballast new cuts. Contractors agreed to co-operate, but at the same time did not feel themselves bound by their contract to remove all the gravel in the cut above and below the pound lock accumulated by the late flooding. In 1867, the Thames Conservancy built a new stone lock at a cost of £4,700; this structure lasted until the building of the new, modern and much larger lock in the winter of 1973–4.

Penton Hook Lock

The present weir stream forms a considerable horse shoe. Before the lock cut was excavated, and the chamber of the lock constructed in the narrow neck of land at the top of the horse shoe, flood water surging down from Staines tended to cut through this neck and on occasions the breach made it possible for barges to pass through. The bank here was being repaired at regular intervals, whilst the land was built up. John Rennie, the renowned civil engineer (1761–1821) proposed the building of a lock at this point way back in 1809. The City of London (remember we are now downstream of the 'City Stone') started negotiating for the site in 1813, the enabling Act was passed in 1814 and by August of that year work was under way. Excavation for the chamber posed problems due to the great ingress of water. The lock, which was the highest upstream of any of those under the jurisdiction of the City, was opened in 1815. The new lock at Penton Hook was completed during 1909. Like many other locks, at one time it had 'rollers' which enabled sculling boats and other light craft to be quickly and easily conveyed up, or down, suitable ramps from one level to another.

Chertsey Lock

A survey for a lock in this area was carried out in 1793 by Robert Whitworth, who was a pupil and son-in-law of James Brindley. Parliament disallowed this scheme. Then in the later part of 1805 John Rennie planned a cut from the southern end of Penton Hook to a little upstream of Chertsey Bridge; this cut would have been around 2,500 yards in length, containing a pound lock with a 5 foot 6 inch fall. This cut would have avoided Laleham Gulls. Land proprietors objected to the scheme and won the day. Then in 1809 Rennie proposed a weir, a little above the tail of Chertsey Abbey Mill, which was intended to pen the water over Laleham Gulls with a cut on the north side containing a pound lock. The lock was authorized by an Act in 1810 above the infall of the Abbey River. Later in the same year the Thames Commissioners proposed that the City should build the lock against the Surrey bank; In August of that year the present site was surveyed. In the next year

Lord Lucan asked to have the lock sited as far away from his outlook as possible. Finally the lower, and present, site was authorized in 1812. The lock was built straight away and opened in September 1813. The lock was re-built by the Thames Conservancy in 1912–13, being re-opened for traffic by Easter 1913; it was divided by additional gates, similar to those on some other locks. In May 1955 the weir 'blew' and in order to carry out emergency repairs *all* the lock gates were winched open so that the main flow charged straight through the lock. The ropes holding back the downstream left-hand gate parted, causing it to swing outwards, where it hung in a precarious and 'out of true' position. Fortunately it was not damaged and the timber resumed its normal shape when the lock returned to regular use.

In May 1955 Chertsey Weir 'blew'. To effect repairs the whole flow of the Thames had to be directed through the lock. For this purpose all the gates had to be winched open and roped back. The rope holding one of the lower gates parted, with dramatic results as shown.

Shepperton Lock

The weir stream at Shepperton forms the most southerly point of the Thames. The configuration of the site is not unlike Penton Hook, with the same phenomenon of flood water breaching the small neck of land at the top of the ox bow. However most bargemasters were not worried about travelling round the great bend, for many had business with the Wey Navigation, or goods

to load or unload at Weybridge. Those no[?] ing to stop off often made use of the [?] mentioned breach if conditions were favo[?] – although many a chance and great risl[?] taken. The breach was known as Stoner['?] ('gut', see glossary), and as far as can be [?] tained is just about the site of the presen[?] Our old friend John Rennie, in 1805, prop[?] lock in a 1½ mile long cut below Chertsey [?] the fall being approximately 5 feet. Due t[?] opposition (nothing new!) the schem[?] dropped. Then in 1809 Rennie came up w[?] idea of a lock in Stoner's Gut. This schem[?] ahead but with some further excavation [?] alignment of the 'cut'. The lock was ope[?] January 1813. An early lock keeper/fer[?] was a Purdue, a family name that is a[?] known in the district today as it was 50[?] ago. Like most locks it was re-built – in [?] by the Thames Conservancy. In 1940 th[?] house was damaged by enemy action. Th[?] was mechanized in time for the 1963 s[?] after undergoing major repairs the year [?] ously.

Sunbury Lock

Before the lock was built in 1811, severa[?] had been erected at Sunbury, and one f[?] down on the Middlesex side of Platt's [?] (Timber from the remains of the latter m[?] excellent fireside curb for the author's [?] These weirs were virtually low stops of [?] and piling, so as to direct the flow into, [?] scour out, the normal barge course. Renn[?] suggested a lock in 1805 in a long cut [?] Halliford bend, which would have tied u[?] his suggestions for Shepperton and Chert[?] 1809 he proposed a further scheme whicl[?] ahead a year later. This lock, like others o[?] period, was of timber construction; that [?] sides of the chamber were built up with ba[?] timber, retaining piles were left projecting [?] the uppermost horizontal baulks, in or[?] prevent craft lodging on the grass banks [?] the water was up. Within 40 years the lo[?] become very down at heel, with much [?] timber in a decaying condition; the buildi[?] new lock was put in hand, this being const[?]

at the tail of the cut, because the eddy caused by the confluence of the main flow brings silt and gravel into the entrance, so forming a bar. If this is just below the lock it can be flushed away by drawing the lock sluices. If there is a length of cut the flash of water from the sluices pretty well loses its impetus by the time it reaches the bar. The footbridge was also built about this time. In 1838 Sunbury Lock pre-dated many others in having a second pair of gates, so as to conserve water when smaller craft were passing; this largely came about with the general use of smaller barges. In 1866 the lock was provided with boatslides ('rollers') to facilitate the passing of small pleasure craft without opening the lock. The lock was re-built in 1886. The construction of the new lock alongside the old one was carried out in 1925.

Molesey Lock

Charles Truss, Clerk to the Corporation of the City of London, first put forward a proposal for a lock late in 1802 'to hold up the water over the shoals at Kenton Hedge and Sundbury Flatts above'. Nothing happened, but then by 1809 Rennie was urging the construction of a lock and weir, but 5 years were to pass before action began; however by August 1815 all was completed and in use. In 1864 the fishladders were added to the weir whilst the lock was endowed with boatslides in 1871. The lock was re-built in 1906 at a cost of approximately £14,000, being re-opened on June 2nd of that year. The new lock house was built in 1925 and due to the cessation of commercial traffic in the form of coal lighters for the waterworks at Hampton and Abbs Court, 24-hour manning of the lock came to an end on January 1st, 1980.

Teddington Lock

In the late 1700s various structures were put up to try and direct water into the barge channel, rather like the efforts at Sunbury. It was the clerk, Truss, who suggested a lock. It was built by the Corporation of the City of London after their Act of 1810. This lock was 150 feet long by 18 feet wide and was opened in 1811. Fourteen years later the lock required major repairs which

were put in hand by the City Corporation, who decided to re-build the lock with an additional little lock for small pleasure craft; this work was completed by the newly formed (1857) Thames Conservancy and opened for public use on May 8th, 1858. So the last lock on the upper Thames became one of the first major projects of the Thames Conservancy. In 1869 they re-built the much repaired Teddington Weir – a weir that was critically damaged by ice in 1827, on which occasion it seems that nature exerted even more power than Hitler's bombs upon the weir in the last war.

The weir was considerably enlarged in 1883. By 1899 Teddington Lock was proving too small to deal with the quantity of barges and tugs that worked up with the tide and reached there at almost the same time; plans were prepared for a new lock, 650 feet long by 25 feet wide to take a tug and tow of six barges, calculated to meet all requirements of traffic. The new barge lock was opened by the then Chairman of the Board, Sir F.D. Dixon Hartland, on June 11th, 1904, in the presence of some 3,000 people. It required 800,000 gallons of water to fill and the sluices were so designed that this could be done in 7 minutes. In 1953 flood lighting and an electrical system of light signals to control river traffic were installed; certainly the Conservancy was moving with the times, little realizing there was going to be a great decline in commercial traffic. Teddington Weir is the point where the flow of the Thames is very precisely monitored and recorded.

Due to limitations of space it has not been possible to give information on locks long since removed such as Folly Bridge, those above Oxford or the few downstream such as Chalmore Hole and Hart's near Goring. Likewise details of lock maintenance and repairs, from routine painting to the building and hanging of new gates, together with the mechanization of all locks has to be left to the imagination; sufficient to say that the latter scheme covering all locks from Iffley to Teddington was completed in 1968. Work on weirs, almost a perpetual job for the engineers, goes hand in hand with lock maintenance and improvement. The significant work of recent years has not only been the re-building programme, but the fitting of electrically operated gates at all major weirs, some of which are equipped with automatic gear controlled by rise and fall of river levels.

The smallest Thames lock, although not in official lists, is on the Abbot's Brook at B End. It is positioned at the tail of the within a short distance of the main rive enables craft up to the size of the tradi Thames skiff to gain access to private mo on the adjacent residential estate.

GLOSSARY

RIVER, IN PARTICULAR THAMES, TERMS

Ait or **Eyot** (with earlier variations in spelling) An island.

Ballasting An old term for dredging. Goes back to the days when sand and ballast required for building was removed from the river bed.

Bargewalk Old-fashioned, and at one time popular slang for towpath.

Bucks Large paddles, or floodgates, integral with the weir; they fitted into slots in the vertical timbers, and were raised and lowered by means of chains which wound round a drum rotated with a handspike in a similar manner to eel bucks.

Campshedding The protection and retention of a river bank with a sheathing of timber, or in modern times interlocking steel sheets. 'To campshed' is a variation of the 18th century term 'to campshot'. Many theories have been put forward with regard to this quaint name; however the logical answer is that it originated in the days when Dutch water engineers were working in this country and 'side boarded' watercourses, which in their native tongue was 'Kant schot'.

Cutwater The pointed shape of masonry, or concrete, at the base of bridge piers to spread the water. Also known as 'splitwater'.

Deeps Spaces in the river 200–300 yards in length granted by the Corporation of the City of London to towns and villages between Staines and Richmond to be preserved exclusively for angling (no net or 'engine' being allowed). The deep was granted to the village against which it lay. Deeps are mostly a natural phenomenon but some were formed by ballasting.

Drawdock A creek or inlet in the bank of a navigation into which barges can be run to load and unload cargoes or lie in the mud at low tide. On the upper Thames 'drawdock' usually refers to a 'parish wharf'; occasionally these were excavated at right angles to the bank such as at Lechlade, Radcot, Remenham and Bray.

Flash or **Flush** A rush of water downriver. To draw weir tackle so as to release penned up water to increase the level in the reach below to relieve grounded barges. Or in some cases to direct a surge of water to scour a barge channel.

Flat A punt-like craft of hard chine construction, i.e. sides being vertical and at right angles to the bottom. Used for ballasting, ferrying horses and vehicles, river maintenance work and numerous duties. Built in a wide range of sizes; sometimes referred to as 'ballast punts'.

Gull or **Gutt** Is a part of the river where the water is shallow and fast flowing. It can refer to a section that has been hollowed out by the action of nature in the form of 'freshes' (see Landwater). It also refers to shoals that have been swept away by similar action.

Ham or **Hamm** A peninsular formed by the meander of a river; sometimes the river breaks through the neck of the ham to transform it into an island.

Hard or **Hythe** A public landing for passengers and merchandise.

Hole A short section, or area, of the river where the water is exceptionally deep. Often caused by the action of eddies and/or underwater currents acting on a soft stratum in the river bed. Modern holes have been made by bombing raids in the last war.

King pile A timber pile, set at about 6 foot centres, for holding the waling and point cill which in turn retains the timber sheathing used for containing a river bank.

Landwater A quick run-off into the river after very heavy rain or a quick thaw; resultant sudden increases in flow being known as 'freshes'.

Meander Is the way in which a river winds about in its course. Derived from the Latin *maeander*. The Romans named a river thus in Phrygia (Turkey). There is also a River Maeander in Alberta.

Paddle Other than in the propulsion of canoes or the 'blades' of a mill wheel or paddle steamer, it refers to the boards or coverings of the openings of weirs and so on. They are mounted at the end of a long shaft, fitted with a 'T' shaped handle to facilitate the raising

and lowering required in the contr water.

Riparian Proprietor of a river bank (Lati a bank).

Ryepeck A very stout pole, often of larch but alder sometimes used due to it being ily available. Bottom end fitted with shaped prong forged from iron and abo feet long including socket. Ryepecks and are now to a very limited extent, u boat moorings, holding fishing pun station', serving as 'markers' at aquatic and maintaining barge mounted pile and ballasting machines accurately in

Rymer or **Rimer** Post in a weir in or on v 'paddle' rides up and down.

Starling Elliptical projection of m around bridge piers, not only giving s but providing 'cutwaters', sometimes 'splitwaters', to guide the flow and too much water impinging upon the f of the bridge.

Tumbling bay Overspill from a river, also the pool into which the water fl

West country 1. The name for th bottomed swim-headed barges that upon the upper Thames. 2. Bargeme ing 'beyond the flux of the tide' were be travelling 'West Country'.

BOATING TERMS

Terminology varies from one part of the river to another; for example, where Constable of Hampton would have referred to the uppermost plank as the 'top strake', Claret of Eton would have called it a 'saxboard'. To boatmen in some areas the so-called 'duck-boards' in a punt would be called 'gratings' whilst in other places they would be 'hatches'; so be prepared for odd, and sometimes conflicting names!

Bermudan rig Modern racing rig. Mainsail tall and triangular with no throat or gaff; head of sail goes to masthead and foot to the boom.

Luff is kept tight to mast by runners i track or groove in mast.

Burden board Floorboard.

Carvel Planking of boat laid edge to stout framework giving smooth exte ish.

Ceiling The inside planking of a barge; a floor in domestic terms, whilst o floors are the lower portion of a tr frame, usually a vertical section e from centre line of bilge from inner bottom.

Centreboard A wooden board lowered

a slot in the keel of a sailing boat; this is to help a boat sail closer to the wind; it is raised when running before the wind or in shallow water. If made of iron it is termed a centreplate. 'Leeboards' perform the same function; they are suspended (and pivoted) over the sides of flat-bottomed vessels, also canoes, and the board on lee side is lowered so as to sail closer to wind.

Chine   The intersection of a straight side with a flat bottom.

Cleat   A wood or metal fitting with two arms on which a rope may be belayed (made fast with turns).

Clinker or **Clincher**   A boat built with overlapping planks fastened with rivets that are clenched by hitting and burring their ends over into a roves (cup shaped washers).

.Fairlead   A metal fitting through which a rope can be run in any direction without chafing rope or boat.

Foresail   In a small craft with two sails it is the foremost one.

Gunter **rig**   A sail bent (fastened) to a gaff (spar) slung from a strop about two-thirds along, the head of the gaff being hoisted almost perpendicular. Although the sail used is four-sided it appears almost triangular.

Gunwale or **Gunnel**   Strengthening piece at the top of the hull fitted all round the boat, so holding timbers and top strakes. Name comes from the days when guns were pointed from the upper edge or wale.

Huff   The upward slope of the bows of a lighter, or early Thames barge.

Knee   Angular section of timber usually 'grown', that is, cut from a suitable branch giving the required shape, for use in bracing the hull.

Mast step   The recess into which the mast is located.

Painter   The mooring ropes of small craft.

Quarter   The side of a craft between midships and stern.

Rabbet   A groove cut lengthwise in a piece of timber. (In naval slang 'rabbit' refers to an article that is smuggled ashore having been obtained illegally.)

Reefing   To reduce the sail area by rolling, or tying up part of the sail(s).

Spritsail   A fore-and-aft sail supported and extended by a sprit, which is a boom set diagonally across a sail from the mast up to the peak.

Strake   Line of planks, or plates, running the length of a vessel. Garboard strake is the one next the keel, whilst top strake receives the gunwale.

Tholes   Hardwood pegs within a crutch on the gunwale to contain sculls or oars. Crutch is the same as a fixed rowlock. Rowlocks often of gunmetal or bronze with a shaft sliding into a socket affixed to gunwale. Some boatmen refer to these as 'rowlocks', others 'swivels'.

Thwarts   Seats placed athwartships (across) a boat upon which scullers or oarsmen sit.

Till   The decked portion of a punt.

Tingle   A temporary patch of copper or thin mahogany placed over a hole, or leak, in a boat and secured with copper boat nails.

Transom   The athwartship timbers of a craft bolted to the sternpost. The transom shapes the buttocks and holds the planking.

BIBLIOGRAPHY

Books

Adams, Thompson and Fry, *Survey of the Thames for Middlesex and Surrey County Councils* (St Dominic's Press, 1930)

Bolland, Reginald R., *Victorians on the Thames* (Midas, Tunbridge Wells, 1974)

Bowen, Frank, *100 Years of Towage* (Private publication, 1933)

Boydell, John and Joshua, *History of the River Thames* (1796)

Chaplin, Peter H., *The Thames Valley Welcomes You* (C. & D. Constaple, 1959)

Chaplin, Peter H., *The Thames at Hampton* (Dibb, 1967)

Chaplin, Thomas W., *The Narrow Boat Book* (Whittet Books, Weybridge, 1978)

Cook, T.A., and Guy Nickalls, *Thomas Doggett Deceased* (Constable, London, 1908)

Council for the Preservation of Rural England, *Thames Valley – Cricklade to Staines* (1929)

Dickens, Charles, *Dictionary of the Thames* (Chas. Dickens and Evans, London, 1891)

Ekwall, Eilert, *English River Names* (O.U.P., Oxford, 1928)

Gabor, Mark, *Houseboats* (Ballantine, New York, 1979)

Hansard, Henry, *Report from the Select Committee of the River Thames Preservation* (1884)

Ireland, Samuel, *Picturesque Views of the River Thames* (Egerton, London, 1791)

Motor Boat Manuals (1904–   )

Pitman, C.M., *The Record of the Un Boat Race* (T. Fisher Unwin, London

Rivers of Great Britain, The Thames (\ Cassell, London, 1889)

Robertson, H.R., *Life on the Upper '* (Virtue Spalding, London, 1875)

Searle and Sons, *Oarsmen's Guide* (18.

Taunt, Henry, *Illustrated Map of the* (Simpkin Marshall, London, 1880s)

Thacker, Fred, *Stripling Thames* (Fred ` Kew, 1909)

Thacker, Fred, *Thames Highway, Gene tory* (Fred Thacker, Kew, 1914)

Thacker, Fred, *Thames Highway, Lo Weirs* (Fred Thacker, Kew, 1920)

Thames Conservancy Acts 1857 to 18

Magazines and journals

Architectural Review, 'The Linear Park' by Eric de Mare (July 1950)

Lock to Lock Times (from June 9th,

Motor Boat (later *Motor Boat and* \ (Temple Press, from 1904)

Thames Boating News, an excellen (Thames Boating Trades Associatio

Thames Illustrated, weekly (Newnes,

Thames (later Thames & Medway) (`

Thames Topics, bi-monthly (River Th ciety, 1975–9)

Handbooks and maps

Bennet's Map and Guide to the Thames (Bennet, London)

Bowles, Carrington, Map of the Thames (1788)

Chaplin, Peter, *The Thames Book*, an annual publication (Link House, Croydon)

Salter's Guide to the Thames, an early prolific publication; by 1910 it had reached its 13th edition (Alden, Oxford)

Smith, W.H., Reduced Ordnance Map of the Thames (2 miles to the inch) (c. 1880)

INDEX

References in italics are to page numbers of illustrations

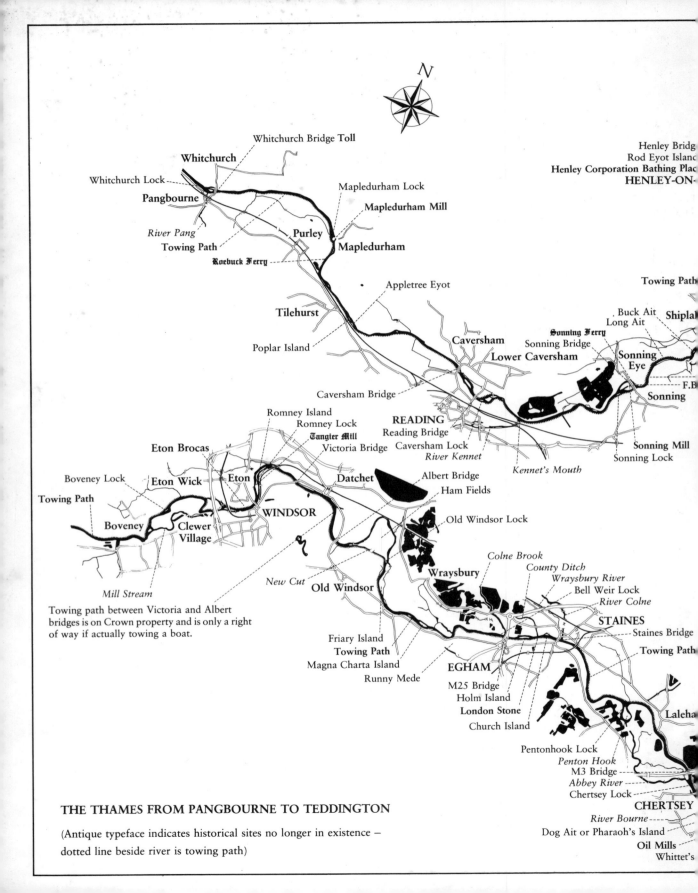

THE THAMES FROM PANGBOURNE TO TEDDINGTON

(Antique typeface indicates historical sites no longer in existence –
dotted line beside river is towing path)